Robin Murray

Selected Writings

Lawrence Wishart Selected Writings series

1. Stuart Hall (2017)
2. Robin Murray (2020)

Robin Murray

Selected Writings

Edited by Michael Rustin

No. 2 in the Lawrence Wishart
Selected Writings series

Lawrence Wishart
London 2020

Lawrence and Wishart Limited
Central Books Building
Freshwater Road
Chadwell Heath
RM8 1RX

Typesetting: e-type
Cover design: River Design
Cover artwork/photo credit: © Bethany Murray
Printing: Imprint Digital

First published 2020
Introduction © Michael Rustin 2020
Robin Murray (1940-2017): A friend's appreciation © Stephen Yeo
All other essays © Estate of Robin Murray

British Library Cataloguing in Publication Data.
A catalogue record for this book is available from the British Library

ISBN 9781912064496

Contents

Note on the text

For reasons of space, some material in this book has been abridged and lightly edited – where this is the case, it is indicated on the first page of the chapter, alongside original publication details. For ease of reading, ellipses have not been inserted. Some explanatory notes present in the original texts have also been omitted, for the same reasons.

Acknowledgements

The editor would like to thank Frances Murray, Bethany Murray and Julie Caulier-Grice for their help in preparing this collection.

Glossary of acronyms

ASTMS	Association of Scientific, Technical and Managerial Staffs
CAD	computer-aided design
CA	civic amenity site
CHP	combined heat and power
CICs	community interest companies
CRN	Community Recycling Network
Dinkies	double income, no kids (yet)
EEC	European Economic Community
EETPU	Electrical, Electronic, Telecommunications and Plumbing Union
EMS	European Monetary System
EU	European Union
FAO	Food and Agriculture Organisation
GLC	Greater London Council
GLEB	Greater London Enterprise Board
GPO	General Post Office
HP	hire purchase
IMF	International Monetary Fund
IRC	Industrial Reorganisation Corporation
LETS	local exchange trading schemes
LIS	London Industrial Strategy, published by the Greater London Council, 1985.
LT	London Transport
MMC	Monopolies and Mergers Commission
MRF	materials recovery facility
MOOC	massive open online course

MSF	Manufacturing, Science and Finance trade union, 1981 to 2001
NEB	National Enterprise Board
NFDP	Not For Distributed Profit
NFFO	non-fossil fuel obligation
NICs	newly industrialised countries
OECD	Organisation for Economic Co-operation and Development
PRN	Packaging Recovery Notes
PSBR	public sector borrowing requirement
SRB	single resolution board
TGWU	Transport and General Workers' Union
UMIST	University of Manchester Institute of Science and Technology
UNCTC	United Nations Centre on Transnational Corporations

Introduction

Michael Rustin

Robin Murray was unusual in having been both an influential writer and intellectual, a political economist and a practical innovator and an activist over many years.[1] He wrote significant articles and papers and took part in social and political initiatives in every phase of his working life, each usually arising from and intersecting with the other. Indeed, theory and practice were joined up in his life and work to an exceptional degree, from the first activities he was engaged in, in the 1960s, to the last, not long before he died.[2]

Guiding all his writing was his interest in the economy and its consequences and meanings for the larger society in which it existed. His writings have been influential in several spheres of debate. These include:

- The critique of both social democratic and state socialist economic models as these had come to dominate the left's economic thought.
- The idea, which he derived from Marx, that primary attention needed to be given to the sphere of production over those of circulation and distribution, in devising economic programmes.
- His analysis of the economic system Gramsci called 'Fordism', and his advocacy of what he believed to be the emergent system of 'post-Fordism', with 'flexible specialisation' at its core.
- The new model of locally based economic development he first theorised as Chief Economic Adviser at the Greater London Council in the early 1980s (the programme was published as the *London Industrial Strategy*[3]).

- The international focus of his work is a consistent thread through his writing, from his work on multi-national companies, through his research and consultancy with the Institute of Development Studies, to fair trade.
- The 'fair trade' model of economic relationships with agricultural producers in developing countries became the basis of a significant social movement.
- The idea of 'zero waste', based on his critique of standard systems of waste-disposal, and his advocacy of recycling which would mobilise the voluntary commitment of citizens and householders to end the pollution of the environment.
- The renewal of cooperative principles and practices, both in Britain and in developing countries, drawing on his critique of both state- and market-dominated systems, to develop decentralised and democratic modes of production.
- His early explorations of the nature of the 'platform economy', or as he called it: 'post-post-Fordism'.

This book presents a selection of Robin's writings, making some of his best work available in an accessible form, and also tracing the development of his thinking and political imagination over the decades. His written work is extensive, in both its published forms and in the voluminous unpublished notes and correspondence which he produced.[4] Although he worked for many years in universities, in particular at the University of Sussex's Institute of Development Studies, and valued scholarship highly, he was not an academic in his approach to writing and publishing. He always wrote with a sense of political and social purpose: he was not interested in developing formally accredited 'research outputs' in economics or any other discipline; instead his writing was always addressed to the different communities involved in the different political spheres where he took an active, and often, a leading role.[5] His most important published works were not scholarly monographs or treatises, but reports that he wrote for public institutions, networks of activists, and interested general readers.[6]

Robin published influential papers and articles in political journals and multi-authored volumes: these were often interventions in ongoing debates. In his two decades (1972-1993) at the Institute of Development Studies at the University of Sussex he wrote many consultancy reports for different governments and agencies, often offering specific applications of the model of post-Fordist economic development – 'flexible specialisation' – which he had developed in his succinct but pathbreaking papers in *Marxism Today*.[7]

Unfortunately, until very near the end of his life, Robin gave little consideration to gathering his own work together in collected volumes, nor did he seek to trace and analyse the significant evolution of his thought, leaving that task to those who survive him and who value his contributions. This introduction gives particular emphasis to Robin's focus on processes and forms of production, though there are myriad points of view from which one could approach his work.

Biography

Robin was educated at Bedales, a progressive co-educational private ('public') school, and at Balliol College Oxford, where he read history, and where he was taught by Christopher Hill, the great Marxist historian of the seventeenth century, whom Robin greatly admired, perhaps in part for his attention to the experience of his subjects. Robin's mother Margaret, an architect, came from a prominent Quaker family. His father, Stephen, was a left-wing lawyer in London before he decided to become a landowner and farmer in Cumbria. His father had a somewhat paternalist cast of mind and Robin's character contained in it something of this heritage. Nevertheless, he had a boundless and inspirational belief in what people whose origins were more modest than his own could achieve given the opportunity to associate with one another, and to think and act together. There was an almost Tolstoyan aspect to Robin's enthusiasm for popular democracy and its emancipatory potential.

After leaving Oxford, Robin studied European Studies at the College of Europe in Bruges between 1962 and 1963, before deciding to read economics at the London School of Economics (LSE). He wanted to understand better the dynamic forces that shaped societies and their development.[8] Perhaps even at the outset he saw the need to engage with what became a principal ideological enemy, within its own lair.

At the LSE, he encountered neoclassical economics, with its doctrinally driven commitments to both abstract economic theory and highly mathematicised but, in Robin's view, largely useless, econometric techniques. This was an intellectual approach at the furthest possible distance from the historical method – particularising, attentive to subjective experience, seeking to explain holistic changes in economy and society – that he had learned reading history at Balliol. While he disliked the kind of economics that was dominant at the LSE – I remember his many denunciations of 'the neoclassicals' – he nevertheless learned a lot about what its theory had to teach, about the key categories of scarcity, exchange, value, price, rent, profit, and wages. The problem was how to understand the economic universe in terms distinct from the discipline's fundamentalist belief in markets. At this time Robin became involved in socialist discussions leading to the publication of the *May Day Manifesto*.[9] The editors of the Manifesto – Stuart Hall, Edward Thompson and Raymond Williams – had been founding figures of the first New Left.

After the Manifesto's publication in 1968 Robin became interested in the writings of the German Marxian economist and philosopher Alfred Sohn-Rethel, on intellectual and manual labour.[10] In the early 1970s he became an active member of the Conference of Socialist Economists, and a keen reader of Marx's work through a *Capital* reading group that met in Brighton where he lived and worked.

Robin's relationship to Marxist economic ideas was a highly individual one. He jointly (with Mary Kaldor) taught a course on Marxist economic theory at the Institute of Development Studies (IDS) at the University of Sussex, at a time when quite arcane debates on Marx's theory of value were raging. These focused on the so-called 'transformation problem', the question of how Marx's idea that value was determined by the contribution of labour power to production could be reconciled with prices as they were manifested in market exchange. This seems to have been the central point of contradiction – the hinge – between the classical economic paradigm to which Smith, Ricardo and Marx were the main contributors, and the so-called 'marginalist revolution', in which value and price were determined by market exchange alone.[11] Although Robin engaged in these debates – he wrote a two-part substantial paper on the theory of rent – these meta-theoretical arguments were not of the greatest interest to him.[12]

Robin interpreted Marx's 'law of value', and frequently made reference to it, not so much as an intractable theoretical problem, but rather as a determining constant of capitalist economic life, according to which the powers of capital pressed down inexorably on labour, and on other elements in the productive process, to enable enhanced profits to be made through the 'ruthless' (as Robin would say) driving down of costs. Within capitalism, as Marx had shown, all economic actors were required to compete in terms of their relative costs of production, if they were even to survive. It was in part through the labour process that this law of value was enforced upon producers and, in particular, on the workforce.

An important contribution to these debates in the 1970s, and to the Conference of Socialist Economists and its journal *Capital and Class*, was Harry Braverman's book *Labour and Monopoly Capitalism: The Degradation of Work in the Twentieth Century*.[13] Its central argument was that market competition tended to drive down labour costs, by deskilling the labour force and replacing scarce skilled workers with cheaper unskilled ones. Historians such as Edward Thompson had written about this process in relation to the dire consequences of mechanised production for the handloom weavers.[14] Braverman argued that this tendency had become difficult to resist. Much of Robin's work in this period was dedicated to developing models of the labour process that offered a positive alternative to this view.

Keynesianism and monetarism

A distinguishing feature of Robin's work as an economist was his insistence on the priority of the sphere of production over those of circulation: distribution, exchange and consumption. This was the basis of his rejection of the neoclassical paradigm, in which value was determined in the process of market exchange, and not by the inputs of the factors of production of land, labour and capital, as set out in the 'classical' economic models of Adam Smith, David Ricardo, and Karl Marx, whose explanatory paradigm Robin preferred. (Robin's 1978 paper on rent argued for Marx's view over Ricardo's.)

Robin used these long-established conceptual distinctions to critique dominant theories of economic life, and the policy prescriptions to which they gave rise. His critique was not only of the 'ultra' free-market perspectives of the monetarists, with their models or fantasies of self-equilibrating, output-maximising perfect markets. He equally rejected the Keynesian framework of thinking and policy which for some decades had displaced the monetarist orthodoxy of the pre-war years.[15] The ideas of monetarism's most important thinker, Friedrich von Hayek, had become intellectually almost defunct in this period – or so it appeared, until it became evident, with the arrival of Thatcherism, that they had retained a devoted and ultimately influential following, not least at the Institute of Economic Affairs.[16] Although Robin had no time for monetarism, there is perhaps some affinity between Robin's commitment to decentralised and distributed systems, and Hayek's extreme scepticism about centralised state planning.

Keynesian theory had sought to remedy the defects of the free-market model, and the economic practices it gave rise to, by means of intervention by governments in the spheres of distribution and demand – that is, mainly through counter-cyclical fiscal and monetary policies. However, the post-war economic system entered a severe crisis during the 1970s. After the election of 1979, and its defeat of the 'corporatist' strategies to resolve the crisis, mainstream economic debate became dominated by the onslaught on the Keynesians by the Thatcherite market fundamentalists. The Keynesians lost this battle, with the defeat of the 'wets' in Thatcher's first Cabinet, and following her second election victory of 1983, after the Falklands War. This battle was fought and lost again, with the adoption of programmes of 'austerity' after the 2007-8 financial crisis, and its consequences are felt to this day.

Robin's belief was, however, that both sides in this monetarist-Keynesian argument were wrong, because of the priority they both gave to the domains of markets, exchange and consumption. Robin based his argument on Marx, noting that that the beginning of *Capital* is about the production process. Here, he said, Marx:

> offered a theory of production and its relationship to the sphere of exchange. Here for the first time we saw placed at the centre of economic concerns not the declining marginal utilities of some abstract individual, but the concrete details of production, the nature of work, the length of the working day, the drive for productivity and mechanisation, for time economy and ever more extensive controls by capital over labour in the factory. Here, too, was a long-run theory of technical change and accumulation which was self-evidently richer and more explanatory than the formal growth models of neoclassical and Keynesian thought.[17]

Robin's argument was almost as much with the limitations of social democracy as with free-market conservatism. He believed that Labourism in Britain had failed to remedy Britain's economic problems, or do more than scratch the surfaces of inequalities of power, income and wealth, because of the belief that it could achieve its goals largely through interventions in the sphere of circulation (through fiscal and tax policies) while leaving the sphere of production to the market.[18] Anthony Crosland had been the most influential advocate of this view in the Labour Party, with his insistence (contrary to the foundational doctrine that the party had inscribed as Clause 4 of its Constitution) that ownership of the means of production was irrelevant to the pursuit of Labour's goals.[19] Robin disagreed with this neo-Keynesian view and sought to develop a different economic model.

He had begun to formulate this alternative in his contribution with Michael Barratt Brown and others for the 1968 edition of the *May Day Manifesto*, which insisted that Britain's economic problems needed to be addressed not piecemeal but as those of an entire system, requiring holistic remedy.[20] But it was later, in the 1980s, after the failure of Labour's 1970s governments, that Robin's alternative model was set out, in the context of a larger critique of both Thatcherism and its ideology, and of the inadequacies of the conventional social democratic and indeed more left-wing responses to them, including in the *London Industrial Strategy* (LIS) and Robin's *New Directions* article for the Fabian Society, which is part of this collection.[21]

Marxism Today

These critical arguments were first set out in the Communist Party's monthly journal *Marxism Today* (hereafter MT), which obtained a wide circulation and visibility in Britain between 1978 and 1991.[22] The journal was produced by a group that included Martin Jacques, Stuart Hall, Robin Murray, Doreen Massey and Andrew Gamble. Its work was deeply influenced by the ideas of Antonio Gramsci (1891-1937), the Italian Marxist who died in Mussolini's prison but whose key *Prison Notebooks* were only translated into English in 1971.[23] Crucial was the distinction Gramsci had made between political strategies appropriate to the circumstances of centralised author-itarian regimes, like that of tsars in Russia, and those adapted to struggles in pluralist societies which facilitated the peaceful pursuit of what Gramsci termed ideological hegemony and political power.

Many of *Marxism Today's* contributors, including Robin, had never been Communist Party members, and it was remarkable that *Marxism Today* was allowed by the Party to expound and campaign for its revisionist positions, no doubt in part because of the wide visibility and political influence which it achieved for several years. The Eurocommunist project to which *Marxism Today* was broadly affiliated foundered in Italy in the late 1970s, bringing great damage to its larger influence, with the failure of its leader Enrico Berlinguer to achieve the 'historic compromise' of entry into national government in coalition with Christian Democrats. The historic compromise partly failed because of disruptive interven-tions by the far-left Red Brigades, who kidnapped and murdered the Christian Democrat leader Aldo Moro in 1978, and forceful opposition by the United States to Communist entry into Italy's national government.

It was in *Marxism Today* that Robin published several articles whose arguments were central to this important phase of his work and remained significant in its later development.[24] In these articles, three of which are reprinted in this selection (see Chs 1-3), Robin developed his analysis of post-Fordism, and his account of the mode of production he called 'flexible specialisation'. This emerging system was supplanting Fordist systems of mass production and mass consumption and was also making the 'mass' and bureaucratic forms of state welfare which had become pervasive during the post-war era seem outmoded and oppressive. The origin of Robin's argument lay in Gramsci's prescient paper, *Americanism and Fordism*, written in 1939 and published in English in the *Prison Notebooks* in 1971. This first noted the modernising and progressive significance (from Gramsci's perspective in the 1930s) of the revolution in methods of production which had been brought about by Henry Ford in his manufacture and distribution of cars for a mass market. Ford had introduced the methods of scientific management developed by Frederick Taylor (and hence Taylorism is often equated with Fordism). Gramsci, whose contrasting point of reference was the parasitic rentier economy of southern Italy and its cities such as Naples, noted the rationalising and disciplinary impact of Fordist methods, and the transformation of the habits and mentalities of the workforce which it required.

Gramsci argued that Ford had persuaded his American workforce to subject themselves, in an implicit bargain, to the soul-destroying routines of the assembly-line, in return for higher wages which enabled them to become purchasers of the automobiles they were manufacturing. Robin and others recognised that Gramsci's description of Fordist production and its concomitants could be extended. Not only cars were being produced and distributed by these methods, but many other manufactured commodities also. (The post-war Italian economy thrived through its production of 'white goods'.) The dynamics of an entire social system could now be understood as one in which a 'modern' mode of production, based on electro-mechanical and internal combustion technologies, had brought about the creation of mass-markets. Accompanying and sustaining this were forms of welfare provision (education and health services for example) and systems of governmental regulation. Their functions were to reproduce the entire system of production and its working and consuming population and maintain its political stability.[25] During a post-war period of a continuing rise in levels of production and consumption, what in France were called 'Les Trente Glorieuses' (in Macmillan's terms in Britain, these were the years when 'you've never had it so good'), this system was in its own terms successful. This was the case across much of Western Europe and North America, under governments whose politics we would now describe as of both the centre-right and centre-left. The most substantial account of this model of development came from the French Regulation School, whose writings had a considerable influence on Robin's thinking.[26]

However, Robin and his fellow-writers in *Marxism Today* were writing about this system not during its period of growth and stability, but in the light of its virtual breakdown following the inflationary, industrial relations, and broader social upheavals of the late 1960s and 1970s. At the time of this revisionist phase of *Marxism Today*'s work, from 1980 to 1991, a radical revolution was being accomplished by ideologues of the New Right, under the governments of Thatcher in Britain, and Reagan in the USA. Neoliberalism, we can now say, had begun its long advance to global supremacy. Stuart Hall and his colleagues' book *Policing the Crisis* had developed an insightful analysis of what had taken place, and had anticipated, before the 1979 election, the effectiveness of the Thatcherite response to it.[27] The project of *Marxism Today*, in which Robin's writing was influential, was to understand the reasons for this defeat and to identify potentials for positive development in this critical situation.[28]

It is notable that 'Fordism' came to be theorised as a historically specific system or regime only in hindsight, at the point of its disintegration and overthrow. 'The Owl of Minerva' (as Hegel wrote) 'spreads its wings only in the falling of the dusk', in this instance as in others. A widespread and understandable reaction on the left to its defeat by the Thatcherites was to do all that was possible to defend the gains which had been achieved in the postwar welfare settlement, and to resist the waves of attacks on it from the right. (Anti-trade union legislation, privatisation of publicly owned assets, council house sales, financial deregulation, attacks on the autonomy of professions etc.) The miners' strike of 1984-5 can be seen in these terms as an essentially defensive action, even if Arthur Scargill's aspirations were more radical. This was an embattled defence from the left of the positive elements of the post-war Fordist system and the compromises between capital and labour, mediated by the state, on which it had rested.

Robin's model of 'post-Fordism', and *Marxism Today's* critique of Labourism were based on the view that the Fordist regime had collapsed under its own contradictions, and that to merely attempt its restoration was futile. Thatcherism was even grudgingly admired by Stuart Hall and other MT writers, because of its success in capturing dynamic aspects of the present situation and in devising its own hegemonic strategy. From MT's point of view, the necessity was for a 'New Left' (this was the post-1950s tradition from which MT had evolved) to achieve a revolution in socialist theory and practice comparable to that which the New Right were accomplishing. It is notable how much of MT and Robin's critique was directed against what they saw as regressive and unthinking aspects of 'Labourism' – for example, its top-down model of nationalisation, its complacency about working class identifications, its bureaucratic methods of government and service provision. They not only attacked the possessive individualism and authoritarianism of the right; Labourism, they held, had manifested many of the deficiencies of the Fordist system in which its politics had achieved their greatest success, and this now accounted in part for its loss of popular support. Many on the 'old left' were critical of MT's positions, holding that Hall and others were mistaken in representing Thatcherism as a new formation, and that they were over-estimating its popular support. There was an argument to which Hall responded, that Hall and his colleagues were too 'culturalist' in their approach and were insufficiently attentive to persisting conflicts of material interests.[29] However, the long hegemony of neoliberal ideology which followed the early breakthrough of the 'New Right' suggests that Thatcherism's first analysts had correctly understood its powers.

There were some affinities between the critique of 'old left' assumptions and beliefs which were set out in MT, including in articles by Robin, and the criticisms set out by New Labour of old labour and the traditional left. Indeed, MT's critiques provided some unintended legitimation for New Labour's programme. For example, there were parallels between the ideas of 'active welfare', put forward by New Labour's leading theorist and public intellectual, Anthony Giddens, and the critique of 'Fordist' models of welfare advanced by Robin and others.[30] After 1997 there was an estrangement between New Labour and some of the leading members of the MT group, who became among New Labour's severest critics. (The cover of the post-closure MT Special Issue in 1998 featured a photograph of Tony Blair and the word WRONG). However Robin, though no doubt agreeing with much of this critique, remained at a distance from these sometimes bitter exchanges, and indeed continued to work productively with some of those, such as Geoff Mulgan, who held a significant position in the Cabinet Office of the New Labour government, as well as with its critics.

Robin's argument for an emergent 'post-Fordist' mode of production and consumption attempted to redefine the politics of the left in terms relevant to the present. It sought to outline a progressive alternative to a Fordist system which it held to be in long-term decline, in opposition to the counter-revolutionary alternative to it which had taken command. The model of 'flexibly specialised production', among whose pioneers, in Robin's view, were the Toyota car manufacturing corporation in Japan, and Channel Four's devolved commissioning system for television programme-making, enhanced the diversity and quality of goods, and also involved a more active and participative engagement of workers in their making, compared with Taylorist systems of production. It had become advantageous to manufacturers to recognise the capabilities and engagement of their workers as critical assets to be developed, rather than viewing them as quasi-robotic cogs in a machine. Hence the Toyota and Volvo invention of 'Quality Circles' to make use of the expertise of their workforce. (The idea of active work-force participation became central to Robin's later economic thinking and practice, in virtually every field of his work.) This model was Robin's response to the de-skilling thesis which Braverman had advanced, which had presupposed, without using the term, a Fordist mode of production.

Another key influence on Robin's work was the description of the modes of production in the 'Third Italy' that was set out in Charles Sabel and Michael Piore's book, *The Second Industrial Divide*.[31] This described the form of enterprise which had evolved in central

Italy, in the production of various kinds of consumer product, for example ceramics, furniture, and leather goods. Central to this model were forms of 'co-operative competition' between firms located in proximity to one another in industrial districts, and making shared use of specific services (research, marketing etc.) which it was not feasible for individual companies to provide for themselves. These were often family-based firms, employing a core of highly skilled workers on a long-term basis. Robin saw that autonomous productive cells could be enabled to function success-fully in a larger system, if support functions were shared within a consortium. The local and regional governments of this region of central Italy had been largely Communist, since the war, and the 'Third Italy' was an example therefore not only of relatively benign and mutually-supportive relations between labour and capital, but also of the enabling role of the local state.

Robin observed in the 'Third Italy' not only a 'post-Fordist' model of capitalist production, but also of fully co-operative enterprises, which became an increasingly important focus in his work. In writing about social innovation and social enterprise he refers to examples such as the Third Italy, the Grameen group of companies in Bangladesh, and to the large Mondragon cooperative system in Spain.[32] In his *Co-operation in the Age of Google*, a report written in 2010 for Co-Operatives UK, he described the exemplary Mondragon development at some length.[33]

Another important influence on Robin's work arose from the contexts in which he chose to study and work after his encounter with neoclassical economics. These included not only centres for collec-tive learning such as the LSE, but also the College of Europe where he studied European Studies in 1962-63, and the London Business School where he taught economics between 1966 and 1970. Central to the curricula and teaching methods of Business Studies are case studies, often of firms and their strategic problems, distinct from the more abstract and generalising approaches of the economics discipline. Leading business schools, such as those of Harvard and Stanford University, now make their exemplary case studies avail-able online. Between 1970 and 1993 Robin worked for the Institute for Development Studies at Sussex, where much of his work consisted of economic consultancy to governments and non-governmental clients in Cyprus, Ethiopia and Jamaica, and many other developing countries, for which he wrote many research papers. He was always notably internationalist in his outlook – his pioneering work on multi-national companies and their transfer pricing policies was another aspect of this.[34] The fair trade movement, in which he was a leading figure, can be understood as a radical democratic response to the problems which had been left behind by colonisation. Later he became a mainly freelance researcher and consultant, conducting investigations, writing reports, and providing advice and guidance to many different associations and organisations. He was also a social entrepreneur, co-founding Twin and Twin Trading,[35] through which the fair trade brands Divine Chocolate, Cafédirect and Liberation Foods were developed. There are affinities between the case-study methods of business studies and consultancy practice, and the approach to historical study, with its respect for particulars and the historically specific, which Robin may have absorbed while reading history at Balliol.

In fact, particulars, examples and 'cases' appear in nearly all of Robin's writing, as readers of this book will see, and demonstrate the close link between his professional practice as a researcher, teacher and consultant and his ongoing involvement as a participant and activist. This is to be seen in his work with Frances Murray and others in Brighton in the 1970s, where they set up QueenSpark, an East Brighton community association. This had many activities, including oral history-writing by local residents, a campaign against the Brighton Marina, and a book documenting the effects of austerity on Brighton.[36] When he later moved to the London Borough of Hackney in the 1990s, he campaigned to reverse a council decision (in 2000) to close the Haggerston Public Baths, which had first opened in 1904. This campaign failed – the baths were not reopened under the council's 2017 restoration plan. The last community action in which Robin engaged with great feeling before he died was a campaign to convert the threatened local post office in Hallbankgate, near his family home in Cumbria, into a co-operative. Robin's work always involved visits to and research in a specific 'field' or place.

His writing, reports and recommendations would emerge from innumerable conversations and interviews, as well as extensive reference to data. He brought an admirable warmth, interest and enthusiasm to his encounters. This was his practice in all his spheres of work, as Chief Economic Adviser at the GLC, in the fair trade movement, in his support for farmers in developing countries, in the campaign for recycling and zero waste, and in his work with cooperatives. In his advocacy of alternative forms of production, social action, or organisation, he would usually describe examples of where something similar or relevant was being done. For this reason, as readers of this collection will see, Robin's writings are usually full of illustrative detail and are often inspirational for this reason.

However, this method of developing arguments from cases, however numerous and vivid these are, has its limitations as well as strengths. By referring to many examples of particular practices, Robin was well able to demonstrate how innovative a particular approach had been. But to show the admirable qualities of a practice, or indeed that it actually exists and thrives, does not in itself establish its larger applicability. For example, 'flexible specialisation' is undoubtedly an important form of production and can bring benefits both to producers and consumers. But how extensive or dominant as a mode of production is it, compared with others with which it must compete? The contention of Robin's argument was that post-Fordism was not merely one variant among several competing forms of production but was becoming the *dominant* form in our time. However, no amount of examples can, by themselves, establish its *relative* importance in an economy. Similar issues of method arose when Robin came later to write about emerging forms of cooperative and social economies. One can be convinced that they are exemplary and inspiring, but that is different from assessing their potential role in the larger system, in their unavoidable competition with conventional economic forms.

A considerable amount of Robin's work, especially in the years before the mid 1990s, was written to influence political debate. This was the case for his early work with the *May Day Manifesto*, as Director of Industry and Employment at the GLC from 1982 to 1986, and as Special Adviser to the Minister of Economic Development and Trade in the Government of Ontario from 1993 to 1995. Much of his consultancy work during his two decades with IDS in Sussex was undertaken to advise or influence governments, for example in Jamaica, Honduras and Cyprus, and in post-Communist Eastern Europe. He produced many reports of this work in many countries. Robin's earlier articles were published in journals and collections which had an explicitly socialist commitment (e.g. *Capital and Class*, *Marxism Today*, Spokesman Books, Fabian Essays), while his later work most often appeared in publications associated with 'social movements', social enterprise, and projects of 'social innovation'. But there are many connections between these phases of his work, and no repudiation of his earlier commitments.

In this earlier phase of Robin's work, the theory of 'post-Fordism', which had its foundations in his reading of Marx, was central. Robin sought to articulate the conception of a 'post-Fordist' mode of production and to support it as a practice. His aim was to empower workers, enhance the quality of products and their use, and establish alternatives both to the authoritarian individualism of the right, and to the outmoded forms of social democracy of the traditional left. He also critically described the 'Fordist' approach to production which dominated the Soviet and East European economies.[37] At the GLC, he supported industrial restructuring at a firm-by-firm level, popular economic planning, design-led innovation, and the adoption of new technologies, in the interests of the workforce as well as of firms' owners. The aim of these many interventions was to support development from below. His approach was an economics based on practice. However, *Marxism Today*'s project failed in its larger political purpose, as New Labour took its own different and more neoliberal path. The GLC was abolished in 1986, having had far too little time (four years only) under Livingstone's leadership to be able to achieve much of economic substance.[38] Its legacy was to be an example of what an inclusive and enabling democratic municipality was capable of achieving, if it were given the opportunity, and Robin describes many initiatives of the GLC which anticipated future developments.[39] These included the inclusion of women, ethnic minorities, and sexual diversity in its programmes. Its focus on distinct sectors of production as the key to economic strategy – for example in its recognition of the importance of the cultural and food industries to London – shows what was lacking during the years of New Labour government.

After these significant defeats, the focus of Robin's work shifted somewhat. Work with regional and local governments continued, with the SEEDS local authority consortium in south-east England, with the Government of Ontario in the 1980s, on waste management with Nicky Gavron and the London Mayor's Office in the 1990s, and in consultancy projects for IDS, and with the City of Seoul in the 2010s. But during this period Robin became more active in social movements whose primary activities lay outside the governmental sphere. These included the fair trade movement, the zero waste campaign, and various initiatives concerned with social innovation, undertaken with Nesta and the Young Foundation, and a large study for the Co-operative Movement intended to stimulate its rejuvenation.

Several chapters in this collection describe this work. Robin also taught at the Schumacher College, an institution committed to decentralised social initiatives. Continuities with his earlier work are to be seen in the importance in all of them of quality of labour processes. For example, in his anti-waste campaigns, Robin counterposed the centralised and polluting technology of incinerators (Robin did not hate many things, but incinerators were one of them) with a model of domestic waste-collection in which householders would voluntarily undertake the sorting of their own waste. In the fair trade movement, some of the competitive advantage which he hoped 'fair trade' producers could gain were to come from a labour process in which farmers would produce higher-quality products, with cooperative methods of production and marketing. The ideas of co-operation, social innovation and a 'social economy' have as their essence work based on community benefit, rather than on private profit for individuals. Yet such work, in the contemporary economic environment, had to be undertaken in relation to markets.

This change of context gave rise to a partial theoretical reorientation in Robin's work. While this continued to be informed by his 'post-Fordist' perspective, another tradition, associated with Karl Polanyi and E.F. Schumacher rather than Marx, became important to his thinking. Polanyi's *The Great Transformation* was a history of capitalism which described the destruction of an earlier 'moral economy', and the supplanting of a pre-industrial system organised according to norms of social responsibility, by one of amoral and predatory individualism.[40] This transformation had always been an important theme in the writings of socialist historians, for example in Edward Thompson's work on the 'moral economy'.[41] It is evident too in Christopher Hill's descriptions of the normative changes brought about by capitalism (the imposition through the Puritan religious influence of work discipline and the curtailment of the religious and social customs of communities) and Richard Tawney's ethical socialist perspective.[42] Robin was also influenced by Stephen Yeo's work on the defeat of institutions of working-class co-operation by the rise of the state, and the domination of the Labour Party by the Fabian tradition.[43] Robin's engagement with Polanyi's work brought a more ethically-focused and 'voluntarist' emphasis to his writing and practice. If governments and political parties were not of themselves going to bring about major changes, Robin concluded, then one must look to voluntary and co-operative movements for initiatives. But this is, after all, where Robin had started, with the QueenSpark community activities in Brighton in the 1970s, and, in support of independent trade union action, his analysis of the Upper Clyde Shipbuilders bankruptcy.[44]

'Post-Fordism' was originally viewed by Robin in Marxist terms (in its Regulation School form) as a new phase of capitalist development, possessing competitive advantages over its Fordist predecessor, as well as preferable in its relational aspects. But his commitment to initiatives such as fair trade, zero-waste, cooperation, and social innovation based on improved design[45] and enhanced participation rested on their intrinsic desirability, as much as on any competitive advantages they might bring in a market system. Their benefits were formulated in holistic, collective terms. A zero-waste system of total recycling is beneficial and necessary for entire societies, but it is not motivated by goals of market advantage such as Toyota and Benetton hoped to gain a 'flex spec' mode of production.

Robin nevertheless believed that co-operative methods and labour processes which released the creativity of workers, could enable producers to hold their own in market environments. He remained a realist and did not believe that the 'law of value' could be completely ignored in the global economy, as it now is. He tried to introduce co-operative institutions – in Britain and abroad – to modern methods of production and distribution to enable them to sustain their practices and their values within modern market environments. He thought that adaptation to Fordist methods of production had in fact greatly damaged co-operation as an approach to work, reproducing hierarchy and standardisation as the price of commercial survival. He believed that post-Fordist approaches to production and distribution could be a means to co-operative renewal.

Nevertheless, it should be noted that the forms of economic activity which Robin supported often seemed to depend on a measure of public altruism to sustain them. Fair trade and Twin Trading products, like the co-operative farmer-owned Divine Chocolate and Cafedirect, were designed to be of good quality, but their marketing approach invited purchases to pay a small 'ethical premium', to support fairer forms of exchange between developing country producers and their western customers. Commercial retailers with little intrinsic interest in these principles have sometimes added 'fair trade' to their range of brands, seeking to achieve a commercial gain from customer's ethical preferences, while giving little support other than as buyers to the farmers. By contrast Twin Trading helped to sustain the networks which enabled the farmers to produce and trade.

Thus, many of the initiatives in which Robin became engaged were morally constituted and motivated and were often inspiring. He saw in them the seeds of a new 'social economy', based on relational and cooperative principles and empowered by the new information technologies. The revival of the idea of the 'commons' whose enclosure was important in Polanyi's work has become an important theme in contemporary debate. In a 2016 Schumacher podcast (see note 39) Robin compared this phase of their development to that of the small enterprises described by Adam Smith, which had eventually grown to become the dominant economic system of capitalism. Robin had earlier seen the post-Fordist economy in a similar light, as an emerging form of production able to succeed in the market because of the advantage which its technologies and modes of organisation conferred on it. I am not sure whether it is at this point realistic to see the 'social economy' in these terms of potential competitive advantage, rather than in terms of the aspirations and ideals it demonstrates in a variety of practices.

Robin remained keenly interested in these larger issues, alongside his activist commitments. His belief that a new social or civil economy might have a socio-technological as well as a moral basis drew on the work of Carlota Perez and her view of 'long-wave' economic developments, which derived from the writings of Schumpeter and Kondratieff.[46] He addressed these issues in his articles 'Danger and opportunity' (2009) and 'Global civil society and the rise of the civil economy' (2012), and in his interview with Jeremy Gilbert and Andrew Goffey in *New Formations*, reproduced as Chapters 8, 9 and 12 of this collection.[47] In this interview, Robin discusses the appearance of what he called 'post-post-Fordism', the phenomenon of the platform economy whose dominant players include Amazon, Google, Facebook, and Netflix.

The technologies in question here are information-based, allowing (perhaps) disseminated modes of small-scale production, linked 'horizontally' with one another and directly with consumers, and able to dispense with 'middlemen' or wholesalers, and the control they exercise over markets, and the value they extract from transactions. These technologies do make possible, through electronic ordering, distributed storage, and production on demand, a greater diversity of products and thus extended consumer choice. Whereas earlier forms of mass production offered only highly restricted ranges of products, first 'flex spec' and now the platforms enlarge this range in almost unlimited ways, since the new means of supply and distribution overcome many limits of space and time. (This is the so-called 'long tail effect', extending the 'shelf-life' of many products.) For many kinds of 'information goods', supply can be virtually instant. Thus, Airbnb will find accommodation in a flash, booked in one part of the world to be to be occupied in another. Online newspapers can be read all over the world. Many information-based products, such as music, software or written work can be virtually costless to reproduce and distribute (the phenomenon of zero marginal costs). But this has not stopped most published academic journal articles being accessible only at prohibitive prices, or via the exclusionary privilege of university library memberships. Among the ideas and practices which greatly interested Robin in this later phase of his work were those of Michel Bauwens, and his conception of peer-to-peer (PtoP) production, together with the development of the commons,[48] and Laloux's analysis of different forms of organisation, including Fordism and post-Fordism, and the Buurtzorg model of neighbourhood home care in the Netherlands.[49]

In some ways this 'post-post-Fordist' system, which Jeremy Gilbert refers to as 'cognitive and communicative capitalism', does enfranchise publics.[50] Democratic radicals have argued that this makes possible new forms of mobilisation, with nearly-instantaneous communication through social media taking the place of slow mechanisms of printed circulations of documents, face-to-face meetings, and delegated representation. The more sceptical point out that the unrestricted communication and freedom to choose it makes possible is also an agent of the fragmentation of publics, allowing people to avoid, rather than engage, with lifeworlds of others. A celebration of the political potential of the new media was Paul Mason's acclamation of the popular revolts of the Arab Spring, which in those instances ended badly in the face of the resistance of coercive forms of power.[51] But other political movements, such as Extinction Rebellion and strikes for climate action by school-children seem to be doing much better, having in the shortest imaginable time enabled a young Swedish girl, Greta Thunberg, to become the inspirer of global activism.

Robin once recommended that I learn about the 'zero marginal cost economy' (the title of a book by Jeremy Rifkin) as a glimpse into a possible future.[52] This is the hypothesis that modern methods of computer-guided production may drastically reduce the costs of production of many commodities (as it has reduced the real cost of disseminating information) to virtually zero. 3-D printing is one element of this – the idea that citizens may become able to 'print out' (just as now happens in factories) many of the products and commodities that they might wish to possess. This would be a further extension of a 'prosumer' economy that, as Robin states in the *New Formations* interview (see Chapter 12), has already come into being, dissolving the boundaries between production and consumption as households and associations could provide for their own needs. We can customise our own Dell computer or car online, and order it as we would like it to be; assemble our own furniture in flatpack form, design our own holidays (contributing to the end of package holiday firms like the 184-year-old Thomas Cook) and can find guidance online from anonymous fellow-citizens which can tell us how to solve innumerable practical problems.

Some believe that this development signifies the decline and fall of the capitalist mode of production. Will it mean it will no longer be possible to extract surplus value and thus capitalist profits from people, if fewer and fewer people will need to be employed as wage workers to produce goods and services for sale? Does a post-post Fordist mode of production mean the virtual end of capitalism as a social system? But wage-labour seems rather unlikely to disappear, although perhaps its preponderance as a mode of economic life may diminish. It will, in an optimistic view, be displaced by forms of voluntary and co-operative social exchange. Or in a more dystopian perspective, it could give rise to widespread redundancy and social exclusion – large populations that will at best find themselves pensioned off.

The development of the 'platform economy' discloses another extremely serious problem, and another source of inequality and exploitation, distinct from the potential control of information by multinational digital corporations. This is the return of rent as the primary means through which disproportionate amounts of wealth are sequestered by the owners of assets, and which then become the main cause of inequalities. Given Robin's writings from the seventies about the theory of rent this is surely an issue that he would have taken serious note of. Rents are defined as extracted flows of income larger than those needed to secure supply. They arise from closed and monopolised access to resources of different kinds. The principal corporations of the platform economy appropriate enormous rents in return for access to their digital platforms. There is rent extraction that arises from the ownership of land and real estate, and of financial assets. And from closed access to intellectual property, such as the patented medicines owned by the pharmaceutical companies, which determine what medicines are produced and to whom they are made available.[53] An economy dominated by the extraction of rent may become even be more unequal and pernicious than one dominated by invested capital, since capitalist relations of production necessarily confer at least *some* power on those who labour in return for wages.

Thus, on the one hand, one sees the emancipatory effects and possibilities of enhanced information and its productive power. But on the other, there is the potential for an extreme polarisation between a minority of those who own and monopolise scarce assets, and a majority of displaced persons who own nothing, and whose labour-power has no value. Nor is to be taken in the least for granted that the 'means of information' will be in common supply, taking into account the oligarchic ownership of many forms of communication. Or that the larger part of the world's population will be enabled to obtain the kinds and qualities of education which will enable them to gain access to information and to make use of it.

This is the critical contemporary situation which one would have very much liked Robin Murray to help us to understand and act upon.

Notes

1 I am grateful to Julie Simon for her valuable advice on this introduction.
2 Fine descriptions of Robin Murray and his influence on some of those who worked with him can be found at https://www.nesta. org.uk/blog/celebrating-the-life-and-work-of-robin-murray/. In an interview at the Schumacher College, 2016, Robin Murray gives an account of his own development, including his work at the Institute of Development Studies, at the GLC, and with cooperative and other social movements. The podcast can be found here: https://www. shareable.net/podcast-late-environmental-economist-robin-murrays-views-on-creating-a-new-economy/.
3 Greater London Council, *LIS: London Industrial Strategy*, GLC, 1985. An open access version of the strategy can be viewed here: https:// ecommons.cornell.edu/handle/1813/45891 (hereafter LIS).
4 Much of Robin's unpublished writing has being gathered and edited for publication in an online archive: www.robinmurray.co.uk. A full bibliography of his work is at https://en.wikipedia.org/wiki/Robin_ Murray (economist).
5 There are some parallels between the purposes and methods of Robin Murray's work, and those of Stuart Hall, whose *Selected*

Political Writings, London: Lawrence and Wishart, 2017, preceded this collection in a book series dedicated to prominent left thinkers associated with Lawrence and Wishart. Stuart Hall, as Director of the Centre of Contemporary Cultural Studies, and Professor of Sociology at the Open University for many years, was far more fully embedded in university environments, and influential within them, than Robin, who worked across so many different spheres.

6   LIS; Greater London Council, *London Labour Plan*, London: GLC, 1986; SEEd Association of Local Authorities, *Re-inventing Waste: Towards a London Waste Strategy*, Ecologika, 1998, *Creating Wealth from Waste*, Demos, 1999, *Zero Waste*, Greenpeace, 2002; *The Fair Trade Revolution*, London: Pluto, 2010; *Co-Operation in the Age of Google*, Co-operatives UK, 2010.

7   Three of Robin's ground-breaking contributions to *Marxism Today* are reproduced in this collection: 'Benetton Britain: The new economic order', *Marxism Today*, Nov 1985, pp28-32; 'Life after Henry (Ford)', *Marxism Today*, Oct 1988, pp8-13; 'The state after Henry', *Marxism Today*, May 1991, pp22-27.

8   Robin said that one inspiration for this was his interest as an undergraduate in the economy of the medieval monasteries.

9   Stuart Hall, Edward Thompson and Raymond Williams, *The May Day Manifesto*, 1967. The manifesto was republished a year later under the editorship of Raymond Williams. Available open access: https://www.lwbooks.co.uk/sites/default/files/free-book/Mayday.pdf

10   See for example Alfred Sohn-Rethel, *Intellectual and Manual Labour: A Critique of Epistemology*, New Jersey: Humanities Press, 1978.

11   S. Clarke, *Marx, Marginalism and Modern Sociology: From Adam Smith to Max Weber,* Basingstoke: Palgrave Macmillan, 1991; M. Mazzucato, *The Value of Everything: Making and Taking in the Global Economy*, London: Allen Lane, 2017.

12   Robin Murray, 'Value and theory of rent: Part one', *Capital & Class*, Vol 1, No.3, 1977, pp100-122; 'Value and theory of rent: Part two', *Capital and Class*, Vol. 2, No. 1, 1978, pp9-33.

13   H. Braverman, *Labour and Monopoly Capitalism: The Degradation of Work in the Twentieth Century*, New York: Monthly Review Press, 1974.

14   Edward Thompson, *The Making of the English Working Class*, London: Victor Gollancz, 1963.

15   'The state after Henry', *Marxism Today*, May 1991, pp 22-27 (Chapter 3 of this collection).

16   F. Hayek, *The Road to Serfdom,* London: Routledge, 2008 [1944].

17 Robin Murray, 'New directions in municipal socialism', Chapter 15 of Ben Pimlott (ed.), *Fabian Essays in Socialist Thought,* Fabian Society, London: Heinemann, 1984, reprinted in this volume as Chapter 4, p88.

18 It is continuing failures to address problems in the sphere of production, and the economic weakness which has followed from this, which explains Britain's vulnerability to financial crises.

19 A. Crosland, *The Future of Socialism,* London: Jonathan Cape, 1956.

20 Raymond Williams, *The May Day Manifesto,* Harmondsworth: Penguin, 1968.

21 Robin Murray, 'New directions in municipal socialism', in B. Pimlott (ed.), *Fabian Essays in Socialist Thought,* Heineman, 1984 (Chapter 4 in this book) (Hereafter: *New Directions*).

22 The open access archive is available on the Amiel-Melburn Trust website: http://banmarchive.org.uk/collections/mt/index_frame.htm

23 A. Gramsci, *Selections from the Prison Notebooks of Antonio Gramsci,* edited and translated by Quintin Hoare and Geoffrey Nowell Smith, London: Lawrence & Wishart, 1971.

24 'Benetton Britain: The new economic order', *Marxism Today,* Nov. 1985, pp28-32; 'Public sector possibilities', *Marxism Today,* July 1986, pp28-32; 'Life after Henry (Ford)', *Marxism Today,* Oct 1988, pp8-13; 'The state after Henry', *Marxism Today,* May 1991, pp22-27.

25 I. Gough, *The Political Economy of the Welfare State,* Basingstoke: Palgrave Macmillan, 1979.

26 The Regulation School developed a model of capitalism's historical development, identifying its different phases, one of which they defined as Fordism. They were influenced by structuralist approaches in which the economy is understood as but one element (even if 'in the last instance' the decisive one), in a complex social system. Their influence on left thinking paralleled that of Gramsci and Althusser in the 1970s and 1980s: see B. Jessop and S. Ngai-Ling, *Beyond The Regulation Approach: Putting Capitalist Economies in their Place,* London: Edward Elgar, 2006; M. Aglietta, *The Theory of Capitalist Regulation: The US Experience,* London: Verso, 1979; A. Lipietz, 'Towards global Fordism', *New Left Review* 1/182, March-April 1982; R. Boyer, *The Regulation School: A Critical Introduction,* New York: Columbia University Press, 1990.

27 S. Hall, C. Critcher, T, Jefferson, J. Clarke, B. Roberts, *Policing the Crisis: Mugging, the State and Law and Order,* Basingstoke: Palgrave Macmillan, 2013 [1978].

28 Two of Robin Murray's articles – *Fordism and Post-Fordism* and *Benetton Britain* – have a scene-setting place in a key *Marxism Today*

anthology edited by Stuart Hall and Martin Jacques, *New Times: The Changing Face of Politics in the 1990s*, London: Verso, 1989, pp39-64.

29 B. Jessop, T. Ling, S. Bromley, K. Bonnett, 'Authoritarian populism, two nations, and Thatcherism', *New Left Review* 1/147, 1984; 'Thatcherism and the politics of hegemony: A reply to Stuart Hall', *New Left Review*, 1.153, 1985; S. Hall, 'Authoritarian populism: A reply', *New Left Review*, 1/151, 1985.

30 A. Giddens, *The Third Way: The Renewal of Social Democracy*, Cambridge: Polity Press, 1998 set out this perspective; it came out at the same time as a Fabian pamphlet by Tony Blair with the same title.

31 M. Piore, C. Sabel, *The Second Industrial Divide: Possibilities for Prosperity*, New York: Basic Books, 1984.

32 'Post-Post-Fordism in the era of platforms: Robin Murray talks to Jeremy Gilbert and Andrew Goffey', *New Formations*, 84/85, 2015, pp5-19 (Chapter 12 in this volume).

33 Robin Murray, *Cooperation in the Age of Google*, Co-operatives UK, 2010.

34 Murray, *Multi-National Companies and Nation-States: Two Essays*. Nottingham: Spokesman Books, 1975.

35 Twin Trading began its life at the GLC, as the Third World Information Network (TWIN).

36 QueenSpark Rates Book Group, *Brighton on the Rocks: Monetarism and the Local State*, Brighton: QueenSpark Books, 1983.

37 A. Joffe, R. Murray, S. Sips, 'Fordism and socialist development', Institute of Development Studies, University of Sussex, 1990.

38 There may have been element of contingency in the GLC's abolition. Thatcher had won an election in 1983 and was now powerful enough to implement her full programme. The GLC was both defiant and provocative, displaying banners with London's unemployment figures on the roof of County Hall opposite the Houses of Parliament. The Miners' Strike had just been defeated. The Provisional IRA's Brighton Hotel bombing, aimed at Thatcher and her entire government, had killed five Conservatives in 1984, while Livingstone was known to be sympathetic to Sinn Fein, and of course had advocated the process of dialogue which led to the Good Friday Agreement of 1998, at a time when such contacts were off the official agenda. Even then, there was wide resistance to the abolition of a major tier of government. In less exceptional circumstances, such an arbitrary act by a government would hardly have been politically feasible.

39 Murray, 'Creating a new economy: Interview at Schumacher College', 2016. Podcast at https://www.shareable.net podcast-late-environmental-economist-robin-murrays-views-on-creating-a-new-economy/

40 K. Polanyi, *The Great Transformation: The Political and Economic Origins of Our Time*, New York: Beacon Press, 2002 [1944]. Robin Murray refers to Polanyi's discussion of counter-movements to nineteenth-century market liberalism in his discussion of contemporary co-operatives and community economic developments in 'Global civil society and the rise of the civil economy' in M. Kaldor, H. Moore, S. Selchow (eds), *Global Civil Society 2012: Ten Years of Critical Reflection*, Basingstoke: Palgrave Macmillan, 2012, pp144-64. (Reproduced as Chapter 9 of this collection.)

41 In E. Thompson's *The Making of the English Working Class* and in an influential paper: E.P. Thompson, 'The moral economy of the crowd in the eighteenth century', *Past & Present*, Vol. 50, Issue 1, February 1971, pp76-136.

42 C. Hill, *Society and Puritanism in Pre-Revolutionary England*, London: Verso, 2018 [1964]; R.H. Tawney, *Equality*, London: Unwin Books, 1931.

43 S. Yeo (ed.), *New Views of Co-operation*, London: Routledge, 1988.

44 Robin Murray, *UCS: The Anatomy of Bankruptcy*. Nottingham: Bertrand Russell Peace Foundation, 1972.

45 Robin worked for the Design Council for a year in 2004-05 using design principles to improve the quality and effectiveness of health and other services.

46 C Perez, *Technological Revolutions and Financial Capital: The Dynamics of Bubbles and Golden Ages*, London: Edward Elgar, 2003.

47 The *Global Civil Society Yearbook* series published annually since 2001 and edited by Mary Kaldor and others, is a key source of writings on the civil economy, and on issues of global governance more broadly.

48 M.Bauwens & V.Kostakis, *Network Society and Future Scenarios for a Collaborative Economy*, London: Palgrave Pivot, 2014.

49 F. Laloux, *Reinventing Organisations*, London: Nelson Parker, 2016.

50 Jeremy Gilbert and Andrew Goffey interview with Robin Murray in 2015 (see Chapter 12).

51 P. Mason, *Postcapitalism: A Guide to our Future*, London: Allen Lane, 2015.

52 J. Rifkin, *The Zero Marginal Cost Society: The Internet of Things, the Collaborative Commons and the Eclipse of Capitalism*. New York, Palgrave, 2014.

53 The significance of this emerging economy of rents is discussed in a review by John Grahl in *New Left Review* 113, Sept-Oct 2018, of Philippe Askenazy, *Tous rentiers! Pour une autre répartition des richesses*, Paris: Odile Jacob, 2016.

Robin Murray (1940-2017): A friend's appreciation

Stephen Yeo

From the first time we met as history undergraduates in Oxford in 1959, I delighted in Robin's company. He was lucky enough to be studying with Christopher Hill at Balliol. We had both been through phases of wanting to do a degree in English: too much pure pleasure! I later learned that Robin had been a fine Hamlet at school. He was to move through history to a committedly historical engagement with economics and Marxism, an engagement manifest in this book. I was to move through Oxford history to engage with the social history of labour movements and 'history from below', inspired by History Workshops and continuing my professional life at Ruskin College and then at the Co-operative College.

The term 'professional life', I would suggest, doesn't quite fit Robin's trajectory: *poiesis* is better. This is the Greek word – in origin as material as woodwork – for 'making'. It is where the English word 'poetry' comes from. One of Robin's most-favoured words was 'production'. In this brief appreciation – part of a longer whole – I will concentrate on two phases of the *sui generis*, productive life he lived: a period in Brighton in the 1970s and 1980s, and then onto the period of his illness during 2016 and (until his death) 2017, when breath and voice, pivotal to his presence in the world, became difficult. Even then, he never lost his capacity to listen patiently, to take and give ideas with anyone, however young, and to laugh out loud – in wonder rather than anger – while continuing to talk.

Towards the end of his life, thinking aloud with spontaneous clarity took over, for example on the nature of money or the social economy emergent within morbid capitalisms. He would talk and ask about what character of cells – forms of association – would be needed if socialism was ever to in-form the whole body, economic and political. Having discovered that *hematopoiesis* is the medical term currently used for the process through which the body manufactures blood cells, I now connect this line of enquiry with Robin and Frances Murray's commitment to an alternative, rather than allopathic, approach to human disease.

Throughout his life, enquiring and listening, being fully present with the diverse others he co-operated with, projecting onto, while celebrating them (us), were skills he had in abundance: in a word, mutuality, *The Making of ...* mutuality. Robin had no condescension in him and, like the working class in Edward Thompson's celebrated preface to *The Making of the English Working Class*, he was fully present at everyone's 'own making'.

Robin was a *social* materialist, in the strongest, early-nineteenth-century, Owenite sense of *social*. Like the Rochdale Pioneers in the 1840s, he was committed to 'arranging the powers of production, distribution, education and government' by labour in its own class interest, against capital. He put the last two – education and government – on the same plane as the first two, foregrounding *agency* (hence arranging rather than nationalising) within and beyond, in and against structure and system.

The system or -*ism*, capitalism with its 'law of value', was out there, well understood as such. But it was to be infringed, warranted, displaced and replaced, reasoned within and beyond on a daily, local (located) basis. 'The reproduction of daily life' was a phrase used in the Murray household. How to do things differently? Material production and distribution included meanings and associational forms: literary, cultural, communicative, political, edible – every *thing* (including wellbeing) being seen also as a *relation*.

How to succeed the commodity form? How to replace the 'real subordination of labour'? Subordination was not Robin's thing, home or away. How to make capital a servant of labour here and now, in the short term, as well as elsewhere in the *longue duree*. Practical answers meant tactical acceptance, preparing to speak truth to the powers that be, tomorrow, next week, as well as strategically rejecting their would-be-permanent, proprietorial claims to 'take power', whether by election or revolution.

Following meetings in London in 1967 and 1968, working towards the Penguin edition of the *May Day Manifesto*, we got to know each more closely – with families, young children and mutual friends – in the Hanover, Queen's Park area of East Brighton where we lived, and at the University of Sussex, where we worked for the following two decades. This is where *QueenSpark* campaigns, newspaper, books, shop and the Hanover Centre grew, animated in large part by women, notably Frances Murray.

I taught history at Sussex between 1966 and 1989 before leaving Brighton for Ruskin College. In the days before the Research Assessment Exercise – and the management of universities as if they were either subject to a Politburo or sought promotion to a World Class Super-League – there was time, in and against the academy, for conception and execution, for heads and hands to work together.

So we used our time, for example in reading groups on *Capital Volume 1*. We were preoccupied with the labour process in Marxist theory, yes, but also with ITT Creed, the telecommunications firm in Brighton. We organised against EMI's bid to Brighton Council to enclose parts of the seashore for profit, for Brighton Marina. (They won, in spite of a three-day inquiry at the town hall, animated by Robin.) We worked on a campaign to Save Our Schools from cuts imposed by East Sussex County Council and on Brighton Council's preference for a casino in a crumbling Regency Spa in Queens Park, as against the local community's demand for a nursery school. (We won, in spite of lukewarm support from Labour).

QueenSpark work teams, made up of students as well as long-term, older, working class residents, came together to make life stories from below by Katherine Browne, Albert Paul, Daisy Noakes, Les Moss, Jack Langley, Bert Healey (the list continues today), deliberately sold door-to-door rather than in bookshops, along with the community newspaper, *QueenSpark*, numbers one to twenty-one. *Brighton on the Rocks: Monetarism and the Local State* by QueenSpark Rates Book Group followed. This was a photo-graphic, experience-based account of the effects of public spending cuts (austerity *avant le mot*) alongside a Robin-esque essay on political economy, plus pointers to specific ways of taking (back?) control.

Robin was full of the possibilities for labour of pre-digital communications technology: 'means of communication as means of production' in Raymond Williams' formulation. I remember one day in the launderette on Montreal Road, East Brighton, Robin conceiving a complete encyclopedia for labour, years before Wikipedia.

'Community politics' remains to be fully 'read' on the left, particularly after Labour's defeat in December 2019. The 'local' remains to be parsed. It still needs to be rescued, alongside 'the women's movement' and the 'voluntary sector' of the same period, from their standing as tributaries rather than as the socialist mainstream that they constitute. 'The community' as abstraction still finds it hard to earth its contradictory being, realising itself against the big Ps of Politics, Party and 'getting into' Power.

Nostalgia? The idea that radical critiques of *now* can run through a channel of *then* among working, so-called 'ordinary' people. John Berger's 'nostalgia for the future' is not an easy idea. It calls for skilful listening followed by self-conscious, associated 'making'. Berger celebrated *Brighton on the Rocks* in the (then) weekly periodical *New Society*. Reformism? Difficult also is the idea that, for mortals, partial, useable allotments of Somewhere – won through sustained, organised *process* by labour for labour – have an absolute value, in themselves. Achieved reforms matter, even while we take part in old (pre-parliamentary) labour's future-present Co-operative Movement, or delight in Morris's *News from Nowhere*, Trotsky's *History of the Russian Revolution* and Ebenezer Howard on the Garden City movement in *Tomorrow, a Peaceful Path to Social Reform*.

False consciousness? Even more difficult, perhaps, is the idea that poets like Brecht (*d*. 1956) articulated with such skill, that it is capitalism as *system* – turning the world upside down each second of every day wherever its 'law' extends – which determines the fact that contradictory ways of understanding the world by working people – so called 'ordinary' – can seldom look scientifically 'correct' as programmes for changing the world.

*

Robin began his work at the Institute of Development Studies (IDS), University of Sussex in 1970. His specialism – if such a word ever fitted his approach to anything – was the multinational company. He kept his fellowship at the IDS until 1993 sustained by creative secondments, for example to the Greater London Council (GLC). He worked as Director of Industry and Chief Economic Adviser to the GLC during Ken Livingstone's mayoralty from 1982 to 1986, as Michael Rustin relates in his introduction to this book.

Robin's GLC activities – alongside the many people he attracted to develop initiatives such as the Popular Planning Unit – is the socialist work for which he is probably best remembered on the left, although his work as an *animateur* of fair trade and of 'zero waste' (his term) was just as generative. The GLC years were far-sighted and opportunist, practical and visionary, enabling and charismatic, of their time and tailor-made for 2020. 'Why don't you join us?' he would ask his friends, as if building a movement rather than recruiting, say, to Herbert Morrison's London County Council fifty years earlier. Robin's approach was socialist construction hand-in-hand with Marxist theory. Or, as he would say when he came to write *Co-operation in the Age of Google*[1] for Co-ops UK, accumulation for labour. The GLC's presence was such that it *necessitated* abolition in 1986 by the Thatcher government, by means of a *Local* Government Act! When activists are told by policy managers that they cannot 'abolish' public schools or outlaw non-resident, billionaire ownership of land, newspapers, human habitations and football clubs, it is good to recall that County Hall was summarily *sold* by 'government' to the family-owned Shirayama Shokusan Corporation for £60 million. 'Ruthless' was one of Robin's words for the agents of capital, uttered with traces of wonderment in his face: how can we match it?

He had the *chutzpah* – gathering facts at speed, thinking on his feet, encouraging his associates to exceed their self-expectations, careless of his personal 'prospects' – to argue with and get results from waste contractors in the East End of London; the Ethiopian Derg; large-scale corporates like EMI; the Planning Inspectorate; Brighton Corporation and East Sussex County Council; management at the IDS with its 'points system' to measure the productivity of fellows. A complete list would be as endless as a long line in Walt Whitman's forever growing *Leaves of Grass*. By the way, Robin loved

Darwin's final scientific work, *The Formation of Vegetable Mould through the Action of Worms* (1881) reading it in, *mais oui,* 'from below' political terms.

Knowing it in our bones as well as in our heads, there was much collective *making* across and between classes and generations during the 1970s and 1980s in Brighton. Some of this was enabled through what Robin called the grant economy. Following arguments between the Federation of Worker Writers and Community Publishers (FWWCP) and the Arts Council over whether 'community writing' constituted 'literature' – a story well told in *The Republic of Letters*[2] – and, in the case of *QueenSpark*, differences between us and South-East Arts over whether an 'unincorporated voluntary association' was a grant-worthy associational form, *QueenSpark* books got some public funding. There was locally federated work: with a nearby Centre for the Unemployed; with an Adult Literacy Centre in a mid-town Quaker Meeting House and former Adult School; with Queens Park Jaguars' little-league football club; with Brighton Print Centre in a former Congregational chapel; and with Brighton Trades Council for a series of tape-recorded life stories with former activists. All this was seen as prefiguring a transformed state (of affairs) at least as much as protesting against the current one. All-night teach-ins in reaction to external political and funding threats; *workshops* for everything, including for writing at the much-maligned local comprehensive school; popular-memory 'Sparchives' in *QueenSpark* newspaper; Free and Easy readings in the Hanover Centre; published collections of poems by first-time writers. In a word, *poiesia* as production.

Of what? Glyn Maxwell, brought up in Welwyn Garden City, ends a poem in his *Selected Poems*[3] called 'We billion cheered' with these lines:

> Don't forget
>   Nothing will start that hasn't started yet
> Don't forget
>   It, its friend, its foes, and its opposite

Poiesis and its many compounds has recently joined the socialist lexicon, particularly among active practices and theories relating to commoning and 'the commons'. In his book *The Web of Life*,[4] Fritjof Capra uses *autopoiesis* to describe self-making, living systems, biological and social. An entire 'moral economy' – its land, labour, law, currency, dwellings, digital platforms, public and private spaces – is being reclaimed and reimagined among radicals. This is the countryside (in pre-1949 Maoist terms) which creative young people (not always 'socialist', not always even 'political') are culti-vating in order to get to the cities. Can we get something, a *different* set of social relations together, in and against the deeply destruc-tive, anti-social, capitalist relations now threatening nature as well as society? Can we make commons, be commoned, produce and circulate value co-operatively? Can we move beyond the fragments presently, transitionally, only connect by drawing so many hori-zontal lines that they turn the vertical upside down?

Having worked on Twin Trading (one of the longest-lasting legacies of the GLC) and as an *animateur* of fair trade in coffee, chocolate and nuts in Ghana, Kerala and elsewhere, Robin took a full part in such positive questioning. He was preoccupied for years with the problem of 'rent' in political economy. He excitedly introduced me and others to the work of Michel Bauwens, Elinor Ostrom and David Collier. He designed and taught alternative and oppositional curricula with Tim Crabtree at Schumacher College. He helped John Restakis and Pat Connaty to bring the *Synergia* network into being, designing MOOCs and participating in sessions in the Italian co-operative regions of Emilio Romagna and Trento. He encouraged the ambitions of the Co-operative College to initiate a Co-operative University. 'Have you read'? 'Do you know about?' – Robin's socialist practice was to communicate and share, teaching and learning simultaneously, reinforcing, never rebuking or being patronising.

As Mike Rustin's selection of essays in this book shows, during decades of London-based, global acting and local thinking, Robin's focus was on commissioned, for-the-moment, written and practical interventions. The big book was not his favoured mode, although the *London Industrial Strategy*, a summation of his work at the GLC, was the size of a London telephone directory.[5] He died knowing that he had a book on the social economy in his head. Anticipations of this appeared in publications from the Young Foundation and from

Nesta (the National Endowment for Science, Technology and the Arts), in collaboration with Geoff Mulgan and Julie Caulier Grice. Robin's friends had long projected onto him no less a burden than the *Capital Volume 4* they wanted from him.

Meanwhile, his characteristic forms of co-operative and mutual communication were more-than-daily memos, notes of conversations and meetings, lucid notes and think-pieces on his reading, and videoed discussions. These survive. Some of them have been put together, by Frances Murray, with articles, journal essays and pamphlets on the website he liked to anticipate as a legacy form of publication (http://www.robinmurray.co.uk). The website is well-designed as a stopping place – alight here – rather than a sealed train of thought: a socialist rather than an individualist form of production, distribution and exchange of ideas and actions. As well as an overview of Robin's work, it has a full bibliography, including his talks, tributes from his associates and a gallery of images and more episodic interventions.

It is easy to set down, in the manner of a CV, a brief list of 'positions held' by Robin to earn a living. Key elements of this are detailed in Mike Rustin's introduction to this book. After Oxford, an MSc in Economics at the LSE led to teaching that subject at the London Business School; he was a long-time Fellow of the IDS at Sussex; there was the GLC secondment; he was Special Adviser to the Minister of Economic Development and Trade, Government of Ontario (1993-95); Visiting Research Fellow at the Centre for the Study of Global Governance at the LSE (1998-2003); Senior Visiting Fellow at the Civil Society and Human Security Research Unit, also at the LSE, from 2011 onwards; Acting Director of RED, the research and innovation arm of the Design Council (2014-15); Executive Chair of Liberation Foods (formerly the Ethical Nut Company), 2005-9; he worked with the Young Foundation on the Methods of the Social Economy project, and was a Visiting Fellow of NESTA from 2008 to 2010.

But perhaps more interesting than any of this for socialist millennials and older generations, making our precarious ways in transformed, now apocalyptic, political, economic and climatic times, is to draw attention to what Robin did *not* do. His was a life lived rather than a job, or a succession of jobs, done. Even the word 'consultant' doesn't fit professionally, because for much of his doing/making/writing – even when it was contracted – he was seldom paid at, or asked for, more than a minimal rate. He was never good at acting as his own shop steward. What he did not do was to 'carve out a career', 'get promoted', 'hold down a post at...', 'occupy the Chair of...'. At a time of discontinuous (a word Robin often used) changes in the economy, or 'economies', as he pluralised them, such a way of improvising a livelihood in endist times is already a preferred way forward among some late-teen and twenty to thirty-year olds in the age of school strikes, extinction rebellions and Greta Thunberg. What, no, *how,* are you going to *be?*

*

Poiesia found its more plainly poetic, more conventional place during the final months of Robin's life. Listening to music, to radio talks, listening, laughing and being read to, released such enthusiasm in him, of a kind which made him pause for breath. 'We are creatures', as Alice Oswald writes, 'whose prayer is breath'. Oswald's poetry, taken with her writing about it, was an inspiration for more than five years. Robin was himself an insightful critic of words and lines and the *stance* – the alignment and commitment – of any poem or poet, whether published or not. He wrote poems himself. As we had discovered in the *QueenSpark* years, so do multitudes (most?) of over-modest people. Prose, we mused, is a more artificial form than poetry. Poetry articulates (joins) the associative ways all humans think, however un-free we may now find our free-associational capacity has become.

Production *and beyond* ... With his daughter Bethany Murray's help, for many years Robin made a well-produced New Year's Calendar of Poems, thematically connected and circulated among friends. He would have loved the much-published Lemn Sissay's introduction to the 2017 Canongate edition of his selected poems, *Gold from the Stone.* Sissay plays with the private and the public, the occasional and the universal, the 'for you' and 'for everyone' in a way which would have launched a great conversation:

> The best poems are unseen and unheard by anyone other than the person who wrote them and the persons they were intended

for. They are read at funerals or between lovers or between daughters and fathers. They are kept within the family. Writers, audience, performer, performance and applause. It is the perfect journey for a poem: beginning, middle and end. The closest to that is a reader and a book.[6]

In Robin's private-publication calendars, Kathleen Raine, a poet who had lived in his native Cumbria, found favour, as did William Blake from his adopted city of London. Robin loved to tell his own stories, past and present, acting the gestures and accents of as many of the *personae* as possible. He seemed to enjoy communicating in this register with as much insight, verve and uninhibited passion as he spent in the more formal essays selected for this book. We particularly enjoyed Louis MacNeice's 'The Kingdom' (*c.*1943) together, with its roots in the extraordinary nature of the 'ordinary', roots which took us back to *QueenSpark* and to Raymond Williams' signature essay, 'Culture is Ordinary'.

The longest prose piece Robin and I read together was Alice Oswald's 'The Universe in time of rain makes the world alive with noise', published in a Poetry Society booklet edited by Sarah Maguire in 2000.[7] Oswald's essay included a section on 'Sound' and another on 'Work'.

Robin's reaction to these was immediate, in words something like 'Look here! I've been going on about *production* all these years, but this is something else... the labour process indeed!' His freedom of mind and willingness to soar skywards, taking interlocutors with him to sites they had not dared to acknowledge before will be remembered, as will his way with *talk,* in his case at least as powerful a 'means of communication as means of production' as print. His voice only ever raised when denouncing an outrageously capitalist act, Robin was patient with the impossible: 'give me half an hour...'.

Oswald's essay celebrates the routes and roots of originality which run (in her case) between the labour and listening of gardening and the making of poems. Her writing method as she once described it is to conceive (hear, feel, think, see) a poem whole, then do research (be in place, walk, revisit night and day, talk and pick up ways of talking among Others) and only then set down lines in sequence. 'Very Dartington' said Robin when I described this, taken from a talk I had just heard Oswald give. 'Not unlike how you go about your written pieces', I said to him, 'always looking first for *the run of the argument*'.

We continued to delight in this essay, reading aloud her paragraphs on 'Sound':

> When I'm writing a poem, the first thing I hear is its shape somewhere among all that noise.
>
> I try to avoid conventional metre in favour of this metre that is already actual. I try to keep listening, letting each line grow slowly out of the landscape. I have my left hand cupped like an ear and it feels as if I'm holding my mind in my right hand and a garden in my left. And I can hear two ranges – the range of real sound out of which the poem's melody emerges; and further down, where hearing joins forces with speaking, I can hear sentences, distinct grammatical waves coming off things like waves of energy...

Her poems, she continues:

> are nothing more than a series of extended names spoken together; a kind of complex onomatopoeia, or 'naming through listening'. It doesn't matter how a poem is made. What's important is that listening, and gardening as a form of listening, is a way of forcing a poem open to what lies bodily beyond it. Because the eye is an instrument tuned to surfaces, but the ear tells you about volume, depth, content – like tapping a large iron shape to find if it's full or not. The ear hears into, not just at what surrounds it. And the whole challenge of poetry is to keep language open, so that what we don't yet know can pass through it.

Oswald then describes her search for 'a form establishing and breaking itself as it goes'.

Is this a form for adequate future-socialist association – Auden's 'a way of happening', Thompson's 'being present at our own making' – as well for the next authentic poem? 'For this reason',

Oswald continues, 'I build poems out of discrete blocks of sound and grammar with huge gaps in between them. But it's not always clear to readers what I'm doing' ... Is it for this (or at least a cognate) reason that activists continue to build prefigurative cells of a future-imperfect socialist body, economic and political, i.e. fully social-ist but in an *associational*, as opposed to a merely *collectivist* or *statist*, sense of socialism? Robin's essay on 'The three socialisms', drafted for an early issue of the *Conference of Socialist Economists Bulletin*, was formative for me.

Back to Oswald on poetry, and a 'work-world': 'all long unstable rhythms and dissonance':

> Every job has its dialect. Salmon fishers talk of the 'voler', the unique clean line a salmon makes through water. Most of us don't see the line because we don't know the word.
>
> One way of expressing this attitude to meaning, that it always operates within a work-world, is to suggest, through the notation of poetry, a series of separated frames – something like Emerson's circles: 'the natural world may be conceived as a system of concentric circles, and we now and then detect in Nature slight dislocations, which apprise us that this surface on which we now stand is not fixed, but sliding.'

Is this how the seemingly natural social – now terminally anti-social 'western' capitalist world – might now be re-presented, undermined or souveyed (one of Robin's words) ready for change as well as surveyed, for the purpose of understanding? 'A system of concentric circles' telling us 'that this surface on which we now stand is not fixed but sliding'.

Notes

1   Robin Murray, *Co-operation in the Age of Google*, Cooperatives UK, New Insight 5, 2010.

2   David Morley and Ken Worpole (eds), *The Republic of Letters: Working Class Writing and Local Publishing*, Comedia, 1982.

3   Glyn Maxwell, *One Thousand Nights and Counting: Selected Poems*, Picador, 2011.

4 Fritjof Capra, *The Web of Life: A New Scientific Understanding of Living Systems*, Anchor, 1997.

5 Greater London Council, *LIS: London Industrial Strategy*, London: GLC, 1985.

6 Lemn Sissay, *Gold from the Stone: New and Selected Poems*, Edinburgh: Canongate, 2017, p.xxv.

7 Alice Oswald, 'The Universe in time of rain makes the world alive with noise', in Sarah Maguire (ed.), *A Green Thought in a Green Shade: Poetry in the Garden,* Milton Keynes: Poetry Society, 2000, pp35-45. All the ensuing quotations from Oswald are taken from this essay.

Post-Fordism

1

Benetton Britain:
The new economic order

First published in Marxism Today, *November 1985, pp28-32. Reproduced with permission.*

Keynesianism doesn't work anymore. But what to put in its place?

If there is one economic lesson we should have learnt from the last twenty years, it is the limits of Keynesian policy. Whether in this country or abroad – in Spain, France, Greece or Australia – social democratic governments have come in on a platform of expansionism and redistribution, only to traumatise both their electorates and themselves by introducing cuts and deflation. In this country such turning points occurred in 1966 and 1976. The election of 1983 was a trauma of a different kind, but with a similar lesson. Labour fought monetarism with Keynesianism, and lost both the economic argument and the election.

In spite of this, Labour's current economic policy is still predominantly in the Keynesian mould. Its main axes are reflation, redistribution and balance of payments control – in short, the management of markets. A few Labour politicians may still believe that such measures will restore full employment. Most have lowered their sights to what they think Keynesian orthodoxy can deliver. But in the movement as a whole there is a deeper ache, a sense that what has happened to Mitterrand will happen here. As a result, there is a real openness to new policies, without any clear idea along which path a credible alternative actually lies.

Part of the problem is that progressive alternatives to Labour orthodoxy have shared a similar Keynesian outlook. Reflation has been a common starting point. What has divided the left and right has been the extent of reflation, and the severity of controls necessary to complement it. The size of the public sector borrowing requirement (PSBR) has become an index of economic progressiveness: the higher the braver. The larger the deficit, the more severe must be protection and exchange controls, and the more extensive the internal control of the economy. Around the Keynesian problematics of expanding demand and protecting the national economy, there is a continuity which runs from the Alliance on the right to virtually all versions of the alternative economic strategy on the left.

Three weaknesses

There are three weaknesses in this general approach. First, as Roy Hattersley is himself acutely aware, there will be balance of payments and inflationary pressures even with an injection of the £5 billion into the economy that he is currently proposing. With the collapse of so many sectors of British production, an increase in consumer demand and capital investment cannot but help draw in imports in the short- and medium-term – however severe the protection. To take a recent example from the Enterprise Board's work in London. The Board has been backing an attempt to move the leading electric bicycle design from prototype to mass production. It could find no firm remaining capable of manufacturing the frames in this country. The designer has turned instead to Italy and the USA.

Strategies of reflation aim to counter this problem by concentrating their short-run plans on activities with a low import content (like construction) or on labour-intensive projects (like job creation schemes). But there will still be import pressures when the new wages are spent and there will still be inflationary bottlenecks in sectors like construction. Taking London again: there are already skill shortages reported in the engineering and building trades, reflecting the departure of skilled labour from those industries and the decline in the number of apprentices to replace them. As with a person who has been starved, there are limits to which the British economy can be force-fed.

The key issue is under what conditions and at what speed 're-industrialisation' could take place. All the evidence we have from the GLC's firm and sectoral studies of the London economy is that many sectors are unlikely to recover, even with protection, without profound restructuring.

The second weakness of the Keynesian approach is that the power of any government to control the national economy through macro measures has been seriously eroded by the growth of multi-nationals and the openness of the British economy. In the late 1930s imports accounted for a tenth of the UK market for manufactures. Today the figure is nearer a third. Four-fifths of all UK exports are accounted for by multinationals, much of it transferred between affiliates within the same company. Industrial and banking multi-nationals also dominate flows on the foreign exchanges. Changes in tariffs and exchange rates do affect the pattern of multinational trade and investment, but in different ways and over different time periods than they did in the days of more integrated national economies.

The third, and perhaps the most significant, weakness of Keynesianism is that it has no direct purchase on the major economic issue of our time, which is the restructuring of produc-tion. The central fact of the present era of capitalism is that Fordist production (mass production of standardised goods, using specially designed machinery, production lines, and a semi-skilled workforce) began to run out of steam in the 1960s. Its earlier spread had been the basis of the postwar boom, but as markets became saturated, profit rates fell. Expansions of credit and government-financed consumer demand slowed down but did not reverse this process.

From Fordism to neo-Fordism

The major counter-tendency has come from another quarter – the introduction of a quite new stage of capitalist production. In the USA it is referred to as 'flexible specialisation', in France as 'neo-

Fordism'. It consists of applying computer technology not only to each stage of the production process, from design to retailing, but also to the integration of all stages of the process into a single co-ordinated system. As a result, the economies of scale of mass production can now be achieved on much smaller runs, whether small batch engineering products, or clothes, shoes, furniture and even books. Instead of Fordism's specialised machinery producing standardised products, we now have flexible, all-purpose machinery producing a variety of products. Computers have been applied to design, cutting down the waste of materials, and to stock control. Distribution has been revolutionised, as has the link between sales, production and innovation.

A good example of the 'new production' is that of the Italian clothing firm Benetton. Their clothes are made by 11,500 workers in Northern Italy, only 1500 of whom work directly for Benetton. The rest are employed by subcontractors in factories of thirty to fifty workers each. The clothes are sold through 2000 tied retail outlets, all of them franchised. Benetton provide the designs, control material stocks and orchestrate what is produced according to the computerised daily sales returns which flow back to their Italian headquarters from all parts of Europe. Similar systems are at the heart of the success in the UK of the 'new wave' clothiers – Burton's, Next and Richard Shops.

In industry after industry a parallel restructuring has been taking place. Japan has been the home base for the new production, together with Germany, Northern Italy and parts of the Scandinavian economy. The UK and the USA, mostly deeply bound into Fordism, have been slowest to respond (the car industry is a notable example), though the USA is now changing rapidly. Policies which are restricted to managing markets, providing finance, or merely changing formalised control, do not begin to address these issues. What is needed is for the labour movement to shift the whole focus of policy, from money and markets, to production. It is the crisis in production which is at the root of the world recession and the British slump, and it is the way in which the labour movement addresses restructuring which should be the central matter of economic debate.

The 'Japanisation' strategy

What are the alternatives? The first is a 'Japanisation' strategy which would aim to restructure industry in the interests of British-based capital. It would require a central restructuring institution – in the tradition of the Industrial Reorganisation Corporation, and on the scale of the Japanese planning ministry MITI. It would also need a source of long-term finance, as well as specific government policies of protection, research funding and state support, that would be linked to the individual industrial plans and financial packages. There are traces of such a 'Japanisation' project in alliance policies and in parts of Labour's economic programme. But in both cases industrial policy is obscured beneath the shadow of Keynesianism.

Socialists have been understandably wary of restructuring proposals along these lines. Such restructuring is merely another word for rationalisation, involving loss of jobs, and the undermining of labour's position in the workplace. It recalls the 'Mondist' movement of the 1920s and 1930s, which was concerned with the introduction of Fordist methods of production with the consent of the trade unions.

In the case of Japanese-type restructuring, the dangers go well beyond the workplace, as the Benetton example shows. For the establishment of single integrated systems of production and distribution has permitted the break-up of large factory complexes and the growth of a subcontract and franchise economy. In Japan, the resulting dualism is particularly sharp. On the one hand, there is a central core accounting for a third of the workforce (with the celebrated corporate welfare systems, high skill levels and jobs for life). On the other, there is a peripheral subcontract and sweated economy, casualised, low paid, weakly organised and restricted to a grossly inadequate public welfare system.

We should certainly be suspicious of such trends. But we cannot ignore them. For already they are taking root in the British economy. Subcontracting has expanded. So has franchising. Private welfare systems, from health to pensions, to job security and even to housing, are growing as the welfare state is being run down. There is a deepening dualism in the labour market. The problem is that in the market sectors of the economy, the failure to match the new flexible production systems, has meant the destruction of many of the manufacturing strongholds of the labour movement.

The point was brought home to us in London by the experience of one of the Greater London Enterprise Board's clothing factories. GLEB bought it from the receiver, re-equipped it, improved the plant layout and the flow of work. The company slowly raised wages, and has been developing an enterprise plan. But when it bid for one public contract, it found itself undercut by quotations which were from 18-36 per cent below its own direct labour and materials costs. Initially, GLEB thought that the competitors must have been relabelling imports from South East Asia. But they found that their rivals had set up flexible systems in this country, linking design, production, distribution and sales. The lower bids reflected the large increases in efficiency that resulted.

Differences of this magnitude are common in other industries. Ford Europe, for example, found that their Japanese associate, Mazda, was able to produce an Escort in Japan £1000 per car cheaper than Ford. A top-level Ford management team were astonished when they discovered that only 10 per cent of the difference could be accounted for by labour factors (wages, running along the line and so on). Ninety per cent was due to factors of flexible specialisation.

Another path?

Such findings show up the futility – even from capital's point of view – of the present government's cheap labour solution. But they also pose as great a problem to the left as did Fordism to the Bolsheviks after 1917. What policy should socialists adopt towards the most advanced forms of capitalist technology? Lenin's answer was to embrace the principles of Fordism and scientific management. Trotsky argued along similar lines, that if socialism failed to adopt the most modern technology and narrow the gap between domestic and world prices then, at some point, internal political opposition would emerge, arguing for imports. Hence he supported and organised the massive import of western technology as a means of restructuring Soviet manufacturing on Fordist lines. Henry Ford's largest tractor plant in the world was built in the Soviet Union.

All socialist countries have faced the force of the world market. However strong the protection, a Labour government would face it here. This means we cannot avoid having a policy on restructuring. If we do not have such a policy, the market and its managers will settle it for us. Some version of 'Japanisation' will take further hold of the British economy, with British factories being increasingly confined to the periphery – as sub-contractors, assemblers, finishers, the screwdriver plants of the world economy. But while agreeing with Lenin and Trotsky that we cannot ignore foreign technology, the question we must pose is whether there is an alternative path of restructuring to that offered by the Japanese model? Can we have restructuring in the interests of labour rather than of capital? Can we take over the advantages of new computer systems of production, without the deskilling, fragmentation, and dualism that goes with it? Can we talk of a strategy of alternative production?

I believe we can, though its outlines are hazy. In this, as in so many other fields, Brecht's maxim 'truth is in the concrete' applies. Our answers will necessarily be in the details of particular sectors. Take retailing for example. The modern superstores, hypermarkets and out-of-town shopping centres have pioneered the new principles of flexible specialisation. But they have done it in such a way as to destroy local shops. They have made access to shopping harder for the immobile and for those without cars. They have followed a policy of employing casual, part-time, largely female labour, and have failed – in the food sector – to transform the nutritional quality of food and its conditions of production, in line with their extraordinary advances in systems of physical distribution and stock control. The conditions and wages in meat product factories in London, for example, are atrocious.

The transformation of retailing need not be like this. The technology could be developed to bring the advantages of the supermarket to local corner shops. There is wide scope for improvements in food quality, and in the provision of fresh food using the 'just in time' systems of stock control. Supermarkets could provide creches and independent nutritional advice centres. Many of these policies may conflict with the market. They do not conflict with need.

Or take software. The computer programs that are written to control the new systems of production are geared to control labour rather than emancipate it. There is no necessity in this. Bus-workers in Leeds, for example, found that computerised bus schedules could be rewritten (with the help of a friendly programmer) in a way which was just as efficient in time terms, but which took into account their own (and the passengers') needs in a quite different way. Professor Rosenbrock's human-centred lathe and automatic factory systems – designed to extend traditional engineering skills rather than dispense with them – provide another example.

Britain has great strength in programming. But the private software economy is about to be swamped by US mass-produced programs. Software, like retailing, is one of the new commanding heights of the present phase of capitalism. Its effects have already gone deep into market production. The next phase of expansion is to be directed at public services. It is therefore critical, in terms of a strategy of alternative production, that a public software capacity is secured to develop the alternative computer programs on which the advances in production will be based.

Some lessons learnt

I have given examples of how computer systems can be applied in the interests of need rather than merely of profit. But their implications go beyond this. If, for instance, such systems are developed for the furniture industry, and if they are applied in plants under social control, then those plants will have a competitive advantage. It is this advantage which will give scope for those things that have been driven out by the market economy: adequate wages, training, full access for women and for black people (in an industry where the workforce is still almost entirely white and male), designs that take into account those needs which have no power in the market (like those of the disabled), planned imports from progressive third world countries that are desperate for foreign exchange. The scope will be wider, too, for an extension of real control by the workforce. I say 'real' as well as 'formal' since real control requires the development of confidence and strategic skills, and this takes time, resources and groups of support workers.

All these we have been trying to put into practice, in conjunction with the trade unions, through the Greater London Enterprise Board in London and the GLC. In one factory, one thing will work, but not in another. We have learnt as much from the failures as from successes. But there are four overall conclusions:

a) There is enormous scope for public intervention in the restructuring of production. Many sectors in which medium-sized firms are significant have been or are being destroyed by imports, and have shown themselves quite incapable of innovating on the scale required. In sectors where large, multi-national firms predominate, some have found it difficult to escape from their Fordist traditions. In others, particularly those involved in military production, there is an appalling waste of technological capacity which could be applied to civil markets and to social need. Local enterprise boards cannot take on these giants, though councils have supported trade unionists in pressing for alternative plans. It is here that a National Enterprise Board – committed to a strategy of alternative production – is needed.

b) The main constraint in extending public intervention is people: people who have managerial skills (to turn round a factory, for example) and who, at the same time, are sympathetic with the strategy. Because of a lack of such staff, the enterprise boards have often been forced into joint ventures with private owners. For GLEB at least, the relationship has again and again been unsatisfactory, compared to those cases where there has been full, or majority, municipal control.

c) There is a need for new systems of investment appraisal and social accounting. These must shift the emphasis from short-term financial returns to the longer-term questions of the product, its relative strength with respect to other products, and the extent to which it can meet non-market, as well as market, needs. As the Japanese have found, restructuring of any kind often takes a long time. They have geared their institutions and methods of assessment accordingly.

d) That the robustness of the strategy depends above all on the involvement of the workforce. Strategic plans have been developed not by economists divorced from production, but by researchers in conjunction with those working in the industry, who again and again have provided a level of deep knowledge, and a sense of what practicably could be.

The enterprise boards have intervened in market sectors. What local councils have also been sharply aware of is that there are restructuring issues – usually on a much larger scale – in public services themselves. As with market production, there are clear alternatives in restructuring. Some of them are not confined to issues of flexible specialisation. In energy for instance, there is a choice between nuclear power on the one hand, and conservation on the other. This cannot be settled on financial grounds, but rather on the basis of employment, ecology and political considerations. With London Transport (LT) on the other hand, the battle between the alternatives did involve questions of how new systems were put into practice (as well as fares). The growing strength of the progressive alternative led to the government 'nationalising' LT. Similarly, with cable – which will provide the basic infrastructure for the electronic era – there are wide options about how fibre optics will be introduced and controlled.

In each of these cases restructuring is taking place. There is no one way in which it has to happen. The alternatives have very different implications for labour, and the choice that exists cannot be settled by comparing rates of return. It is rather a question of social and political choices. There are even some cases where the options which are desirable socially, are greatly superior on narrow cost grounds as well (preventative health care, for example).

A strategy of alternative production

My argument then is this. The present economic crisis should be seen first and foremost as a crisis of restructuring. It is a restructuring which is taking place at great cost. The priority for the left should be to intervene in this restructuring in order to change its course. This requires detailed popular planning, sector by sector and firm by firm, and the development of a material capacity for intervention at a national, as well as a local, level. This is what I mean by a strategy of alternative production.

There are implications for political as well as economic strategy in all this. Policies which enter from the Keynesian end, or from the end of abstract systems of control, concentrate the mind on the need to take state power. For it is the state which can alter the interest rate, and taxation, and who owns what. Part of the problem with this is that, for many people, it all seems abstract and far away from their immediate abilities to act for themselves.

An alternative production approach is different. It starts from where people are: the particular plant, or shop, or office; the kind of food on sale at the local supermarket; or the programme on television. Not only can alternative plans start from there, but something can almost always be done. It will be limited and difficult, but will have that one overwhelming political virtue of practicality. And the limits, soon felt, lead to new connections, more general demands and, before long, to detailed practical policies which only a progressive government can deliver. Instead of the state being seen as the 'great deliverer' and the focus of power, it becomes the supporter of initiatives begun and fought for elsewhere by trade unionists, communities and municipalities. And, paradoxically enough, a movement developed in this way provides a stronger, not a weaker, foundation from which a progressive government can build.

I say all this not as a litany of wishes, but as a reflection of what has happened over the last fifteen years. That great flowering of local alternative action in the 1970s, through a myriad of community papers, women's groups, trade union support units, peace groups, legal advice centres, tenants' groups, trade union branches, and combine committees, all these have been the basis for a change in municipal politics. In London it came first at the level of boroughs (like Wandsworth), and then in 1981, at the GLC. And the GLC in its turn, like other councils, has tried to see itself as giving strength to, and not merely drawing strength from, the innumerable groups from which it sprung.

What is now possible is for all this to be extended to the national level. In the field of economic strategy, groups of local authorities have already got together to produce national alternatives for the clothing industry, for Ford's, for steel, cable television and combined heat and power. Each has the detail and the organised support necessary to make a strategy of national industrial intervention a serious possibility.

The development of national company and sectoral plans is, I think, the most urgent task for the next two years. It is only when these are in hand that the Keynesian measures, left or right, will become credible and capable of supporting a programme of progressive restructuring. Without such plans, the Keynesian interlude will be short-lived, and will do nothing to protect British labour from the gathering embrace of 'Japanisation' and all that follows in its wake.

2

Life after Henry (Ford)

First published in Marxism Today, October 1988, *pp8-13. Reproduced with permission.*

What is post-Fordism and what does it mean?

During the first two centuries of the industrial revolution, the focus of employment shifted from the farm to the factory. It is now shifting once more, from the factory to the office and the shop. A third of Britain's paid labour force now work in offices. A third of the value of national output is in the distribution sector. Meanwhile 2.5 million jobs have been lost in British manufacturing since 1960. If the Ford plants at Halewood and Dagenham represented late industrialism, Centrepoint and Habitat are the symbols of a new age.

The right portrayed the growth of services as a portent of a post-industrial society with growing individualism, a weakened state and a multiplicity of markets. I want to argue that it reflects a deeper change in the production process. It is one that affects manufacturing and agriculture as well as services, and has implications for the way in which we think about socialist alternatives. I see this as a shift from the dominant form of twentieth century production, known as Fordism, to a new form, post-Fordism.

Fordism is an industrial era whose secret is to be found in the mass production systems pioneered by Henry Ford. These systems were based on four principles from which all else followed:

a) products were standardised; this meant that each part and each task could also be standardised. Unlike craft production –

where each part had to be specially designed, made and fitted – for a run of mass-produced cars, the same headlight could be fitted to the same model in the same way.

b) if tasks are the same, then some can be mechanised; thus mass production plants developed special-purpose machinery for each model, much of which could not be switched from product to product.

c) those tasks which remained were subject to scientific management, or Taylorism, whereby any task was broken down into its component parts, redesigned by work study specialists on time-and-motion principles, who then instructed manual workers on how the job should be done.

d) flowline replaced nodal assembly, so that instead of workers moving to and from the product (the node), the product flowed past the workers.

Ford did not invent these principles. What he did was to combine them in the production of a complex commodity, which undercut craft-made cars as decisively as the handloom weavers had been undercut in the 1830s. Ford's Model T sold for less than a tenth of the price of a craft-built car in the US in 1916, and he took 50 per cent of the market.

This revolutionary production system was to transform sector after sector during the twentieth century, from processed food, to furniture, clothes, cookers and even ships after the second world war. The economies came from the scale of production, for although mass production might be more costly to set up because of the purpose-built machinery, once in place the cost of an extra unit was discontinuously cheap.

Many of the structures of Fordism followed from this tension between high fixed costs and low variable ones, and the consequent drive for volume. First, as Ford himself emphasised, mass production presupposes mass consumption. Consumers must be willing to buy standardised products. Mass advertising played a central part in establishing a mass consumption norm. So did the provision of the infrastructure of consumption – housing and roads. To ensure that the road system dominated over rail, General Motors, Standard Oil and Firestone Tyres bought up and then dismantled the electric trolley and transit systems in forty-four urban areas.

Second, Fordism was linked to a system of protected national markets, which allowed the mass producers to recoup their fixed costs at home and compete on the basis of marginal costs on the world market, or through the replication of existing models via foreign investment.

Third, mass producers were particularly vulnerable to sudden falls in demand. Ford unsuccessfully tried to offset the effect of the 1930s depression by raising wages. Instalment credit, Keynesian demand and monetary management, and new wage and welfare systems were all more effective in stabilising the markets for mass producers in the post-war period. Hire purchase (HP) and the dole cheque became as much the symbols of the Fordist age as the tower block and the motorway.

The mass producers not only faced the hazard of changes in consumption. With production concentrated in large factories, they were also vulnerable to the new 'mass worker' they had created. Like Taylorism, mass production had taken the skill out of work, it fragmented tasks into a set of repetitive movements, and erected a rigid division between mental and manual labour. It treated human beings as interchangeable parts of a machine, paid according to the job they did rather than who they were.

The result was high labour turnover, shop-floor resistance and strikes. The mass producers in turn sought constant new reservoirs of labour, particularly from groups facing discrimination, from rural areas and from less developed regions abroad. The contractual core of Taylorism – higher wages in return for managerial control of production – still applied, and a system of industrial unions grew up to bargain over these wages levels. In the US, and to an extent the UK, a national system of wage bargaining developed in the post-war period, centred on high-profile car industry negotiations that linked wage rises to productivity growth, and then set wage standards for other large-scale producers and the state. It was a system of collective bargaining that has been described as implementing a Keynesian incomes policy without a Keynesian state. As long as the new labour reservoirs could be tapped, it was a system that held together the distinct wage relation of Fordism.

Taylorism was also characteristic of the structure of management and supplier relations. Fordist bureaucracies are fiercely hierarchical, with links between the divisions and departments being made through the centre rather than at the base. Planning is done by specialists; rulebooks and guidelines are issued for lower management to carry out. If you enter a Ford factory in any part of the world, you will find its layout, materials, even the position of its Coca Cola machines, all similar, set up as they are on the basis of a massive construction manual drawn up in Detroit. Managers themselves complain of deskilling and the lack of room for initiative, as do suppliers who are confined to producing blueprints at a low margin price.

These threads – of production and consumption, of the semi-skilled worker and collective bargaining, of a managed national market and centralised organisation – together make up the fabric of Fordism. They have given rise to an economic culture which extends beyond the complex assembly industries to agriculture, the service industries and parts of the state. It is marked by its commitment to scale and the standard product (whether it is a Mars bar or an episode of *Dallas*); by a competitive strategy based on cost reduction; by authoritarian relations, centralised planning, and a rigid organisation built round exclusive job descriptions.

These structures and their culture are often equated with industrialism and regarded as an inevitable part of the modern age. I am suggesting that they are linked to a particular form of industrialism, one that developed in the late nineteenth century and reached its most dynamic expression in the post-war boom. Its impact can be felt not just in the economy, but in politics (in the mass party) and in much broader cultural fields – whether American football, or classical ballet (Diaghilev was a Taylorist in dance), industrial design or modern architecture. The technological hubris of this outlook, its Faustian bargain of dictatorship in production in exchange for mass consumption, and above all its destructiveness in the name of progress and the economy of time, all this places Fordism at the centre of modernism.

Why we need to understand these deep structures of Fordism is that they are embedded, too, in traditional socialist economics. Soviet-type planning is the apogee of Fordism. Lenin embraced Taylor and the stopwatch. Soviet industrialisation was centred on the construction of giant plants, the majority of them based on Western mass-production technology. So deep is the idea of scale burnt into Soviet economics that there is a hairdresser's in Moscow with 120 barbers' chairs. The focus of Soviet production is on volume and, because of its lack of consumer discipline, it has caricatured certain features of Western mass production, notably a hoarding of stocks and inadequate quality control.

In social-democratic thinking, state planning has a more modest place. But in the writings of Fabian economists in the 1930s, as in the Morrisonian model of the public corporation, and Labour's post-war policies, we see the same emphasis on centralist planning, scale, Taylorist technology and hierarchical organisation. The image of planning was the railway timetable, the goal of planning was stable demand and cost-reduction. In the welfare state, the idea of the standard product was given a democratic interpretation as the universal service to meet basic needs, and although in Thatcher's Britain this formulation is still important, it effectively forecloses the issue of varied public services and user choice. The shadow of Fordism haunts us even in the terms in which we oppose it.

Fordism as a vision – both left and right – had always been challenged – on the shopfloor, as in the political party, the seminar room and the studio. In 1968 this challenge exploded in Europe and the US. It was a cultural as much as an industrial revolt, attacking the central principles of Fordism, its definitions of work and consumption, its shaping of towns and its overriding of nature.

From that time, we can see a fracturing of the foundations of predictability on which Fordism was based. Demand became more volatile and fragmented. Productivity growth fell as the result of workplace resistance. The decline in profit drove down investment. Exchange rates were fluctuating, oil prices rose, and in 1974 came the greatest slump the west had had since the 1930s.

The consensus response was a Keynesian one, to restore profitability through a managed increase in demand and an incomes policy. For monetarism, the route to profitability went through the weakening of labour, a cut in state spending, and a reclaiming of the public sector for private accumulation. Economists and politicians were refighting the battles of the last slump. Private capital, on the other hand, was dealing with the present one. It was using new technology and new production principles to make Fordism flexible, and in doing so stood much of the old culture on its head.

In Britain, the groundwork for the new system was laid not in manufacturing but in retailing. Since the 1950s, retailers had been using computers to transform the distribution system. All mass producers have the problem of forecasting demand. If they produce too little, they lose market share. If they produce too much, they are left with stocks, which are costly to hold, or have to be sold at a discount. Retailers face this problem not just for a few products but for thousands. Their answer has been to develop information and supply systems which allow them to order supplies to coincide with demand. Every evening, Sainsbury's receives details of the sales of all 12,000 lines from each of its shops; these are turned into orders for warehouse deliveries for the coming night, and replacement production for the following day. With computerised control of stocks in the shop, transport networks, automatic loading and unloading, Sainsbury's flowline 'make to order' system has conquered the Fordist problem of stocks.

They have also overcome the limits of the mass product. For, in contrast to the discount stores which are confined to a few, fast-selling items, Sainsbury's, like the new wave of high street shops, can handle ranges of products geared to segments of the market. Market niching has become the slogan of the high street. Market researchers break down market by age (youth, young adults, 'grey power'), by household types (dinkies, single-gender couples, one-parent families), by income, occupation, housing and, increasingly, by locality. They analyse 'lifestyles', correlating consumption patterns across commodities, from food to clothing, and health to holidays.

The point of this new anthropology of consumption is to target both product and shops to particular segments. Burton – once a mass producer with generalised retail outlets – has changed in the 1980s to being a niche market retailer with a team of anthropologists, a group of segmented stores – Top Shop, Top Man, Dorothy Perkins, Principles and Burton itself – and now has no manufacturing plants of its own. Conran's Storehouse group – Habitat, Heals, Mothercare, Richards and BHS – all geared to different groups, offers not only clothes, but furniture and furnishings, in other words, entire lifestyles. At the heart of his organisation in London is what amounts to a factory of 150 designers, with collages of different lifestyles on the wall, Bold Primary, Orchid, mid-Atlantic and the Cottage Garden.

In all these shops the emphasis has shifted from the manufacturer's economies of scale to the retailer's economies of scope. The economies come from offering an integrated range from which customers choose their own basket of products. There is also an economy of innovation, for the modern retail systems allow new product ideas to be tested in practice, through shop sales, and the successful ones then to be ordered for wider distribution. Innovation has become a leading edge of the new competition. Product life has become shorter, for fashion goods and consumer durables.

A centrepiece of this new retailing is design. Designers produce the innovations. They shape the lifestyles. They design the shops, which are described as 'stages' for the act of shopping. There are now 29,000 people working in design consultancies in the UK, which have sales of £1600 million per annum. They are the engineers of designer capitalism. With market researchers they have steered the high street from being retailers of goods to retailers of style.

These changes are a response to, and a means of, shaping the shift from mass consumption. Instead of keeping up with the Joneses there has been a move to be *different* from the Joneses. Many of these differences are vertical, intended to confirm status and class. But some are horizontal, centred round group identities, linked to age, or region or ethnicity. In spite of the fact that basic needs are still unmet, the high street does offer a new variety and creativity in consumption which the left's puritan tradition should also address. Whatever our responses, the revolution in retailing reflects new principles of production, a new pluralism of products, and a new importance for innovation. As such it marks a shift to a post-Fordist age.

There have been parallel shifts in manufacturing, not least in response to the retailers' just-in-time system of ordering. In some sectors where the manufacturers are little more than subcontractors to the retailers, their flexibility has been achieved at the expense of labour. In others, capital itself has suffered, as furniture retailers like MFI squeeze their suppliers, driving down prices, limiting design, and thereby destroying much of the mass-production furniture industry during the downturns.

But the most successful manufacturing regions have been ones which have linked flexible manufacturing systems, with innovative organisation and an emphasis on 'customisation', design and quality. Part of the flexibility has been achieved through new technology, and the introduction of programmable machines which can switch from product to product with little manual resetting and downtime. Benetton's automatic dyeing plant, for example, allows it to change its colours in time with demand. In the car industry, whereas General Motors took nine hours to change the dyes on its presses in the early 1980s, Toyota have lowered the time to two minutes, and have cut the average lot size of body parts from 5000 to 500 in the process. The line, in short, has become flexible. Instead of using purpose-built machines to make standard products, flexible automation uses general-purpose machines to produce a variety of products.

Manufacturers have also been adopting the retailers' answer to stocks. The pioneer is Toyota, which stands to the new era as Ford did to the old. Toyoda, the founder of Toyota, inspired by a visit to an American supermarket, applied the just-in-time system to his component suppliers, ordering on the basis of his daily production plans, and getting the components delivered right beside the line. Most of Toyota's components are still produced on the same day as they are assembled.

Toyota's prime principle of the 'elimination of wasteful practices' meant going beyond the problem of stocks. His firm has used design and materials technology to simplify complex elements, cutting down the number of parts, and operations. It adopted a zero-defect policy, developing machines which stopped automatically when a fault occurred, as well as statistical quality-control techniques. As in retailing, the complex web of processes, inside and outside the plant, were co-ordinated through computers, a process that economists have called 'systemation' (in contrast to automation). The result of these practices is a discontinuous speedup in what Marx called the circulation of capital. Toyota turns over its materials and products ten times more quickly than Western car producers, saving materials and energy in the process.

The key point about the Toyota system, however, is not so much that it speeds up the making of a car. It is that in order to make these changes it has adopted quite different methods of labour control and organisation. Toyota saw that traditional Taylorism did not work. Central management had no access to all the information needed for continuous innovation. Quality could not be achieved with deskilled manual workers. Taylorism wasted what they called 'the gold in workers' heads'.

Toyota, and the Japanese more generally, having broken the industrial unions in the 1950s, have developed a core of multi-skilled workers, whose tasks include not only manufacture and maintenance, but the improvement of the products and processes under their control. Each breakdown is seen as a chance for improvement. Even hourly-paid workers are trained in statistical techniques and monitoring, and register and interpret statistics to identify deviations from a norm – tasks customarily reserved for management in Fordism. Quality circles are a further way of tapping the ideas of the workforce. In post-Fordism, the worker is designed to act as a computer as well as a machine.

As a consequence, the Taylorist contract changes. Workers are no longer interchangeable. They gather experience. The Japanese job-for-life and corporate welfare system provides security. For the firm it secures an asset. Continuous training, payment by seniority, a breakdown of job demarcations are all part of the Japanese core wage relation. The EETPU's lead in embracing private pension schemes, BUPA, internal flexibility, union-organised training and single-company unions are all consistent with this path of post-Fordist industrial relations.

Not least of the dangers of this path is that it further hardens the divisions between the core and the peripheral workforce. The costs of employing lifetime workers means an incentive to subcontract all jobs not essential to the core. The other side of the Japanese jobs-for-life is a majority of low-paid, fragmented peripheral workers, facing an underfunded and inadequate welfare state. The duality in the labour market, and in the welfare economy, could be taken as a description of Thatcherism. The point is that neither the EETPU's policy nor that of Mrs Thatcher should be read as purely political. There is a material basis to both, rooted in changes in production.

There are parallel changes in corporate organisation. With the revision of Taylorism, a layer of management has been stripped away. Greater central control has allowed the decentralisation of work. Day-to-day autonomy has been given to work groups and plant managers. Teams linking departments horizontally have replaced the rigid verticality of Fordist bureaucracies.

It is only a short step from here to subcontracting and franchising. This is often simply a means of labour control. But in engineering and light consumer industries, networks of semi-independent firms have often proved more innovative than vertically integrated producers. A mark of post-Fordism is close two-way relations between customer and supplier, and between specialised producers in the same industry. Co-operative competition replaces the competition of the jungle.

These new relationships within and between enterprises and on the shopfloor have made least headway in the countries in which Fordism took fullest root, the USA and the UK. Here firms have tried to match continental and Japanese flexibility through automation, while retaining Fordist shopfloor, managerial and competitive relations.

Yet in spite of this we can see in this country, a culture of post-Fordist capitalism is emerging. Consumption has a new place. As for production, the keyword is flexibility – of plant and machinery, as of products and labour. Emphasis shifts from scale to scope, and from cost to quality. Organisations are geared to respond to rather than regulate markets. They are seen as frameworks for learning as much as instruments of control. Their hierarchies are flatter and their structures more open. The guerrilla force takes over from the standing army. All this has liberated the centre from the tyranny of the immediate. Its task shifts from planning to strategy, and to the promotion of the instruments of post-Fordist control – systems, software, corporate culture and cash.

On the bookshelf, Peters and Waterman replace F. W. Taylor. In the theatre, the audience is served lentils by the actors. At home, Channel 4 takes its place beside ITV. Majorities are transformed into minorities, as we enter the age of proportional representation. And under the shadow of Chernobyl even Fordism's scientific modernism is being brought to book, as we realise there is more than one way up the technological mountain.

Not all these can be read off from the new production systems. Some are rooted in the popular opposition to Fordism. They represent an alternative version of post-Fordism, which flowered after 1968 in the community movements and the new craft trade unionism of alternative plans. Their organisational forms – networks, workplace democracy, co-operatives, the dissolving of the platform speaker into meetings in the round – have echoes in the new textbooks of management; indeed capital has been quick to take up progressive innovations for its own purposes. There are then many sources and contested versions of post-Fordist culture. What they share is a break with the era of Ford.

Post-Fordism is being introduced under the sway of the market and in accordance with the requirements of capital accumulation. It validates only what can command a place in the market; it cuts the labour force in two and leaves large numbers without any work at all. Its prodigious productivity gains are ploughed back into yet further accumulation and the quickening consumption of symbols in the post-modern marketplace. In the UK, Thatcherism has strengthened the prevailing wind of the commodity economy, liberating the power of private purses and so fragmenting the social sphere.

To judge from Kamata's celebrated account, working for Toyota is hardly a step forward from working for Ford. As one British worker in a Japanese factory in the north east of England put it, 'they want us to live for work, whereas we want to work to live'. Japanisation has no place in any modern *News From Nowhere*.

Yet post-Fordism has shaken the kaleidoscope of the economy, and exposed an old politics. We have to respond to its challenges and draw lessons from its systems.

First there is the question of consumption. How reluctant the left has been to take this on, in spite of the fact that it is a sphere of unpaid production, and, as Gorz insists, one of creative activity. Which local council pays as much attention to its users as does the market research industry on behalf of commodities? Which bus or railway service cuts queues and speeds the traveller with as much care as retailers show to their just-in-time stocks? The perspective of consumption – so central to the early socialist movement – is emerging from under the tarpaulin of production; the effects of food additives and low-level radiation, of the air we breathe and surroundings we live in, the availability of childcare and community centres, or access to privatised city centres and transport geared to particular needs. These are issues of consumption, where the social and the human have been threatened by the market. In each case the market solutions have been contested by popular movements. Yet their causes and the relations of consumption have been given only walk-on parts in party programmes. They should now come to the centre of the stage.

Second, there is labour. Post-Fordism sees labour as the key asset of modern production. Rank Xerox is trying to change its accounting system so that machinery becomes a cost and labour its fixed asset. The Japanese emphasise labour and learning. The left should widen this reversal of Taylorism, and promote a discontinuous expansion of adult education inside and outside the workplace.

They should also provide an alternative to the new management of time. The conservative sociologist Daniel Bell sees the management of time as the key issue of post-industrial society. Post-Fordist capital is restructuring working time for its own convenience: with new shifts, split shifts, rostering, weekend working, and the regulation of labour, through part-time and casual contracts, to the daily and weekly cycles of work. Computer systems allow Tesco to manage more than 130 different types of labour contract in its large stores. These systems, and employment and welfare legislation, should be moulded for the benefit not the detriment of labour. The length of the working day, of the working week and year, and lifetime, should be shaped to accommodate the many responsibilities and needs away from work.

The most pressing danger from post-Fordism, however, is the way it is widening the split between core and periphery in the labour market and the welfare system. The EETPU's building of a fortress round the core is as divisive as Thatcherism itself. We need bridges across the divide, with trade unions representing core workers using their power to extend benefits to all, as IG Metall have been doing in Germany. A priority for any Labour government would be to put a floor under the labour market, and remove the discriminations faced by the low paid. The Liberals pursued such a policy in late nineteenth-century London. Labour should reintroduce it in late-twentieth-century Britain.

Underlying this split is the post-Fordist bargain which offers security in return for flexibility. Because of its cost, Japanese capital restricts this bargain to the core; in the peripheral workforce flexibility is achieved through insecurity. Sweden has tried to widen the core bargain to the whole population with a policy of full employment, minimum incomes, extensive retraining programmes and egalitarian income distribution. These are the two options, and Thatcherism favours the first.

Could Labour deliver the second? How real is a policy of full employment when the speed of technical change destroys jobs as rapidly as growth creates them? The question – as Sweden has shown – is one of distribution. There is the distribution of working time: the campaign for the 35-hour week and the redistribution of overtime should be at the centre of Labour policy in the 1990s. There is also the distribution of income and the incidence of tax. Lafontaine's idea of shifting tax from labour to energy is an interesting one. Equally important is the need to tax heavily the speculative gains from property, the rent from oil, and unearned and inherited income. Finally taxes will need to be raised on higher incomes, and should be argued for not only in terms of full employment, but in terms of the improvements to the caring services, the environment, and the social economy which the market of the 1980s has done so much to destroy. Full employment is possible. It should be based on detailed local plans, decentralised public services and full employment centres. It cannot be delivered from Westminster alone.

Third, we need to learn from post-Fordism's organisational innovations, and apply them within our own public and political structures. Representative democracy within Fordist bureaucracies is not enough. What matters is the structure of the bureaucracy and its external relations. In the state this means redefining its role as strategist, as innovator, coordinator and supporter of producers. In some cases the span of co-ordination needs to be extended (notably in integrating public transport and the movement of freight); in others, production should be decentralised and the drive for scale reversed (the electricity industry, education and health have all suffered from over-centralised operations). Public services should move beyond the universal to the differentiated service. Nothing has been more outrageous than the attack on local government as 'loony leftist' when councils have sought to shape policies to the needs of groups facing discrimination. Capitalist retailers and market researchers make these distinctions in the pursuit of sales, and socialists should match them in pursuit of service. If greater user control and internal democracy were added to this, then we would be some way towards the dismantling of mass-produced administration, and the creation of a progressive and flexible state.

Last, there is private industry. In many sectors, both industry and public policy are frozen in Fordism, even as the leading edge of competition has shifted from scale to product, and from costs to strategy. In spite of the restructuring that has taken place in the 1980s, largely at the expense of labour, manufacturing competitiveness continues to decline. By 1984, only five out of thirty-four major manufacturing sectors did not have a negative trade balance.

The left's response to this decline has been couched largely in terms of macro policy: devaluing the pound, controlling wage levels and expanding investment. Industrial policy has taken second place and centred on amalgamations and scale, and the encouragement of new technology. This has been Labour's version of modernisation.

The fact remains that size has not secured competitiveness. Neither has a declining exchange rate with the yen, nor wage levels which have made UK one of the cheap labour havens of Europe. The changes are much deeper than this.

An alternative needs to start not from plans but from strategies. Strategic capacity within British industry is thin, and even thinner in the state and the labour movement. Sector and enterprise strategies need to take on board the nature of the new competition, the centrality of skilled labour, the need for specialisation and quality, and for continuous innovation.

What public policy should do is to find ways of ensuring that the resultant restructuring takes account of social priorities: labour and educational reform is one part of this; industrial democracy another; environmental and energy saving a third; user concerns about quality and variety a fourth. Some of these will require new laws, others incentive schemes, others collective bargaining. They all need to be a part of strategic restructuring.

In each sector there will be giants barring the path towards such a programme. One will be the stock market. A priority for a Labour government will be to reduce the stock market's power to undermine long-term strategic investment (in this we need to follow the example of the Japanese). Another will be multinationals, who dominate so many industrial and service sectors in the economy. The urgent task here is to form coalitions of states, unions and municipalities across the European Community to press for common strategic alternatives at the European level. A third will be the retailers. In some cases, retailers will be important allies in restructuring industry progressively (the co-op has a role here); in others, the conduct of retailers is destructive, and a Labour government should take direct measures against them.

At the same time, Labour needs to develop a network of social-industrial institutions, decentralised, innovative, and entrepreneurial. For each sector and area there should be established one or more enterprise boards. They would be channels for long-term funds, for new technology, for strategic support across a sector, for common services, and for initiatives and advice on the social priorities.

Public purchasing should be co-ordinated and used not just to provide protection in the old manner, but as supporters of the sectoral programme, as contributors to the improvement of quality and as a source of ideas. New technology networks should also be set up, linking universities and polytechnics with the sectors and unions (this is an effective part of Dukakis' Massachusetts programme).

In short, we need a new model of the public economy made up of a honeycomb of decentralised, yet synthetic institutions, integrated by a common strategy, and intervening in the economy at the level of production rather than trying vainly to plan all from on high. The success of the Italian consortia and the German industrial regions has been centrally dependent on such a network of municipal and regional government support.

A key role in taking forward this industrial programme should be played by the unions. Restructuring has put them on the defensive. They have found their power weakened and their position isolated. Few have had the resources to develop alternative strategies and build coalitions of communities and users around them. Yet this is now a priority if unions are to reclaim their position as spokespeople of an alternative economy rather than defenders of a sectional interest. Research departments should be expanded, and commissions given to external researchers. There should be joint commissions of members, and users and other related groups, as well as supportive local authorities. The production of the policy would itself be a form of democratic politics.

Mrs Thatcher has led an attack on the key institutions of Fordism: on manufacturing, on the centralised state, on industrial unions and on the national economy. She has opened up Britain to one version of post-Fordism, one that has strengthened the control of finance and international capital, has increased inequality and destroyed whole areas of collective life.

There is an alternative. It has grown up in the new movements, in the trade unions and in local government over the past twenty years. It has broken through the bounds of the left's Fordist inheritance, in culture, structure and economics. From it can develop – as is already happening in Europe – an alternative socialism adequate to the post-Fordist age.

3

The state after Henry

First published in Marxism Today, *May 1991, pp22-27. Reproduced with permission.*

The events of the last decade have ensured that the organisation of the public sphere has become the central political problematic of the 1990s. Previously the key issue for social democratic as for revolutionary socialists has been how to take state power. Now the question is how to administer it. For what is clear from the collapse in eastern Europe, and from the administrative problems of the public sector in the west, is that the long-standing model of the state is seriously flawed.

At the same time, the introduction of the market and of private capital into areas previously administered by the state has already led to the re-emergence of the problems which the original development of the state was intended to solve. We know, as John Major knows, that congestion will not disappear if you set up tolls on the M1 or privatise the northern line. The traffic gridlock of American cities testifies to that. Nor will homelessness be solved if public housing is sold. The state is far from finished. The question is – and it is a question that has never been more open since the mid-nineteenth-century – what form it should take.

The form of twentieth-century administration was that of mass production. States sought to match the demands of the economy with the need for new services by borrowing the ideas and methods of industrial Fordism. Progressive architects tried to apply Ford's methods to housing, schools and hospitals. They designed basic models, and then standardised the components and the process of construction. The lack of variety was justified in terms of economy and equality and became bound up with the welfare state principle of 'universality', the availability of standard rights and services for all. School dinners, desks, and uniforms could all be produced and purchased as if for the army. This was the Fordist welfare dream.

Alongside the standardisation went the ideal of scale, the bigger the cheaper. London's mental hospitals looked like large factories in the green belt. Schools grew in size, as did airports, and public offices. Boroughs lost services to counties and counties to Whitehall. The argument was always that size allowed greater specialism (Spanish in the sixth form), cheaper supplies, and more economic administration.

The state also borrowed from industry the ideas of F. W. Taylor on work organisation. Tasks were broken down and wherever possible deskilled so that they could be performed by semiskilled labour. There was a strict division between what the Victorians called 'intellectual' and 'mechanical' labour, with the managers laying down how work was to be done. Each job carried with it a detailed job description and its own wage rate, all of them subject to centralised negotiation.

The structure of management followed the same principles. The senior managers planned what was to be done, did the co-ordination between units, and took the decisions. There was little autonomy for subordinate units or links between them. Management decisions were issued via a lengthy hierarchy to those delivering the service. Service information and requests for decisions made their way back up the hierarchy in a sea of memos and multiple copies.

These flows of information and decisions were the pistons of the administrative machine. The accompanying rules and procedures were the casing. Because it was so highly structured and complex it was slow to adapt to external changes and preferred to get its supplies and technical support in-house. It was an introverted form of organisation. Where it did have external dealings, these were done through senior management. Supplies were purchased through detailed contracts and subject to formal tendering procedures.

As for the users of the service, not surprisingly they often felt themselves to be the passive objects of a service machine which deskilled the client as much as the service worker (the control of patients over their own bodies in the health service is a case in point). For its part the public service – say the local swimming pool – had little idea who used its facility, and thus how it might be tailored to meet particular needs. There is then a distinctly Fordist element in the twentieth-century state: standard products; a commitment to scale; a Tayloristic labour process; a centralised and information-heavy administration; which was inward-looking and cut off from the suppliers and users. These are part of the administrative culture of our time, promoted by the Left as much as by the Right.

Yet the public sector has been an awkward territory for Fordism. Many of its services are delivered by skilled professionals – doctors, teachers and social workers – who have resisted the attempts of the 'scientific managers' to fragment their jobs and standardise them. The fact that civil servants have had job security and strong national unions, has made it difficult to impose on them the level of managerial control that has been the rule in private mass production.

If state managers have had less operational control than their private counterparts, they have had more centralised power. Partly this is because ministers are formally responsible to parliament for the conduct of their ministries, and the senior bureaucrats are responsible to ministers. Those at the centre thus have an interest in keeping tight control over those beneath them. Partly, too, it is because the cost of over-centralisation – the delay and poor services – are difficult to measure when the services are not sold. Firms judge a unit's performance by profit. A state cannot do this. Sub-units, like individuals, are judged by their ability to stick to rules and keep to budgets. This encourages centralisation, and a bias towards neglecting the amount and quality of service.

For these reasons, the traditional form of the modern state is best described as semi-Fordist. In the United States where the old order of land and the new order of labour were both weaker, the movement for scientific management faced less resistance. There, as paradoxically in the Soviet Union, Fordism provided an integrated structure for private industry, the military and civilian administration. In Europe, the very size of the public sector provided a political and economic space which was more insulated from the market and which witnessed a continuing tension between a Fordist model of administration and those within the administration who were threatened by it.

The Tory policies of the last decade are to be seen against this background. Their significance should not be underestimated. Previous governments over two centuries have tried to cut back the state and control its costs. But the current changes have been formed by a theory of public administration which is quite new.

The key text of this approach by Niskanen appeared in 1971. It seemed no more than an ideological excursion of orthodox economics into a neighbouring academic field. Within twenty years it stands at the centre of our political stage, as Keynesian generations listen passively to the sound of its axes in the cherry orchard of the state.

'Public choice' – for that is the name given to the new approach – appears to be about introducing the market economy into previously sacred public domains. Its language is that of contracts and competition, of consumption and choice. In this it already decisively changes the traditional points of focus from inputs to outputs. It calls the producers to account on behalf of the consumers and seeks a new democracy of service choice to replace an old corruption of producer interests. Its advocates, like Adam Smith before them, invoke the market against an order of privilege, and in doing so believe they have history in their sails.

I want to suggest that contrary to its appearance the main thrust of Thatcherite policy, inspired by public choice theory, has been to further the Fordist project of the traditional public sector.

It has done this to begin with by using the market and financial controls to extend Taylorism, notably to the work of public sector professionals. Jobs have been broken down and the less skilled parts assigned to lower-paid workers (this has been at the heart of the reorganisation of nursing). Other jobs have been deskilled through automation, or through government grant scales which are only economic for less experienced and lower paid providers (this was the case with training grants in the late 1980s). Job redesign and cash pressure has increased the intensity of public sector work. Systems of reward have been geared to performance, with output being measured, and individual cash payments promoted as the main form of incentive. These policies have been presented as bringing private sector labour practices into previously protected parts of the state. But their significance is that they represent a particular type of labour market regime – that of the scientific management movement.

There has been likewise a restructuring of managerial control. The key innovation has again been output measurement. Instead of senior civil servants and ministers being directly responsible for operations, services are run at arm's length on the basis of a performance agreement. Whether or not the service operators are public or private the mechanism is similar. Thus, the government's Next Steps initiative has divided central government work which cannot be privatised into a small administrative core and some forty new agencies (such as the Stationery Office). Each is issued with a contract, a budget and allowed to get on with it. The same principle is being applied to quangos and to many local government services. Ministerial and senior bureaucratic responsibility is now confined to the issuing of contracts and the monitoring of performance. The state has become a purchaser rather than a provider.

This again runs right against the trend of a century of public administration. But in substance it is no more than the introduction of Alfred Sloan's basic model for a divisionalised General Motors. The agencies, like GM's divisions, are still structured as vertical hierarchies. 'Next Steps' does not change the basic model of organisation but shifts the locus of control. The decentralisation from politicians is counterbalanced by a centralisation within the agencies themselves.

The Thatcher revolution in government is at its core the attempt to impose the control structures of Fordism on the state. In some instances, private sector managers have been employed by the state. In others, the private sector has taken over directly through privatisation or sub-contracting. The purchasers of state assets, and the contractors of state services, have for the most part been the larger companies. They have been the agents for the new order.

The changes have served to confirm other features of Fordism. There is still a clear commitment to scale, reflected not least in the closure of smaller local facilities. As for products the role of large firms in taking over public assets or services has meant that commercial mass products have been substituted for the standard public ones.

But the clearest indication of the continuing Fordist character of the state is the central institution of the new order – the contract. It presupposes arm's length relations between contractor and contracted. The contractor draws up the contract unilaterally and in detail. It may be negotiated with a public agency or submitted for tender. The contract carries a price or budget, and once signed, the contractor agrees to withdraw to the side-lines and confine itself to monitoring. In spite of revision clauses, the contract freezes the service for the agreed period, and is ill-fitted to adapt to changing circumstances. It epitomises inter-Fordist relations.

The point is that the new model state is based on an old model of management. It is a model which shaped the British state, but never fully controlled it. Thatcherism has changed this and shifted the style of state management to a more commercial Fordism. What remains critical is that this old model of management is the one which has been responsible for the problems faced by British and American industry in world markets. Those in the forefront of industrial competition have exhibited a new post-Fordist managerialism whose tenets go right against the policies discussed above and point up the central weaknesses of the new Right's model.

The first weakness concerns quality. Already the control of service quality has been the overriding managerial problems of local authority and central government sub-contracting. It has also been a central problem for private industry. A recent industrial survey in the US suggested that 15-40 per cent of ex-factory cost was accounted for by poor quality, in contrast to the low defect rates in Japanese factories. What the Japanese have found is that quality cannot be imposed from without, as public sub-contracting aims to do. It must be secured and monitored by front-line producers.

The second weakness relates to labour. The new managerialism sees skilled front-line producers as a key not only to quality but to innovation and production control. To be effective they need training, job security, and a commitment to the work. The same applies to white collar workers. It is now a first principle of modern management that a firm's competitivity depends above all on the quality of its labour force. The Thatcherite state goes almost wholly against this – with its emphasis on deskilling front-line workers, cutting their pay, and increasing labour turnover rates to the levels of a mass production factory. An innovative, high quality, economic public service cannot possibly be built with a Taylorised and antagonised labour force.

Third, there is the structure of management. Post-Fordism emphasises decentralisation of control at all levels, to production teams, support units, and the factory managers. It also seeks to limit the upward flow of information, keeping it in the hands of operatives who need it. Technical production staff are given an advisory rather than controlling role. Layers of middle management have been stripped away so that the organisational pyramid is flattened. What preoccupies management is not how to enforce vertical chains of authority, but how to establish functional horizontal links between separate production units, through project teams, information flow and so on.

The new Right state contradicts each element of this model. It has reinforced centralised managerial control and reduced front-line operative autonomy. It has multiplied the quantity of financial and other central information required by senior management, to the benefit of the accounting profession. Most seriously of all, it has scattered the state into fragments between which there are no co-ordinating links. Co-ordination in the past was too centralised. Now, other than the market, there is none at all.

Fourth, the place given by the new Right to 'the contract' is entirely at odds with post-Fordist practice. The aim of the latter is to establish long term working relations with suppliers and customers. The watchword is trust not contract. Japanese firms are known for their 'mutual understandings' of one page where Ford would have a contract of 500. The rationale is that what the purchasing firm wants cannot be specified in a contract. It puts forward ideas, the supplier comes up with others, both are committed to continuous improvement which would outdate a contract before the ink was dry. Suppliers are taken on for their capacity to innovate and work co-operatively not for low prices. Tendering is the antithesis of this type of relationship.

Similarly close relations are sought with customers. A recent study found that over half of a sample of innovations in the US came from customer ideas. In an era of customised products, customers themselves become part of production. The idea of detailed arm's length contracts runs right against the industrial tide.

The above suggest one clear conclusion. The Thatcherite model of the state is deeply flawed as a system of service delivery. It has attempted answers of some of the weaknesses of Britain's traditional semi-Fordist state – its overcentralisation, its rigid occupational structures – but the answers have been Fordist in nature and contradict the requirements of public service organisations.

What of the alternatives? Private post-Fordist management has given greatest priority to the issues of innovation, quality, customised products and the flexible machinery that such customisation requires. These have in turn depended on a skilled and cohesive labour force. They have also demanded an open organisational system which has multiple points of autonomy within it and sees a wide range of working relationships with those outside it. The condition for decentralisation within it is a developed system of control information, and the cohesion that comes from some measure of shared culture. It is a system that centres round social relations rather than exchange.

This is not a description of a Japanese model of management. Not surprisingly, private firms face contradictions in promoting co-operation when ownership is restricted. But any new model for the public realm has much to learn from those places where elements of post-Fordism are emerging in large firms, in localities of small and medium ones, and in some of the successful groups of co-operatives.

As a starting point, post-Fordism encourages us to focus on the front-line producers of state services, on the users and the relationships between them. On these producers will depend the quality of service, and many of the improvements in it. The refuse collector, the bus conductor and the staff at the local library come from the organisational shadows and are recognised as the key points of public contact. Interestingly, the chief executive of Wirral Council (Conservative) has taken to spending time on the council's reception desk for this reason.

What is implied is not merely greater status and permanence for such front-line workers, but delegation of operational responsibility, and training in information gathering, processing and reporting. There have been successful experiments in Sweden with home helps organising their own schedules instead of relying on an office manager. To a Taylorised culture such ideas seem far-fetched, but they are common practice in the best of modern industrial production.

One need is to redefine jobs to include working with users. I say 'users' because the word 'consumer' fails to recognise that the user too produces. Indeed, users often want to be more involved in production, but are prevented from being so by the way services are organised. Consider the change in the user's role in preventative rather than curative medicine, or in programmes of energy conservation rather than generation. There has been a mushrooming of user groups around such issues. In some cases, they may run a quasi-public facility directly – like a community centre. In others they are channels for information and discussion, and a means for pressing the state on the nature of its services.

What is clear from these civic movements is that people are far from the model of individual, passive consumers, who are all-knowing and rational about what they want. We all want to learn and know more, to do things together and have control over our lives. This puts the role of the service worker in a new light, as a supporter, and adviser as much as provider. Take the job of refuse collecting. One local council near Rotterdam in Holland has redefined it to include advising householders on recycling. A whole range of jobs can be redefined in this way from electricity meter reading, to school caretaking or the guarding of museums (and commonly are, unofficially, in ways that privatisation has disrupted).

Professionals also work in the front line. What is striking is that professional training of, say, doctors or university lecturers puts much greater emphasis on technical knowledge than on interpersonal skills, let alone on how people can help heal themselves, or how adults learn. These types of skills and relationships are difficult to measure. They cannot therefore be included in contracts, and the time allowances assumed in public contracts tend to squeeze out such quality time.

Starting with the service providers inverts the normal organisational pyramid, or rather recasts it as a circle with the service workers and users in the middle, and other parts of the public sector – the maintenance crews, the accountants and managers – supportive of them. The difficult question is what should be the structure of the relationships be, between the cells of the service relationship and the wider organisational body? This is one area to which the new Right have devoted great energy. They have shown that the lack of output measurement was a major weakness of the old public regime, since it led to control through costs.

We should all welcome operational figures like how many trains are late, or what percentage of letters arrive on time. We need more of them, particularly about use. How many people use the public library and who are they? What is the occupancy rate of school buildings? Not only should these figures be public, but they should be used to prompt new services, and customise old ones. If cost per user replaced free floating cost as a key indicator, it would place a premium on improving access to facilities (a free bus ride with every swimming ticket) and on expanding services rather than cutting, say, library hours to save on wages.

The Japanese, like the new Right have a thirst for measurement, but they use it not to introduce some quasi-market, but as a means of improving output. Production line workers undertake statistical quality control with a higher level of statistics than an undergraduate economist. These numbers are used as tools of diagnosis and to suggest innovations. What doctor's practice follows its patients progress with one-tenth of this attention?

Productive quantification is a support not a substitute for qualitative assessment. For evaluations, inspectorates, quality commissions, service auditors, student's assessments (indeed user assessments more generally) must always take first place, and like the figures themselves, serve to suggest and stimulate as well as assess.

Such systems of information represent the nerves of any new social economy. Equally important are the terms of the labour contract and what the French call the 'formation' of those who work in it. State work should be craft work not mass work, and the labour contract should reflect this. This implies an idea of apprenticeship and the re-assertion of a sense of career in an extended way. Public sector workers, like the Danish furniture workers who gather experience all over Europe before returning home, should be able to shift between different public sectors (as in French educational employment), and take time out from their contracts to work abroad, or in industry, or in domestic caring.

One lesson from the history of all European bureaucracies is that overriding attention was given to the training of civil service elites. The Indian Civil Service founded its own public school (Haileybury) in 1806. The mid-nineteenth-century civil service reforms were intimately linked to the reforms of the public schools and Oxbridge. In France there were civil service colleges, in Prussia a long period of bureaucratic apprenticeship, after a legal education. In all cases the aim was to create an integrative culture, and to tailor recruitment procedures to those who had that culture, as the key to organisational structure and control. Like the major corporations of today, the nineteenth-century bureaucracies did not take a common culture for granted.

A progressive state needs to pay similar attention to the recruitment and training of all who work for it. Public sector employment should reflect the composition of the society which it serves, which is why the employment of women and minorities is so important an issue today. There needs also to be a common ethic, and a sense of shared social values as a precondition for decentralisation and a redefinition of the 'service relation'. The substance of further education, polytechnic and university education should be reassessed in this light, with a concerned sociology replacing utilitarian economics as a preparation for public work.

A cohesive culture is the first principle of post-Fordist organisation. Another is the need for decentralisation and a lattice network. Production units, like the frontline staff, need a measure of autonomy, clearly marked, within which they decide, and to which sets of users can relate. The decentralisation principle has been key to the shape of modern production and its organisation.

It necessarily challenges arguments for scale. Large technical projects often exhibit diseconomies of organisation. They have been inflexible (the French nuclear power industry is a prime example) and have been promoted by an overcentralised government which cannot deal with small projects. Furthermore, many of the specialist services which have been used to justify amalgamation could be provided through consortia or by separate service units.

What the organisational issues turns on is whether autonomous units can work together effectively, or whether a centralised, controlling management is required. Industrial experience in Italy, Germany and Japan suggests that networking between independent enterprises has been remarkably successful as a way of overcoming the separation of departments in a divisionalised firm – indeed large firms have been encouraging horizontal networking by the sub units within them from the viewpoint of the state this suggests a lattice structure, with a central or local state ensuring that the lateral links are made and unified systems established.

Such organisations are 'open' within themselves, porous, with a necessary variety. Equally their health depends on them being open to the external world. This implies that effective democracy is a prerequisite for any effective public service. Liberalism and socialism have emphasised votes, parties and majorities as the cornerstones of a concept of democracy. The practices of the state have taught us that this is not enough. Representatives (and party workers) are few in number, and dominated by the tyranny of the immediate.

Four things are required. First with the decentralisation of administration, there should be a decentralisation of representation, with users represented in the management structures of operating units and agencies. Second, discretionary public funds should be made available at local and national level to support user groups. Third, the detailed operating information of any service should be publicly available. Fourth, discretionary funds are needed for research on long-term strategy for particular sectors, since it is regulatory structures and integrated production systems – often planned many years ahead – which increasingly limit the scope for any say in the present.

If a strong civil society is critical to an effective public service, post-Fordism suggests that the character and culture of the non-state economy is also significant. Many of the debates in the past have been about the boundaries between public and private. Less attention has been given to the character of each.

I have defined the public sector in terms of a social ethic, a body of skilled public workers, with a commitment to a particular form of service, and subject to various kinds of democratic control. Historically the state represented one way in which the idea of a society could be reasserted within the context of a daily fractured experience. It stood for some sense of collective culture – and although many of its structures have been inadequate – there is still a real sense even today in which teachers, nurses, or doctors identify with their work for its broader social purpose.

Many of these tenets of a social economy are found outside the formal state in voluntary organisations, companies limited by guarantee, co-operatives, community enterprises and so on. These 'not for profits' form a third sector which is one of the most rapidly expanding in the USA. Their operational structures, their producer/user relations and their collective ethic exemplify many of the principles discussed above.

There is scope for extending the idea by changing company law to recognise a new category of private enterprise – the social company – which although privately owned, accepts as part of its practice elements of the social economy I have described. Such companies along with the third sector should be seen as prime partners of any post-Fordist state.

The regressive distributional results of the new Right's reforms have been evident from the first. I have concentrated on what I think are the productive weaknesses. The severity of the results, coupled with the destructive radicalism of the measures themselves, have now produced a particular political moment. It is a moment which offers a real opportunity for the Left to advance an alternative social vision, together with the outline of a new model, at once a productive and democratic post-Fordist state.

4

New directions in
municipal socialism

First published as Robin Murray, 'New directions in municipal socialism',
Chapter 15 of Ben Pimlott (ed.), Fabian Essays in Socialist Thought,
Fabian Society, London: Heinemann, 1984. Reproduced with permission
of the Fabian Society.

I

Fabian economic writing has always been remarkable for its optimism. With the Webbs it was an optimism of detail. For Shaw it was a confidence that state power would grow as a necessary counter to the abuses of landlords and private monopolies. In the 1930s, Dalton, Jay and Durbin retained an uninhibited belief in the capacity of a Labour government to control the private economy through planning, nationalisation and New Deal budgetary policy, and to achieve equality through the redistribution of income and wealth. In the post-war years, the question was not whether a Labour government could control the economy but by what means and by how much.

The events of the last decade have disturbed this optimism. The main pillars of Fabian economic thought have one by one been undermined. The first to be questioned was nationalisation as the answer to private monopoly. In the first *Fabian Essays*, William Clarke had argued that private monopolies, though efficient, needed to be made public for distributional and democratic reasons. The first detailed Fabian discussion of nationalisation was in 1910. By the 1930s it was a prime theme, and Dalton's *Practical Socialism* contained a large section on 'socialisation', the different forms it could take, how to ensure democracy within state-run industries, and the industries where it was most necessary. By the time of the *New Fabian Essays* in 1952, Crosland was calling a halt to 'the further multiplication of public boards on the present model'. Like Clarke he saw nationalisation primarily in redistributive terms – substituting 'fixed interest payments to capital for rising dividends' – and thus not a main line of advance in an economy with government controls and high rates of taxation.

Unfortunately the debates of the next twenty-five years did not centre on the extension of democratic control over nationalised as well as nationalisable industry, but on the multiplication of the 'present models'. As a result, public ownership is now on the retreat. State industries and public services have too often been experienced by both workers and consumers as alien. Authoritarian hierarchy, time-and-motion study, and technology that deskills and controls those who work with it – all these features of private capitalist work organisation from the period of Henry Ford have been increasingly experienced by public sector workers. Similarly, tenants and other public sector consumers have had to campaign for a say in the services that were said to be organised in their name. Indeed it became clear that much of the programme of post-war nationalisation had primarily served to rationalise production for the sake of private industry; that what had been regarded as a socialist project was in the end part of a capitalist project, to restructure the infrastructure of British capitalism.

Not only did nationalisation as such lose considerable consumer support, but when the Tory offensive for privatisation gathered momentum in the 1980s, the public sector trade unions have in many fields found themselves with only limited support from users in their campaigns of resistance. The last five years have therefore been particularly traumatic: not only has nationalisation failed to win mass support as a path for socialist advance, but the ratchet, which Fabians have always believed would guarantee advances already made, has been released and the gains unwound.

To the first evil of capitalism, monopoly, the Fabian answer was socialisation. To the second evil, *laissez faire*, the answer was planning. The early Fabians were more concerned with the inequality of capitalism *distribution* rather than the malfunctioning of capitalist *exchange*. But the latter became a more substantial theme in the inter-war period. Some writers emphasised the failure of market prices to reflect social costs and benefits – and this has been a continuing theme in Fabian economics and the justification for state intervention in the market economy. Others had a more macro concern, using planning as a mechanism to avoid economic crises. During the Second World War, there was a remarkably extended system of physical planning, which was continued in a number of fields, along with a wide range of controls, by the post-war Atlee government.

Again it was Crosland in the *New Fabian Essays* who called for an end to this planned asserting of the market economy:

> Controls over industry should be directed to certain basic planning ends – full employment, the balance of payments, location of industry, utility schemes and the like. Beyond this they should not be multiplied. A complex mass of detailed controls is highly unpopular, bad for industrial efficiency, and distorting in its effect on production.

Although the Labour Manifesto on which the 1964 election was won re-asserted the importance of industrial planning, George Brown's National Plan was an empty indicative plan, without power or purchase. The Department of Economic Affairs was subordinated to the Treasury, and the July 1966 measures confirmed the end of this shallowest of experiments. Even the industrial planning bodies which came later – the IRC and the NEB – had a narrow brief, limited power, and except in the brief period when Tony Benn was Minister of Industry, ignored the concerns of workers and consumers within the industries they attempted to plan. As with the nationalised industries, industrial planning, to the limited extent it was introduced, appeared as an instrument of capitalist rationalisation, rather than being in any way socialist.

The carefully prepared campaign by the monetarists in favour of the free market thus met with little resistance. The stream of Hobart papers and Chicago market ideology spread to every cranny of Britain's social economy. With the notable exception of books like Titmuss's *The Gift Relation* (about the economics of the distribution of blood), planned, non-market distribution had little theoretical defence, or recent practical examples of success at a macro level. As a result, the market has now got an overwhelming ideological hegemony in current economic thought. Viability, competitivity, freedom of choice, balancing the books – this is the vocabulary of economic approval. Subsidy, lame ducks, uncompetitiveness, unproductive – these are the words used to erode the legitimacy of the public economy. All define themselves in terms of market exchange.

The third pillar of Fabian economics was adopted from a Liberal in the 1930s – Keynes. The control of macroeconomic fluctuations through fiscal and monetary policy grew from being one part of a general case for public planning to a separate, and indeed dominant, argument for state intervention at the macro level. The macroeconomic implications of propensities to save and to consume were woven into the older Fabian case for redistribution. The post-war economic boom was linked to Labour policies analysed through a Keynesian grid. Redistribution increased consumption which encouraged investment. In spite of academic doubts that Keynesian policy might increase fluctuations rather than smooth them out, there was for thirty years a confidence that the long economic boom was somehow associated with government economic management.

From the mid 1970s, the Keynesian consensus has been broken. In this country and elsewhere there had been an ever-gathering crisis in the private sector, reflected in a falling rate of profit, and from 1973 a fall in investment. Keynesian theory indicated the use of public spending to maintain demand and thus the rate of profit. But the traditional instruments of macroeconomic management when operated to this end proved incapable of stemming the decline of private profitability, and the rise of inflation and unemployment. Tony Crosland – who had been the symbol of the 'post-capitalist mixed economy' – turned first on the welfare state in his celebrated 1975 speech declaring that 'the party's over'. Denis Healey – himself a contributor to the 1952 *Fabian Essays* – the following year further marked the turn against public spending and wage-earners with what became known as the 'IMF measures'. The post-war confidence that redistribution and public sector expansion would increase growth was now inverted. Unable to attack the private sector crisis directly, Labour economic policy was forced to attack two of the foundations of the social-democratic tradition, the welfare state and the level of wages. In Whitehall it no doubt appeared as though there was no alternative. But to the troops in the field it felt like being fired at by one's own generals.

Into the vacuum of economic policy monetarism marched with the confidence of a zealot. In practice and theory, monetarism has lost every economic argument to the Keynesian repost, lowering inflation only through collapsing the economy as a whole. Yet in the 1983 election, Mrs Thatcher was returned with her historic majority, and the opinion surveys have shown that Labour actually lost the economic argument. This is a measure of the crisis of Labour economic policy. There was clear public evidence that monetarist policies had doubled the severity of the international economic depression as it affected the UK. Keynesian reflation policy offers to halve the effects of the crisis as it stands now. But Mrs Thatcher's appeal rests partly on the fact that she is offering to attach the whole of the problem. And to this the Keynesians have no adequate response.

Swept away as part of this defeat of Keynesianism has been the fourth pillar of the social-democratic tradition – redistribution. Already in the 1960s the post-war welfare settlement was being re-evaluated, as having redistributed income and services within classes rather than between them. In addition there were similar problems to those affecting the nationalised industries: how to make welfare services – both for the servers and the served – supportive rather than controlling, on our side of the fence rather than theirs. On top of this, a decade of cuts has left many of these services in tatters.

Since 1979 there has also been a growing inequality in incomes. Monetarist policy has asserted that it is now inequality that is necessary for growth, providing incentives for the technocrats and managers and an inducement to invest for the property owners and large corporations. The taxation and control of wealth and high incomes have all been discontinuously lowered. For the unemployed, however, the government directs that poverty should rule, as an incentive for the unemployed to look for work, and for the employed to keep at it. Peter Townsend's monumental study shows how deep a poverty still remains.

As with the monetarist drive to privatisation, and the championing of the market against planning, so the reappearance of unemployment and the reassertion of inequality show the unravelling of the post-war social-democratic system. The trauma for Labour economic policy has been not merely the collapse of each of the four pillars of its traditional programme, nor even the destruction of the achievements in these fields by the current Tory government, but the fact that the retreat on all of them has been started by Labour ministers themselves. These ministers were in most cases the architects of the earlier policies, and the bearers of that post-war confidence. It is against this background that Labour economic policy must be reassessed.

II

What is now at issue in Labour thinking is not just particular ideas or policies but the whole framework of economic analysis. Fabian economics has been dominated by neoclassical theory and, since the 1930s, by Keynes. But it has by and large failed to come to terms with Marx. The exceptions were the early Fabians. Their first serious collective discussion took the form of a reading group on Marx's *Capital*. Shaw, Belfort Bax, and later Wells, argued Marx's position. Sidney Webb and the neoclassical economist Edgeworth argued the utilitarian case. Marx lost, Shaw settled for an inelegant – even if amusing – theory of rent, and Wicksteed took on the task of tutoring the Fabians in the principles of marginalism.

Over the last fifteen years there has been a revival of this debate. From the mid-1960s a generation of students came to realise that neoclassical economics not only failed to adequately answer the major issues confronting the labour movement but that it was also an ideology of the right. By the early 1970s, *Capital* reading groups were springing up, arguing about value as the early Fabians had done. What this direct reading of Marx revealed was that the issues debated in the secondary texts, and in many Fabian interpretations of Marx, were far from central to Marx's political economy:

the increasing immiseration of the working class, the inevitable tendency to the breakdown of capitalism, and other 'hypotheses' which those from an empiricist tradition formally 'tested'.

Rather, Marx offered a major critique of classical and vulgar (what later became neoclassical) economic thought. He argued not that they were incorrect, but that they were theoretically inadequate, and in the case of vulgar economics, so superficial that they misspecified the issues. Key to the argument was that we observe economics at work in the sphere of circulation – markets, distribution and consumption. But what happens in circulation is determined by forces whose origin lies in the process of production. In Volume 1 of *Capital* – titled 'Capitalist Production' – he offered a theory of production and its relationship to the sphere of exchange. Here for the first time we saw placed at the centre of economic concerns not the declining marginal utilities of some abstract individual, but the concrete details of production, the nature of work, the length of the working day, the drive for productivity and mechanisation, for time economy and ever-more extensive controls by capital over labour in the factory. Here, too, was a long-run theory of technical change and accumulation which was self-evidently richer and more explanatory than the formal growth models of neoclassical and Keynesian thought.

Against this background, the first thing to say about Keynesian economic thought is that it has been almost entirely concerned with problems of circulation rather than production. The early Fabians emphasised income distribution. The reason they developed a theory of rent was to explain inequality of wealth and income. They defined socialism in terms of distribution. The task of the state was the nationalisation of rent and its redistribution. Redistribution has remained a dominant theme in Fabian thought. 'Socialism is about equality': the words are Crosland's, but they stand for what is still the principle definition of socialism within the social-democratic tradition today.

Exchange has been a secondary theme, strongest among social-democratic economists concerned to argue the case for state intervention on the grounds of the inadequacy of the market. One strand of argument has been based on Marshall's analysis of external economies, that market exchange did not necessarily reflect social costs and benefits. Another strand was provided by Keynes with his analysis of the labour and money markets. In both cases, the state could intervene through the medium of circulation – imposing taxes, providing subsidies, or deficit financing – in order to ensure that the market system would work.

The third aspects of circulation – consumption – has principally entered Fabian economic theory via Keynes, and his treatment of consumption in terms of its aggregate quantitative amount.

As with orthodox economics, these three different parts of economic circulation have by and large been treated separately, unconnected to and unconstrained by production. In this section I want to argue that our starting point should be production, and that only by developing a new economics and politics of production will we be able to understand the changes in circulation. This is the major theoretical change required in Labour's economic thinking. I will briefly sketch out what is involved in an economics of production, and how developments in production affect and constrain distribution, exchange and consumption. In this way I hope to provide some signposts out of the impasse in which the left finds itself as a result of confining the main thrust of its economic policy to the circulation sphere.

The social-democratic tradition has treated production technically. It is seen as a black box into which suitably motivated inputs are fed, and from which outputs somewhat mysteriously arise. As in the Third International's version of Marxism, technology was also seen as technical rather than social. The idea that many people were living a majority of their lives within factories, that these lives were subject to a lawful tyranny as grievous as that of any totalitarian state, that the ensuing battles within the factory affected how and why technology developed – these issues have scarcely merited a footnote.

Indeed it is a constant theme in Fabian writing that capitalism's main contribution is what it has done for production. This is Shaw writing in the 1931 reprint of *Fabian Essays*: the capitalist system 'worked wonderfully well in the sphere of production and trade. It built up our factory system, our power machinery, our means of transport and communication. Unfortunately these unprecedented achievements in production and finance have been accompanied by a failure in distribution so grotesquely inequitable and socially disastrous that its continuance is out of the question'. There is the same optimism that is found in much Communist theory – East and West – that the forces of production were unproblematic and progressive, and were merely being held back by the relations of production.

The last decade has seen the development of a profound challenge to this view. In Italy it started in the mid-1960s around the work of Mario Tronti. In the US, the key point was the publication of Braverman's book *Labour and Monopoly Capital* in 1974. In this country, the change began the following year. What it has involved is a re-interpretation of economic and labour history around the history of production, and the re-examination of the traditions and meanings of science and technology. The black box of production – formerly entered only by sociologists of work, management scientists, and the management and workforce themselves – has been opened and reconnected to socialist concerns for the first time since William Morris. The key distinction was between capitalist relations of production in circulation and capitalist relations of production in production. The former, which has characterised Fabian and much Marxist work, saw the key feature of capitalism as the monopoly control of the means of production by a minority of private capitalists and the enforced working for them of a proletariat separated from their means of subsistence. The relations of production were therefore determined by private monopoly ownership, and they were reflected in distribution. The capitalist received unearned profit (over and above some notional wage of management) while the worker received a wage more or less related to the cost of subsistence. Shaw and a number of later Fabians argued that it was only by 'socialising' the means of production that the unearned income and exploited wealth could be redistributed by the state in an equitable way.

The monopoly control of production also gives the capitalist rights within the factory. By purchasing labour with a wage, the capitalists or their managers have the right to set that labour to work. The history of production is a history of how to enforce that right to the greatest benefit of the capitalist. The key point of transition is the change from manufacture to 'machinofacture', when the skill and control of the labourer is taken away and embodied in management and machines. Instead of the machine being controlled by its operative, it now controls the operative, in pace, direction, and judgement. The rise of scientific management around the practice and principles of Frederick Winslow Taylor from the 1880s marked the turning point in capital's movement from the formal subordination of labour to its real subordination. Henry Ford embodied Taylor's principles in the production line. The key features of Taylorism were the fragmentation of tasks, hierarchy, deskilling, and the drawing of the sharpest distinction between mental and manual labour. These changes in the factory were soon reflected in distribution. Taylor (at the Midvale Steel Company, Pennsylvania) offered workers who would accept his new systems higher wages, and this was one of the characteristics of Fordism as it spread through the assembly industries.

Fordism also produced a new mode of consumption. The higher wages bought the very goods they were paid to produce. The terms of Fordism's contract were that any worker who accepted the tyranny of the production line would be paid enough to transform his or her home with consumer durables. It was this contract which formed the basis for the post-Second World War boom.

Fordism further redefined the nature of exchange. It created a mass market. In Britain this was at first a national market. The growth of the motor industry in the 1930s was largely based on import substitution. After the war, the ever-increasing economies of scale have been the material basis for the development of multi-national corporations, increasingly integrated at the European level, and now – in the case of Ford itself – on the brink of producing a world car. In addition to the extended range of markets and integrated production, Fordism has added market research, advertising and the manufacture of style. It has also added credit, which mushroomed with the boom in order to avoid that Achilles heel of mass production, overcapacity and a steep climb in unit costs.

At the macro level, these changes in production affect the quantitative aggregates in the economy. As the scale of production grows, capital laid out both on machinery and raw materials increases relative to labour, and there is a tendency for the rate of profit to decline. The development of new products and processes raises productivity. This offsets the fall in the rate of profit, and encourages investment. Accumulation proceeds until it has worked out these new seams, and run up against barriers to expansion in existing branches of production.

When this happens there is a major economic crisis. Historically, crises have had three characteristics. First, there is a massive writing down of fictitious capital values, through bankruptcies, bank failures and factory closures, and now with central banks acting as lenders of last resort, through inflation. Second, there is an attack on labour, both to lower wages, and to increase control and the intensity of work in production. Third, there is the introduction of new methods and machinery in order to increase productivity, as well as the shaking out of the less efficient producers and the concentration of economic activity in the hands of the strong. In this way profit rates and the conditions for renewed accumulation have been restored – though not without a severe social and political crisis.

Some of the mechanisms of an economic crisis work within the sphere of circulation. Financial crashes and the devaluation of capital values are one example. The cut in wages (and now in welfare provisions) is another. But central to any economic crisis and the restoration of profitability have been the major changes in production. The more limited these changes, the greater is the attack on wages, and the more severe the decline of markets. But these circulation crises will only lead to a sustained upturn if their effect is transmitted to production. As in all the examples I have given from Fordism, it is the changes in the factories which are primary, and which determine and limit the movements on the market.

III

If we turn now to economic policy, I want to show why it is totally inadequate to base Labour's economic strategy on a perspective of redistribution, managed markets and deficit financing, without a major and dominant programme for transforming production.

First, as far as distribution is concerned, whereas the early Fabians saw distributional issues as quite separate from production, later theorists were well aware of the constraints that accumulation presented to redistribution. Their reaction has been to play down redistribution. Durbin, for example, was by 1940 against further redistribution because he thought it would raise consumption and reduce savings. Crosland agreed, though he couched his argument in terms of redistribution affecting incentives among the better off. More recently – particularly in the Wilson period – increased growth rather than redistribution was seen as the way to improve the position of the less well off. It was offered as a dynamic rather than static approach to poverty. But with the slowdown of growth and with the present government taking this argument to its uninhibited conclusion, by redistributing in favour of the rich and of business, the left has been on the defensive. For it finds itself without an adequate theory of accumulation which would allow growth at the same time as allowing the reduction of inequality.

There are similar objections to policies confined to the public perfecting of markets. There are four common objections made to the market as a means of allocation: the Marshallian argument on externalities; income inequalities, particularly those based on inherited wealth; the existence of monopolies who may follow a price-cutting policy in order to drive out competition; the fact that a growing national industry may need some protection until it is strong enough to match already developed international competitors. In each of these cases, it is not the market as a mechanism which is held to be at fault. Merely that its particular signals are not accurate, and that state intervention is needed to correct them: taxes, subsidies, a wealth tax, anti-monopoly legislation, infant industry tariffs and so on. The market remains the dominant economic nexus. Modifications to it can be made at the level of circulation without reference to production.

But the major current issues concerning the market as an economic nexus are not so easily dealt with. First, an increasing number of major investment decisions – public and private – are so large, and made over so long a timescale that the market is no longer an adequate guide to choice.

Second, a crisis in the process of accumulation, whose causes should be sought in the development of production, nevertheless makes its formal appearance in the sphere of exchange. Inflation, falling demand, financial collapse, a profits squeeze – these are all linked to the market. Managing the market in these circumstances is highly problematic. For a policy must either suspend the full impact of the market on producers – in which case production will remain untransformed – or discipline producers through the market in order to change production. The latter has been the policy of the monetarists who have quite explicitly engineered a deterioration in market conditions. The mechanism used was spelled out before the 1979 election by monetarists at the London Business School; it involved raising interest and exchange rates, squeezing industry between a declining export market and increasing imports, bankrupting the weaker firms, and shifting resources and markets to the strong. Every market price over the last five years should be seen in this context. They have been manipulated for a particular end. The results for British industry have been disastrous. Quite new plant has had to be scrapped. In some cases it is the most advanced firms that have been put out of business (those based on mass production), while the less efficient, but more flexible, have survived. In some branches of production there is no serious base left on which any recovery could be built. Those large British firms who have restructured themselves have tended to make their major new investments abroad. In the British economy, the long-term strategic decisions have again and again gone by default. The monetarist strategy of restructuring production via the market has weakened the British economy so severely that some sectors will never recover.

Third, the use of the market to restructure production involves a direct attack on labour. This was also an explicit aim of the monetarists. By squeezing profits they intended to squeeze labour. In the private sector they have been remarkably successful. Workforces have been set against each other. One after another has accepted redundancies, lower wage settlements, changes in work practices, in order to keep an enterprise afloat. It has been more effective than any incomes policy. But a socialist view of the economy does not take the side of capital against labour. It cannot therefore accept that the market price is the magnetic north around which all else revolves, if that market price is a mechanism which encourages weak labour to replace strong, or part-time, lower-paid, casual work to outcompete those who are working on proper contracts in adequate conditions. Mrs Thatcher has used money and the market as an instrument for weakening labour in production as in exchange.

Fourth, there is no mechanism in the market economy to ensure that the destruction of some jobs will be matched by the creation of others. In other words, there is no mechanism for clearing the labour market. Rather, the history of capitalist development has been one of creating a surplus population. That is how I read the phenomenon of unemployment in the third world. Advanced country technology drove a rapier through artisanal forms of economy in the countryside and in the small crafts of the towns. Much of the resultant profit was then repatriated to metropolitan countries for accumulation there. Advanced country accumulation and full employment were maintained, at the expense of accumulation and employment in the third world. In the current period this mechanism has no longer been sustained. From the early 1970s the decline in levels of profitability led to money capital being exported back to the NICs and to the socialist world. Accumulation in the advanced countries slowed down. New technology further reduced the demand for labour. Unemployment rates have risen dramatically throughout the advanced capitalist countries. Even with an economic upturn there is no longer a likelihood of full employment, particularly in less competitive economies like the UK.

The significance of these four issues is that a socialist economic policy cannot be confined to adjusting the market. In the first case, long-term strategic planning has already moved beyond the market in the private as well as the public sector. Rather, the market is being made to fit in with strategic decisions – through advertising, guaranteed state purchases, protection (as in South Korean economic planning) or tax relief. In the case of labour, the market is a means whereby one group of workers are set against another – consciously and directly so within large corporations who compare performances of different plants and expand or contract accordingly.

As far as economic crisis is concerned, Keynesian measures will be confined in their expansionary effects. This is because an expansion of aggregate demand will have only a limited impact on the central crisis of profitability when its causes are rooted in production. In the short-term such an expansion will allow firms to produce nearer to capacity, lowering unit costs, raising profit and even encouraging some new investment. But in as much as the long-term trend of profitability is downwards, new investment will be limited, and any budgetary-induced expansion short lived. This is what happened in the early 1970s. The advantage monetarism has over Keynesianism is that it is a direct assault on production. It has simulated the mechanisms of restructuring through a classic economic slump, with all the attendant brutality and waste. The only socialist answer is an equally direct intervention in production, but on very different terms to that underlying monetarism. This is the case for industrial planning on a scale unmatched since the Second World War. Given the economic desolation which already exists after five years of monetarism, only an industrial programme of this scope and detail can hope to restore substantial vitality to the British economy. Deficit financing, import controls and national investment banks are not enough if there has not been a major intervention in production which they can support.

Equally, any serious response to long-term unemployment cannot remain at the level of adjustments to the policy levers of market circulation. It is of course absurd to have people working long hours and overtime while others have no work at all. But even if work was redistributed to avoid this, and even if a thirty-five-hour week was generally adopted, it is probable that there would still be significant unemployment.

One possible response to this would be a full employment policy based on the direct planning of the public economy. At the moment, nearly a third of national production is undertaken by the state. This public economy is fragmented, uncoordinated, largely geared to serving the market economy and private accumulation rather than the other way round.

Yet if an input-output table were constructed we would see that this economy had a considerable degree of self-sufficiency. If we take a wage worker in the public sector, for instance, more than half of his or her income may go on state services, through tax, rates, public transport fares, council rents, electricity, gas and the telephone. The remaining income goes to the private sector:

clothes, food, private transport, domestic appliances. As during wartime, it would not be difficult to develop public provision in each of these fields, and pay for 'imports' from the private market economy by 'exports' of public services and taxation. Once such a system of coordination was established, those without a job could be guaranteed one, since the extra cost of employing them in terms of *imports from the private sector* would be small, and could be met by exports of their production to the private sector.

What I am suggesting in the present conjuncture is the direct planning of labour within the public economy rather than in a national framework. Instead of protection for all producers within the national economy, it would be geared to protecting the developing public economy. Public production could not ignore the private economy. Its prices and products would inevitably be compared to those in the private sector. But it would have the advantage that it was able to use productively labour which market capitalism ignores. It is one of the paradoxes of contemporary capitalism that, as an ever more intense drive for productivity increases, capitalism extrudes labour, lowering its productivity to zero, and at the same time has to pay for its cost of subsistence. Because capitalism pays people not to work, a public economy could pay them to work, and their product would – if adequately planned – more than cover the difference between social security payments and a proper wage.

At this point I shall summarise my general argument. Fabian economics has been limited both is theory and practice because it has restricted itself to the economics of circulation. It is from the sphere of circulation that it has taken its main issues of concern and definitions of socialism: inequality, market anarchy, monopoly. In demanding a 'socialisation' of ownership it was demanding a power for the state to counter these inadequacies in the system of circulation. But Fabian economics as put into practice by successive Labour governments has consistently run into the barriers set by the requirements of private accumulation. It is the contradictory character of these requirements as they are found in the process of production that socialist economic policy must address.

What is called for is nothing less than a major shift in the economic agenda of the labour movement. I will list my main suggested items for this agenda as follows:

1. industrial restructuring through planned intervention;
2. the development of a publicly controlled technology and systems design, geared to the skills and concerns of labour, and to social needs;
3. a redefinition of planning, as popular planning for labour in and against the market;
4. the transformation of public services and state corporations, in terms of their internal organisation, their relations with their manual workforce, and with the users of their services;
5. a concern with the quality of consumption rather than its mere quantitative aggregate. The Fordist mode of production has been particularly inappropriate in food, culture, health and education – all key parts of a new mode of consumption, replacing that based on mass-produced consumer durables;
6. the attack on inequalities within production (particularly the division between conception and execution) which feed back into income inequalities, and inequalities between men and women, and between black people and white;
7. the integration and direct planning of the public economy, and its expansion to ensure a job for all those who are currently unemployed.

This does not mean that the economy will not still require a monetary and a fiscal policy, let alone a strategy towards the balance of payments, and towards income and wealth inequality. But it means it will be subordinate and complementary to productive concerns. The changes will be symbolised at the administrative level by the subordination of the Treasury and the Bank of England to the new Ministry of Industry, rather than the other way round.

IV

Since 1979, socialist initiatives in economic policy have shifted from the national to the local level. Faced with large increases in unemployment, particularly in the metropolitan and older industrial areas, more and more Labour councils have been extending their economic role. These councils – because they have no monetary or foreign trade powers – have had to confront the issues of industrial policy directly. Some have followed a strategy of market support. They have provided industrial premises which the market, for one reason or another, was failing to provide. They have given incentives to mobile capital, and a battery of advice services, geared particularly to small firms. Limited as they are to market adjustments, these policies no more than scratch the surface of the problem.

A number of authorities have followed an alternative strategy, geared to medium and larger firms, to state industry and services, and to the interests of labour and consumers within a more general process of industrial restructuring. Lancashire, Sheffield, Leeds, the West Midlands, and the GLC are the most developed examples, together with certain London boroughs such as Hackney and Brent. Their policies have had different emphases, but each has taken on – albeit in a tentative way – the issues arising from the crisis of production which I discussed earlier.

I want to outline four features of the experience of one of these authorities – the GLC – which are of particular relevance to the national discussions.

Restructuring for labour

The premise of the GLC's industrial intervention is that effective intervention can only successfully take place within the context of national and international restructuring. There is little point in bailing out declining firms and industries without transforming them. The market economy has its own means of transformation. The older, less productive operations are taken over or supplanted by the more productive. Rationalisations, write-offs, new investment, amalgamations – these are the instruments used by private (and public) capital in order to restore profitability. The GLC's view is that this restructuring can take place in many different ways, with different consequences for both workers and consumers. One of the main functions of a public body concerned with industrial intervention is to ensure that any restructuring that does take place is undertaken in the interests of labour and not at its expense.

The point is clearest in the case of the utilities and the basic infrastructure. Take, for example, the case of combined heat and power and conservation programmes as alternatives to the current government's nuclear power policy. Detailed studies suggest that the former options would lead to over 3000 more jobs in London, for the same investment as at Sizewell B, and a higher rate of return. In transport, in the telephone network, in the dock industry, as in health care, there are alternative paths of restructuring over the next decade, with quite different implications for those who work in these industries, and who use their products.

The same argument applies to private manufacturing and service industries. Employment in London's manufacturing has fallen by more than a half in twenty years, from 1.4 million in 1961 to 650,000 in 1981. On present trends a further 200,000 manufacturing jobs will be lost by 1990. Some have argued that there is nothing that can be done about this restructuring of the London economy away from manufacturing. But on closer examination of London's traditional industries – furniture, printing, food and engineering – we have found that there is no necessity for such decline.

Take furniture for example. In 1951 there were over 63,000 furniture workers in London. There are now only 12,000. This collapse has taken place against the background of a major restructuring of the European furniture industry. London's industry lost out because it has been weak on design, unintegrated with retailing and, with two or three exceptions, backwards in machinery and technology. Yet it possesses a rich reservoir of skill. Working with the more progressive manufacturers and the unions, the GLC has identified a strategy which is being implemented by the council's Greater London Enterprise Board (GLEB) in conjunction with European technical advice, and international distributors. It not only promises to reverse the trend which has seen furniture imports into Britain climb from 7 per cent in 1973 to 26 per cent in 1983, but to do so on the basis of union labour, with enterprise planning that involves workforces in the organisation and strategic directions of the firms.

I have given an example because one feature of a strategy which starts from production is that it is an economics of detail, of material processes and particular products. A production strategy is as much qualitative as quantitative, concerned with the quality of jobs and products rather than simply their amount. It is in the qualitative sphere that we have to distinguish the alternatives.

In furniture the alternatives involve the dimensions of geography and control within the firm. In food there is the further dimension of the nutritional value of the product. In milk delivery and retailing it is a question of accessibility for those without cars. In publishing, the record industry, and TV and film production there are the issues of minority interests and political control. Sector by sector we can distinguish the ways in which the market and the lodestar of private profitability bend the development of production to a course which ignores the wider interests of workers and consumers.

In important ways trade unions and user organisations have contested these market-determined paths of development. National legislation and local government regulation have supported these initiatives. Inspectorates, subsidies, preferential purchasing and many other instruments have been used to regulate private capital.

As far as industrial policy is concerned, the GLC and GLEB have tried a number of alternatives. In the early days of the administration, when only a small team existed, it was difficult to take over and run enterprises directly. The council therefore signed agreements with private firms, setting conditions for union recognition and enterprise planning. The council and GLEB have also supported many co-operatives, who embody alternatives in their aims as well as the structure of their ownership. But in the larger plants, our experience is that direct ownership and control is necessary to create socialist alternatives. Put more generally, the restructuring of production for (and by) labour cannot be adequately carried out by regulating circulation. It requires direct involvement in and control of production.

Technology

Central to the process of restructuring is technology. We tend to think of technology as so many new machines – word processors, numerically controlled machine tools, robots. But it is equally a question of systems, linking different processes together within production as well as linking production with distribution and sale. The commanding heights of modern capitalism are shifting from the ownership of the means of production to the ownership of the means of conceptualisation. Once the key processes and systems have been designed and developed, production can be contracted out. Clive Sinclair makes arrangements with factories to produce on his behalf – in the manner of subcontractors. He, like many other inventors, will keep control of the design and specification and of the marketing. Production – with its particular problems of controlling labour – is nevertheless relatively straightforward and can be left to others.

The issue for socialist economic policy is how to match capital's control of the new commanding heights – both because this is the key point of the control of profits, and because the use of new technology and the design of systems moulds social relations all the way down the line.

The GLC is a pygmy in the world of multinationals. Yet in its three universities and seven polytechnics, London possesses technological capacities which match those of the largest corporations. In addition there are the research departments of public corporations and of specialist institutions. The challenge is how to link the work of these institutions into the planned reorganisation of London industry.

The policy we have followed is to establish a number of technology networks. These are based in or near one of the research institutions, and are staffed by 'go-betweens', people who know the research community, as well as the needs of industries and communities within London. One network specialises in energy, and involves the South Bank and Central London polytechnics. It links in energy conservation research with local energy campaigns and initiatives, and the development of products.

A second network specialises in new technology, and includes academics from Imperial College, City University, the Polytechnic of Central London and St Thomas's Hospital. It has been involved in the development of a general-purpose robot arm (aimed particularly at those with disabilities), of expert systems for use in the medical field, of computer graphics and design, and of the 'human-centred' lathe and automatic factory systems. The last project – developed by

Professor Howard Rosenbrock at UMIST in association with Mike Cooley, formerly at Lucas Aerospace and now technology director at GLEB – illustrates one of the key points in the underlying approach of the networks. Numerically controlled machine tools have been designed to deskill the operative. Programming the machines is undertaken by 'white-collar engineers', and the old 'tacit knowledge' of the machinist is being lost. The UMIST project designed a lathe which built on the machinists' skill rather than discarding it (the machine was programmed from the manual operations of the skilled operator). This matched, and even exceeded, conventional machine tools in efficiency, but has only recently been taken up in Britain *via Japan*. Rosenbrock is now building an automatic integrated production system based on the same principles.

Other networks are in the process of development, specialising in electric, electronic and mechanical engineering (North London Polytechnic), medical equipment (Thames Polytechnic) and transport. The response during negotiations has been remarkably supportive from institutions who are aware of the gap that exists between higher research and its applications, and the need for a planned integration of London's public knowledge economy with the restructuring of productive employment.

Popular planning

Another word to describe the pre-production phase of modern capitalism is planning. Restructuring has to be planned. Multinationals have to be planned, as do their new products and systems. I used the word 'conceptualisation' to describe these processes, because they have a dynamic and creative element, imagining what is over the next hill from ground level rather than seeing and organising everything from above. Our model of planning has been too much top-down co-ordination of the railway timetable rather than the beyond-the-horizon adventure of the technologist. Capitalism has both, and socialists need to redefine both.

The socialist tradition has tended to juxtapose the market and the plan, equating capitalism with the market and socialism with the plan. This is misleading. The history of capitalism can be read as the development of a contradiction between the market and the plan, or rather between the market and many plans, for in capitalism planning is largely carried out by different private capitals. In the case of corporate planning, plans are constructed *for* the market, with the aim of maximising private profitability. With alternative industrial plans, we are planning *in and against* the market. We cannot ignore the market. But we can insulate production from the market and resist the tyranny which private capital imposes on labour as a result of its drive for maximum profitability as validated by the market.

In a local economy, three kinds of planning are required: an alternative corporate planning at the level of enterprise; industrial planning at the level of the branch; and strategic planning at the level of the locality as a whole. In each case, adequate planning cannot be done solely from above. It is necessary of course to have an eagle's view, but full-time central planners have in the past exhibited distorted vision and have no grasp of the detail which workers and users experience as part of their everyday job. For an adequate socialist planning we must break down the division between mental and manual labour, and between conception and execution. Those involved in the enterprise or industry must be given the time and the support to take the eagle's view. We estimate that up to a quarter of a million people in London are employed in strategy and design work for the capital's planning: software engineers, marketing specialists, financiers, architects, engineers, managers and so on. The labour movement has been starved of both the time and skills to match the detail of this extraordinary complex which comprises London's private mental economy.

At the GLC we have approached this issue from a number of directions. The Labour Manifesto had a commitment to set up a new economic policy group staffed from outside the council to undertake strategic work. This group now has forty-five people working on broader industrial and strategic planning issues. They provide material for the particular corporate and branch strategies required for GLEB's industrial interventions. Within GLEB itself there is a closely related sector strategy division, and a section responsible for enterprise planning within firms receiving GLEB support. There is a programme of grant aid for a network of trade union resource centres which provide research and planning help to trade unionists at a neighbourhood level. There is an Early Warning Unit within the GLC staffed by former industrial trade unionists which has built up an information network designed to find out about prospective closures and redundancies in time for countervailing action to be taken. There is a Popular Planning Unit who work with trade unionists, community organisations and user groups on alternative plans, and who have also funded a popular planning education programme through adult education institutes.

In all, the council funds some 120 people who are working on some aspects of alternative planning, providing just over 4000 hours per week to support alternatives to the plans produced by the 35 million hours of London's private market planners. This is a measure of the imbalance. It means one person working with trade unions and local community groups on an alternative plan for the whole of the retailing sector in London. It means one person working on the alternative to the government's plans for the private cabling of London. For a socialist economic democracy to have substance, we have to recognise the needs for time and skill in development of alternative plans. We need a quite new conception of planning – its scope, its process, and the resources necessary to make it work.

We also need a new conception of the power to implement the plans. In traditional socialist views of central planning it is the state which both plans and implements the plans. This was, I think, the traditional Fabian view. It was certainly the practice of Soviet planning. In advanced capitalist societies, the planning powers of the central state (let alone the local state) are heavily confined. The main power lies with private capital. Not only does private capital have the real control of production, but in its financial form has the decisive power to move out of the country. In the era of multinational corporations – with as much as £30 billion a year of transactions on Britain's foreign exchanges being one form or another of intra-firm transfer – the capacity of a government to control the exodus of capital is increasingly limited.

In these circumstances the power of organised labour to enforce alternative plans is equally important. In the case of Kodak, for example, the unions in Kodak Europe have combined to demand of Eastman Kodak in Rochester [USA] an alternative set of investment plans, that would maintain a proportion of research and development spending and new production manufacturing in Europe. The alternative of a national industry under public control is no longer a short-run possibility, since the know-how and new products have long since been lost. They can be rebuilt and re-acquired but it would take time and substantial resources (Kodak, for example, are spending some $800 million a year on R&D). In the meantime it is the trade unions who, internationally, have the potential power to challenge the priorities and practices of multinationals. The GLC has worked with other local authorities, the European Commission and the European Parliament to provide support to unions in firms like Kodak and Ford who are seeking to develop joint action in defence of their jobs.

In a single plant, the best enforcers of an enterprise plan are again the workforce themselves. They are also the people who can provide the creativity to make the aims of an alternative corporate plan work in practice. Indeed without their full involvement and support, an alternative plan could not adequately be implemented.

Effective popular planning requires an extension of the scope of the trade unions, of collective bargaining and of resources, and it should be one task of local and national socialist administrations to provide material support for these developments.

Transforming the state

The argument about popular planning applies as much to the state as to private industry. At the moment, the gas industry, electricity, coal, public transport, water, the GPO and British Telecom are run as state capitalist concerns. The consumer organisations are weak. The trade unions have limited powers. Even the GLC – as a major metropolitan authority – has found it extremely difficult to get any substantial discussion with the public corporations, let alone influence the direction of their development. In many parts of the country other state services – including local council services – are experienced in the same way. Socialists employed in the public sector have started to talk of working *in and against the state.*

As I argued earlier, it is one of the most urgent tasks for the labour movement to challenge these structures of the state. How we do it cannot be laid down in a blueprint. It is a question of learning from initiatives – those that work and those that don't. At the GLC we have tried a number of alternatives: public hearings on British Telecom and on cable (in the case of cable we supplemented two days of joint hearings with Sheffield City Council with five local hearings in boroughs); involvement in public inquiries on Sizewell B and on the proposed airport in the heart of London's Docklands; regular conferences with trade unionists and boroughs on the privatisation of local government services; popular planning workshops for trade unionists in public services and for manual workers in the GLC. The council also has a grant aid programme which it uses to support workforce initiatives and user groups: it has supported a number of local energy campaigns, the BT trade unions, the postal workers, tenants' groups, and a local consortium of groups campaigning in Docklands.

As a strategic authority, there are limited services under the GLC's direct control. One exception is London Transport, which operates at arm's length, and which the council has had to struggle to get to conform to its transport and employment policies, in the teeth of government opposition, and the bizarre economic interpretations of the House of Lords.

One of the lessons, indeed, of the GLC administration, is the need for a change in the bureaucratic structure. It faced intense hostility from different parts of the bureaucracy to many of its policies – notably those concerned with industry and employment. When there was not hostility, there was too often a lack of drive and imagination, with a bureaucratic caste unable to understand the goals and the spirit for which the administration stood.

Against this the Labour groups have operated pragmatically. They have brought in socialists from outside to carry forward the new policies. They have increased political control of the bureaucracy, and devoted great energy to simplifying the Byzantine grading structure which served to reinforce hierarchical power and rigidity. What has been clear throughout is that the conventional notion of a neutral administrative bureaucracy ready to carry through any policies required of them was quite inappropriate. There are notable exceptions. Some GLC officers sympathised with the new initiatives, but their power was initially curbed. Equally, and for the same reasons, it is not enough to bring in policy advisors. They need to have administrative power. In the field of industry and employment we have learnt that the labour movement needs an alternative bureaucratic strategy to set along-side any alternative economic strategy.

V

Roy Green and John Eatwell argue for a return to theory in the labour movement. I wholeheartedly agree. But I do so knowing that there is an intense suspicion of theory in the movement, and an impatience for action. What I have wanted to establish in this essay is that Labour's economic policy crisis is a crisis of that very action which has been so impatiently pursued by successive Labour governments. The answer then is not to have more of the same – with the degree of progressiveness judged by the number of billions by which you want to reflate, and how many companies you say should be nationalised. Rather it is to step back and recognise that at least part of the problem is the theoretical tradition which has guided economic policy and practice. To re-examine this tradition critically is the first practical task which all those impatient for action should immediately undertake.

I have suggested one line of approach which shifts the emphasis from circulation to production, and implies a quite different agenda to that of the post-war Keynesian consensus. Fortunately much of the theoretical ground for this new approach has been tilled over the last fifteen years. What has not been done is to translate this general approach into concrete initiatives and programmes. This is where the present municipal experiences are relevant. Local councils have been groping towards new economic policies – falteringly, intuitively, and in the face of the most severe attacks by the Tory government. But the achievements they have already made point the way towards the new national economic policies and politics which are so urgently needed.

Some of the major issues of national economic policy local coun-cils can only tangentially touch. Monetary policy would be one. The erosion of national economic controls by increasingly interna-tionalised corporations would be another.

But in other fields, the municipal initiatives have been a laboratory for new economic policies. Direct intervention is a prime example. All the enterprise boards have quickly realised that it is not money but people who are the main constraint. Private capital has the overwhelming monopoly of the skills of restructuring and long-term industrial and corporate planning. They have now added to this their control over the development and application of new technology and new systems of production and co-ordination. If such restructuring is to be done in terms of broader social interests than those of the balance sheet, then it requires people who understand and sympathise with this alternative, but who also possess the skills of the accountant, the management consultant, and indeed the marketing manager. At the GLC we have found that trade unionists are quick to pick up these skills, and there are a few progressive managers. But the numbers are still small when set beside the tasks and possibilities, even within London itself.

Local councils have also experimented with different organisations – notably the enterprise boards. The issue has been how to maintain a political control over a body which needs (and demands) independence on a day-to-day basis. The model of the council making policy and the enterprise board carrying it out has proved unsatisfactory. The politicians need to be involved in the practice in order to learn about the detailed issues at which policy should be directed, while those who are implementing necessarily generate strategies of their own. A variety of devices have been used to maintain political control over the enterprise boards – key to which has been the staffing of the boards themselves. On the basis of this experience, a future Labour government will be able to reconstitute a National Enterprise Board very different from the last.

The concerns with the quality of products and not just their quantity, with popular planning, with human-centred technology, and with transforming the services and the administration of the state – all these are also of central relevance to a new socialist economic policy at the national level. But perhaps most important is the consciousness that the state's power – locally or nationally – is quite limited in the face of the power of private capital. The traditional Fabian theory of the state as somehow set apart from classes, an instrument of power which needs to be patiently captured and then run by experts independent of sectional interests, this theory is in as urgent a need of revision as the economic theory. For when the state attempts to control and supersede private capital, the outcome of the ensuing battle will depend crucially on the extent of popular support any administration can command. It is one of the unintended results of the government's abolition campaign against the metropolitan counties and the GLC that councillors and council workers alike are having to argue the case for their existence to ordinary people. This is a democratic process far more substantial that a four-yearly visit to the ballot box. It involves councillors explaining what they are doing, justifying it and, if they cannot justify it, dropping it in favour of something else. This is one aspect of the necessary link between a socialist administration and the people they represent.

Another is the need to redefine the role of the state as the supporter of others' campaigns and struggles rather than as the universal provider. I discussed this in respect to state support for trade unionists. But it is equally true with respect to discrimination against particular groups of working people – women and black people most notably. Local councils can help directly, through anti-discrimination monitoring of suppliers and of their own practices. But any successful fight against discrimination will depend on the actions of those who are facing the discrimination, and it is one task of a socialist council to support them in their struggles rather than offer to replace them.

Power in short is not centralised in the state, but decentralised. A Labour administration has considerable power, but it is the temporary power of holding an important position on a wider field of battle. Its economic policies will affect the relative strength of others elsewhere on the battlefield. Mrs Thatcher has recognised this in using public economic policy as a means of a direct attack on the power of labour in production. It is important that the labour movement takes at least this lesson from monetarism and develops an economic strategy which will shift the balance of economic power back to organised labour.

Multinational Capitalism

5

Multinationals and social control in the 1990s

Robin Murray gave this paper as the Manufacturing, Science and Finance trade union (MSF) Second Vic Godfrey Memorial Lecture, at Owen Webb House, Cambridge, on 18 February 1989. Reproduced with permission.

Twenty years ago the world woke up to multinationals. As someone pointed out at the time, it was not that multinationals were new. In the third world, the history of imperialism was, in part, the history of multinationals, of the colonial sugar and rubber companies, of the majors in bauxite and copper, in nickel and oil, and great conglomerates like the British South Africa Company pursuing its goals of 'philanthropy plus five per cent'. In the advanced world the processing industries (such as chemicals) and the electrical giants were early multinationals, as were the pioneers of mass production in vehicles and food, and many of the household names associated with the rise of the industrial era we now call Fordism. Indeed, Fordism in the UK was centred in particular on the US firms who set up around London and the West Midlands in the 1930s in order to get behind the tariff barriers that rose along with the depression. Ford Dagenham was opened in 1931; Hoover and Firestone in the same period. The two latter factories, with their magnificent art deco designs, symbolised the twin focuses of early Fordism – the motor industry on the one hand, and the transformation of the home on the other. And as their products spread, so did the demand for the world's raw materials to make them.

In spite of this corporate internationalisation, there remained little recognition of its significance. As late as the 1960s, two of the most celebrated books on corporate power, Galbraith's *New Industrial State*, and Baran and Sweezey's *Monopoly Capital*, made only passing mention of their global reach. Conventional economic theory almost entirely ignored the subject, and what little academic work that was done was in business schools, and those peripheral countries where foreign investors played the central role in local economic life. I first learned about multinationals in the mid-1960s from Norman Girvan, a Jamaican economist, then studying the international bauxite companies for his PhD. They dominated his own, and many other, third world economies. With his help I made sense, for the first time, of the Zambian economy where two copper firms accounted for half the GDP and ninety per cent of the exports, which fact the free market and Keynesian models we were taught at the time marginalised with the help of suitable assumptions. For mainstream economics, and first world politics, multinationals were not an issue.

From the late 1960s all this changed. Academic articles and books appeared. New journals on multinationals were founded. Centres for research into multinationals sprung up. The US government commissioned major investigations on the role of multinationals in its own economy. In 1973 the United Nations set up a UN Centre on Transnational Corporations in New York. In the UK the control of multinationals became a concern of Labour Party policy. In Latin America, six countries came together in the Andean Pact to strengthen their bargaining power vis-a-vis multinationals. The role of ITT in the overthrow of Allende in Chile in 1973 came to symbolise the extraordinary political as well as economic power that multinationals commanded.

The reason for this change should, in part, be sought in the slow-down in growth in the US and the UK, the two centres of Fordism which, in 1966, had alone accounted for 78 per cent of the world's outward foreign investment. In the UK, foreign investment was seen as being a contributory factor to low domestic investment, competitive with rather than complementary to the national economic interest (the Reddaway Report in 1967 had come to mixed conclusions on the issue). In the runs on sterling in the second half of the 1960s, multinationals were seen to be playing a central role, through their control of large quantities of liquid funds, and their capacity to adjust their transfer prices and to lead and lag their payments. The decline of British manufacturing was associated with the closure of large multinational plants about which unions, local communities, and governments could do little.

One of the most vivid cases came in the mid 1970s when Tony Benn was still minister of industry. Litton Industries was an American conglomerate which had bought a whole series of interests in the international typewriter sector. One of these was Imperial Typewriters. Its UK factories in Leicester and Hull produced the old office machine on which I now write. Litton decided to rationalise them, close the British plants down and concentrate production in Germany. Union delegations went to Tony Benn. Rapid studies were done. It transpired that Litton had developed a new electronic machine. They controlled the technology. Were the government or the unions to take over the UK plants, they would have been left with an obsolete product. By this time there was no alternative source of production in Britain around which government policy could focus and whose expansion might, in principle, provide jobs for those displaced by Litton. National government and national labour found themselves powerless to prevent the end of one more sector of British industry.

In the fields then of macroeconomic and industrial policy, multinationals came to be seen as corrosive forces of the power of governments to control their own economy. This, I think, is the important change and it reflected a material reality. For it was one of the key features of the classical Fordist era that it was based on regulated national economies. The high fixed costs of process plant and mass production meant that private capital had an interest in securing a stable and above all forecastable market. One requirement was protection. The home market should be insulated against attempts by overseas competitors to undercut home producers with dumping (or marginal cost plus) prices. The model that emerged was of a series of developed country national fortresses, within which firms could amortise their fixed costs, and a free-for-all based on marginal cost pricing in the rest of the world. Within these national fortresses was a second set of policies to stabilise the domestic market. Policies that came to be called Keynesian and included not only macroeconomic management, but a welfare state with unemployment insurance and a structure of industrial relations which ensured what has been called 'a Keynesian incomes policy without the state'.

Between 1931 and 1958 we can talk confidently about an international economy built on nation states. The foreign investment which had taken place did not cut across this pattern, indeed it reflected it since the investment was made in order to get into protected home markets. Ford UK, in this sense, was a British firm: it had its own R&D; it made its own parts; undertook the bulk of its designs. It even had a substantial British shareholding. When the British government wanted to direct its expansion away from the south east to the regions, Henry Ford flew over from the States and made a compromise: one car plant to Halewood [Liverpool], if the tractor plant could go to Basildon [Essex]. But this was the power of big business within a national economy not, as yet, of a multinational.

1958 was the year of the reintroduction of the international market. Convertibility between national currencies was restored. In Europe the EEC was formed. Economies began to open out. France, which in 1953 exported nine per cent of the value of its traded goods, was by 1963 exporting 18 per cent. There was a quickening in the growth of international trade and in the pace of mergers and takeovers. Fordist firms which had been constrained by the walls of the national fortresses (even where they had operated in a number of them), were the first to benefit. In 1961 Ford bought out its UK shareholders. By 1967 it was organising its operations in Europe on a co-ordinated European basis (from Brentwood). Over the following two decades it developed an international division of labour within its European plants, whose outcome was recently seen in the decision to shift Sierras from Dagenham to Genk [Belgium]. Ford is only one among many: IBM, Massey Ferguson, Caterpillar, Kodak, Peugeot and General Motors.

These multinationals have dismantled the national walls from the inside. As trade has grown, so has their dominance. In the late 1960s, the top 120 firms in the UK accounted for 50 per cent of all exports. By the early 1980s, multinationals were responsible for 80 per cent of exports, with more than 30 per cent coming from foreign subsidiaries alone. In the UK in 1981, 30 per cent of all exports were intra-firm trade – nearly half of them involving foreign-owned multinationals in the UK. In Japan (1983) and the US (1985) the figures are similar (32 per cent and 31 per cent), with 40 per cent of US imports being intra-firm.

What was taking place from the mid-1960s onwards was a transition from national to transnational Fordism, and from national and multinational firms to transnational ones. One condition for this change was the liberalisation of trade and capital movements. Another was the revolution in communications and data processing, which allowed firms to co-ordinate activities over a wider geographical and economic range than had previously been possible. A third factor was the crisis in Fordism itself.

By the late 1960s, the system of national Fordism was running into a series of barriers. The markets for many products were becoming saturated, in the sense that companies found it difficult to maintain the same rate of growth in the bread-and-butter products of the production line. In many advanced countries there appears to have been a growing volatility in demand, and a fragmenting of the market away from the standardised mass product. Within the factory there was a revolt across Europe of the mass-production worker – symbolised in the events of May 1968 in France and the hot autumn of 1969 in Italy. There was also an ecological revolt. Fordism's extensive use of materials and energy was threatening the supply of world resources, and the resulting shortages were one factor in the oil price rise of 1973. Finally, when faced with the resulting general economic fluctuations, traditional Fordism found it difficult to respond without major cutbacks and sharp increases in average costs. These difficulties culminated in the world recession of 1974-75.

One response was geographical. Within countries, decentralising plants from cities to smaller towns – the so-called ruralisation of industry; between countries, establishing an international division of labour in production. It is the latter which underlies one part of the development of transnational Fordism.

The most notable examples were the shift of labour-intensive processes to the third world, and to the peripheries of the first. The 1970s was the decade of growth of the NICs. Just as Volkswagen began sourcing from Mexico and Brazil, and the Mexican border sprouted US-controlled labour-intensive stages of production, so the four tigers of South East Asia came to supply cheap electronics goods, clothing, shoes, toys, and so on, to the department stores and hypermarkets of the developed west. Some of this production was undertaken by subsidiaries of multinationals; other parts were co-ordinated by the western retailers who effectively subcontracted production to local firms. There developed what the French economist Alain Lipietz has called 'peripheral Fordism' and 'bloody Taylorisation', the use of cheap third world labour for those processes which could not yet be mechanised. What was happening in Asia and South America, was in Europe happening on its periphery in Ireland, Spain and Portugal, on the Southern Mediterranean and in Eastern Europe.

This pattern is distinct from the horizontal division of labour established within regional markets. IBM produced nine sections of its computers, each in a different country, and assembled them locally. Kodak produces X-ray films for Europe in France and Kodachrome for Europe in Britain (Harrow). The drive is for specialisation on a European scale.

Yet these have only been one of the relevant developments of the last twenty years. Other responses by capital to the crisis of Fordism have had different and, at times, contrary implications for transnationalisation.

First has been the substitution of capital for labour. In some instances this has increased the size of plant economies of scale, leading to longer runs and the need for wider markets. But, in many cases, minimum plant size has got smaller (the chemical industry, for example, or electric arc furnaces in the steel industry), which has allowed production to become more dispersed. This has been linked to an increased flexibility in machinery, cutting down times between one batch and another, further reducing the size of the economic length of run for any particular product.

Second, and building on the first, there has been a discontinuous cut in stocks through the adoption of 'just in time' techniques. Flexible machinery and closer ties with markets (particularly retailers) have allowed more producers to make to order rather than to produce for stock, and this has applied to final producers and right back to input suppliers. One implication is the need for producers to be close to their markets, so that some sectors have seen the growth of tighter geographical clusters of firms in developed countries. The new wave retailers like Next, Burton, and Richard Shops have, like Marks and Spencer, brought production back home. Burton, for example, have moved from 50 per cent to 80 per cent UK sourcing over the past three years. The same is true of the suppliers to certain car assembly plants, particularly those where there is a regular interaction between assembler and supplier.

Third, the last fifteen years has seen a switch from the extensive to the intensive use of energy and materials. New materials have cut down on raw materials requirements. So has design and improved systems of layout and cutting (using CAD). There have also been major savings in energy; thus electricity consumption in the UK has only now grown back to its pre-1973 level. One consequence is a decline in demand for third world materials, and the slump in prices. Another is a decline in foreign investment in primary products, as the primary and extractive multinationals have restructured themselves around first world synthetics and providing services to what are now commonly third world-controlled industries. There has been a retreat from land.

Fourth, competitivity has come to turn less on manufacturing costs and more on innovation and marketing. Innovation in many sectors does not depend on scale. Whether in software, cultural industries or clothing, small firms have often developed new products, while in those areas where R&D scale is important, there has been a growth of cross-licensing and joint ventures as a way of spreading the risk of new product development. What has been central, however, is that when a successful product has been developed, the producer has the means to globalise its sales. This requires a marketing infrastructure of representatives, advertisers, after-sales networks and specialised outlets. Access to the market is primary. Economies of scope, of transactions and of advertising have been superseding economies of production scale across a range of industrial sectors.

One implication for transnationals is that new international services industries have grown up around these needs – advertising, market research, legal services, trade, and management consulting. Services now constitute 40 per cent of the world's stock of foreign investments and 50 per cent of the flow. Another is the rise to sectoral power of retailers – the new gatekeepers of the economy – who have substituted international sourcing for international investment and have now begun to internationalise themselves. Recently we have seen a spate of takeovers inspired by the control of brand names, or, in the brewing or broadcasting industries, control of distribution outlets. The commanding heights are changing. Manufacturers are becoming subcontractors, whether to innovators or sales networks. As Swasti Mitter has put it, there has been a decentralisation of production, and a centralisation of market control.

The pattern of transnationalisation is therefore becoming more complex. On the one hand some sectors have seen a growth of a transnational intra-firm division of labour in industrial production. This has been primarily on a regional rather than a global scale. On the other hand, there are quite contrary movements, with a de-multinationalisation in raw materials and primary products, as well as in those manufacturing sectors where labour has been substituted by capital, or where 'just in time' production has brought suppliers 'back home'.

What we can see is a transnationalisation of productive systems, where nominally independent enterprises are consciously integrated into a international systems. The exemplary case is Benetton, the largest clothing firm in Europe, which franchises its outlets, subcontracts the bulk of its production to small factories in the neighbourhood of its head office in Treviso, yet dominates this network through control of internal information, design, corporate marketing, and an automatic warehouse and dyeing plant. These points of control are primarily services. But they are services whose control gives power over a combined system of product development, manufacture and sales. It represents what might be called a post-Fordist transnational.

With Fordist and post-Fordist transnationalisation, the pressure is to integrate markets internationally, and standardise and harmonise them to reduce national barriers, formally separated national markets. In part the transnationals have achieved this by circumventing national restrictions. With such a myriad of intra-firm or associated firm transactions – whether of traded goods, of intangibles like know-how and management advice, of design and accounting systems, or the cat's cradle of short- and long-term capital flows – it has proved increasingly difficult to insulate and guide the economy using the conventional tools of macro-management, or to control location and investment within this new transnationalism. This is even more the case when we take account of the financial industry, itself transnationalised, not only in banking but in insurance and financial services. The financial system has been the spearhead for deregulation and the attack on the fortress walls.

A new international economy

The result has been a new system of international economy. First it is a system with much weaker forms of macro-regulation for the reasons outlined above. As national regulatory frameworks have been weakened, the new system has attempted to get international agreements on monetary and exchange rate policies, and on financial regulations. Much has depended on the United States policy of increasing the budgetary deficit, effectively providing a Keynesian stimulus to the world economy, as private financial flows did in the 1970s. The problem arises, however, when there is international conflict, as there now is over the policy towards the American double deficit. There is the growing fear that the fragility of the present system will be exposed, as the decentralised financial system in the United States had been prior to 1934.

Second, the mobility of capital introduces a new form of competition between states. Instead of competing through the exchange of products on the market, countries are competing both for new multinational investment and for the declaration of profit through a mixture of incentives and concessions. Since the mid 1960s, the net tax rate (tax minus grants and concessions) has been bid down, not least by Britain which one tax adviser recently described as the best tax haven in the world for multinational companies. In 1981, for example, of seventeen leading industrial companies who, between them, declared profits of £9.8 billion, only three paid any tax at all, totalling £416 million. Since 1965, the government has granted more reliefs than it has taken in corporation tax. This tax, which, in the late 1960s was bringing in 9 per cent of total tax revenue, was, by 1984, contributing only 3 per cent.

With firms, prices do not, in the long run, fall below the industry's costs. In the case of countries, this is not the case. The basic costs to exchequers vary widely. The smaller the country, the lower the overall level of public expenditure, and the greater the potential incentive that can be offered to international capital to declare its profits there. Large countries cannot easily follow the small ones as net tax rates are bid down. Hence the fact that tax havens are islands or other small countries. They have contributed to this overall lowering of tax on multinational companies.

During the 1980s, the inter-state competition has gone further. Mrs Thatcher has sought to undercut continental countries in order to attract European accumulation to the UK. The recent cut in the higher rates of personal income tax was explicitly aimed at international executives. The deregulation of telecommunications and BT's tariff policy has had the declared aim of making the UK the telecommunications hub of the EEC. Oftel (a former national regulatory body of the telecommunications system) is, in fact, primarily concerned with supporting BT in the bid to undercut its European rivals. In the field of pharmaceuticals, the lightness of the regulations on animal testing has been a factor in attracting international drug research. Similarly, the government's policies in the 1980s to weaken trade unions, dilute employment protection and abolish wage councils and the minimum wage all serve to undermine the social 'floor' within the EEC.

The result of this policy has been a concentration of European-oriented growth in the south east of England. Not only has there been an increase in European headquarters located in the region, but an important part of the region's business service and manufacturing industry has been focused on Europe. One index of this is international business traffic. Between 1982 and 1986, business trips in and out of the UK rose from 5.16 million passengers a year to 6.53 million – a growth of 27 per cent. The bulk of this is focused on Europe and originates from, or is directed to, the south east: 60 per cent of all air movements to and from the south east airports in 1987-88 were European; 74 per cent of all business trips in the UK started in the south east. Seen from this perspective, the recent growth in the national economy (whose rate was twice as fast in the south east as the north, and seven times that of Northern Ireland) is more fragile than at first appears, for it depends less on a newly liberated small entrepreneurial class, as is sometimes suggested, than on mobile international capital which, at any time, may be attracted elsewhere.

The third feature of the new system is that it is consolidating into three regional blocks: the Americas, the Far East and Europe. Of these the most striking developments are in Europe. The pressure for 1992 has come from the Round Table of twenty-eight major multinational industrialists – driven by Philips and Volvo, and including the UK firms GEC, ICI and the Anglo-Dutch Unilever. Their first goal has been the standardisation and harmonisation of markets subject to preferential treatment for European firms over foreign multinationals. The next issues will be the establishment of a more centralised European monetary system, and the inclusion of a social dimension into 1992 – a policy supported by the Round Table but resisted by the British government. The key point is, however, that during the 1990s the EEC is likely to become as integrated an economy as the German and Italian economies became a century ago, within twenty years of their unification in the 1860s.

My argument is that the process of transnationalisation over the last twenty years has led to a sharp disjunction between the social and public institutions which were formed during the era of national capitalism, and the geographical range of the leading units of private capital. There is a territorial non-coincidence between both state and capital, and labour and capital. It was the recognition of this disjunction which led to the growth of concern about multinationals in the late 1960s and 1970s. At that time there was some dispute as to whether, in the words of the American economist Charles Kindleberger: 'the nation state is about through as an economic unit'. It is now clear that he was substantially correct as far as the independent management of the national economy was concerned. The Keynesian state of the period of national Fordism has been irrevocably weakened. Instead its focus has been redirected towards the labour market, industrial strategy and infrastructure.

What is striking, however, is that although the process of transnationalisation has so decisively advanced, the central concern with multinationals has correspondingly weakened. The journals and the study centres are still there. But the fire has gone out of the issue in economic and broadstream political circles. Partly this reflects the dominance of the new right, in this country at least, partly the feeling of powerlessness within the labour movement, when faced with such insistent trends and powerful giants, a feeling only strengthened by the experience of social democratic governments which have tried to resist the trends – as in the early 1980s in Mitterrand's France.

One line of argument – and it is to be heard in the third world as well as the first – is that multinationals are best left alone. The new right view is that their erosion of the powers of national states and national unions is a good thing, for it overcomes imperfections in the international economy, and brings nearer the goal of an unregulated world market. So, too, do the advanced information systems which have accompanied, indeed, permitted, this growth, since the adequate working of the market requires such 'perfect' information. A more dynamic version of this general approach is that markets aside, the multinationals are the most effective agencies for the innovation and restructuring on which economic growth depends. States, communities and unions interfere at their peril, and should instead act together to repair what damage is left behind. This approach suggests a sharp distinction between the social and the economic. In the economic sphere the multinationals should be allowed their head; it was the primary role of the state to operate as an agent of redistribution in the sphere of the social.

I register the case, for it exists – even in some parts of the labour movement. My view is quite the contrary. The trends to transnationalisation have severely weakened the trade unions – not only those in multinational companies, but also those subject to undercutting from the free mobility of capital. It has shifted the balance of taxation from the large firms to the small, and from capital to labour. It has sharpened spatial and income inequalities, particularly in former industrial areas which have been increasingly abandoned. And, in its Fordist form, it has acted to standardise and limit the diversity of the commodities we use, dissolving the distinct cultures which have been so important a part of European social and economic life. Above all it has served to further concentrate economic and political power in the hands of a small number of firms. Consider only that by the early 1980s the top ten European firms contributed as much to Europe's GDP as the entire agricultural sector. Yet, in spite of such power, the effect of its use on the erosion of the system of national regulation has imparted a greater fragility to the system as a whole, a fragility which stands to be seriously exposed in the event of what is termed the hard landing of the American economy.

In making these points I have restricted myself to these companies as multinationals rather than as capital in general. Commonly, multinationals are criticised for actions they take in the course of acting as capital – criticisms which apply equally to national firms and systems of market capitalism. But I have made this limitation simply because that slow historic process of imposing some social control on national economies is in the process of being unravelled. So, too, are the structures of the socialist countries who are now opening their doors to multinationals because of the gathering crises in their systems of planning. For the labour movement in this country, the issue of transnationalisation will become even more urgent in 1992 and beyond.

Policies towards the transnationals

What then can be done? First we must recognise the extent of the disjunction that has developed between the transnational organisation of private capital and our still firmly national institutions. The MSF is in a strong position here since many of your members experience the material fact of transnationality in the course of their work. But I start by re-affirming the point since our culture in Britain remains so deeply insular – we need only contrast the trivialities of the national news with the broader sweep of the BBC World Service. The parochialism of our national culture is reflected in the rootedly national framework of our institutions. It was the Italian greens who invited David Steele to stand for a European seat in Italy; should we not have invited an Italian, or German, colleague to do the same here? We need to develop a whole range of actions to remind ourselves – quite apart from others – that the leading edges of capital are now European, while we still guard the walls of our fallen fortress. This said, the strategic choices are two – either to rebuild the walls where they once stood or make a wider circle around capital's new arena. The first of these fits our national mood and has greater possibilities than I once thought. But I think to win back both national and local economies from the standardising grip of the transnationals needs a different approach to that which has been customarily followed in the labour movement.

The traditional view is that we restore the national economy – Keynesian style, either soft (capital repatriation incentives, independence from the EMS, some protection) or hard (on the wartime model, with strong central planning, exchange controls and an effective monopoly of foreign trade). Where there is a threat of capital flight, public ownership should be extended to further 'fix' the national economy. The greater the number of firms taken over, and the higher and more severe the controls, the more radical the proposals and the proposers. I do not think such an approach is helpful either in solving the problem or as a register of relative progressiveness. Given the degree of transnationalisation already existing, an attempt to build a wall in what Marx called the sphere of circulation will be swiftly destroyed by the controllers of production and of finance. It is like trying to hold back the sea with a rake. And if a new Labour government were to nationalise Ford, or IBM, or Benetton, they would find themselves with a little more than buildings and irreplaceable stock. It is an idealism with no material grounding.

Yet there are industrial alternatives whose significance has emerged with the rise of post-Fordism. In many sectors, Fordist producers have found themselves out-competed by decentralised, yet co-ordinated, local systems of production. In the light industries with which GLEB was involved – food processing, furniture, clothing and shoes – we repeatedly found that UK and continental mass producers were being severely challenged by Italian industrial districts, basing themselves on strong design, skill and flexible production systems. Thus, in shoes, the Italians now export more than the total production of the mass producers of Germany, France and the UK put together; in knitwear and clothing, Italy has between 10-20 per cent of world exports, in furniture up to 30 per cent, in ceramic tiles 40 per cent. Many of these districts are communist controlled, are strongly unionised, and combine the organisational advantages of the small production unit with the scale economies of collective marketing, fashion forecasting, joint finance and so on.

In the UK there are many moves to develop alternatives to the mass food products. France is the leading European example of a country which has maintained its local food economies and has built a world trade on the basis of it.

In the cultural industries there are many industrial districts in the UK – from Soho to Oxford (in publishing), or Liverpool and Sheffield (music). In West Germany it is the high-skill, networked industrial region of Baden-Württemberg which has been outcompeting the mass producers of Massachusetts in textile machinery. The conventional models of mass production are, in short, not the only way. In this country such a proposition is difficult to accept because of the extent to which the Fordist principles have been burned so deeply into our minds. But on the Continent, where Fordism made less headway, the alternatives are clear. Such alternatives cannot be breathed into being with the stroke of a new government's pen. They need to be developed as cultures of co-operation, of skill and creative design. The music of the Beatles cannot be created by law. What is required is a honeycomb of public support organisations, some sectoral, many local. At the same time there needs to be a strict control on the centralisation of retailing. Decentralised retailing has tended to encourage decentralised production, just as hypermarkets and superstores have encouraged mass production.

The point of such economies is not just that they are less transnationalised and more open to control by public bodies. Equally important is that they are less mobile. A district like Modena, or the area around Stuttgart, does not stand to be suddenly abandoned because of the calculations of an accountant and a head office decision. The districts are subject to the market and suffer their own crises. But they have tended to emerge from them on the basis of retooling, and product development, rather than rationalisation and the minimisation of costs. In Britain we still need to understand more fully how these districts and industries work. But what we know of their experience does suggest that there are alternatives to multinationalisation in its Fordist form.

This is a long-term strategy and does not touch the immediate problem of the 1990s, namely the European transnationals. Here, I think, the main challenge rests with the unions. The matter can be put simply. If capital is European and unions are national, then unions will have to become European. This is what happened in the nineteenth century at the national level, when the building of the railways, and the telegraph, allowed national firms to develop and labour eventually had to follow.

In the current period there is a possible alternative to the unions. The European Commission and its Parliament, or the member states in association, could ensure the wages and conditions, and the wider social regime which might otherwise be the subject of collective bargaining. This, too, happened in nineteenth century Britain locally – at least, for those trades in which organisation was weak.

Yet, in the present circumstances, such a strategy seems farfetched. And this because of the matter I am seeking to address – namely that European capital is strong, while European labour is fragmented, and weak. Hence progress within the EEC has been extraordinarily slow during the 1980s. The Vredeling directive, itself a very modest proposal, was successfully stalled. The various successor propositions for more worker participation (from Germany), consultation (from Sweden), access to information (from France), and greater share ownership (from Britain) seem – as things now stand – to have only slim hopes of achieving a consensus. We must trust that the Delors policy of having a social Europe as well as an internal market by 1992 will meet with some success in preventing social dumping. If there were an international economic crisis, the balance of power might become more open, particularly if there was a move to regional protectionism. But, as things now stand, I do not see that the need for European collective bargaining will be substituted by the progress of European public provision.

This brings us back to the unions. There are two possible starting points: either to begin where we wish to end up, or where we now are. Where we end up should be European unions. Their form, and range, and mode of operation will vary, but they must be able to undertake effective collective bargaining with multinationals operating at a European level and, at times, with the European state. I understand that both IG Metall and the EETPU are, from different vantage points, actively considering Europeanisation.

Let me return to where we are. At the moment there are various forms of co-operation: the two I will mention are those operating through the international trade union structure and those that work through associated action at the level of particular firms. I experienced both while at the GLC, as part of the council's attempt to support the unions in forestalling the rundown of Ford Dagenham, Kodak in Harrow, Philips and Unilever. In the case of Kodak, the initiative came from Kodak Pathe in Paris. A meeting was held between Kodak plants in the UK (comprising TGWU and ASTMS members), and a number of French plants. This meeting pooled its information, which was supplemented by research we had done at the GLC. Within half a day it became apparent that Kodak were involved in major international restructuring, shifting from chemicals to electronics, rationalising transatlantic production, and pulling R&D back to America. A set of seven demands were drawn up, a standing conference was formed and a newspaper produced. Four successive meetings were held – two at the GLC, one in Paris and a fourth in Italy, at which some twenty plants were represented. The demands were raised in the European Parliament; a march was held to present the demands at Kodak's head office in High Holborn; and a Val de Marne officer was seconded to the GLC for six months to work further on the background research.

The first conclusion I drew from this, and other similar cases, was the importance of sustained background research on the firm and sector. There were resources neither at the national nor international trade union level to undertake this, not least because the unions were fragmented both nationally and internationally – on the continent, along political lines. I would suggest then that the first step for the trade union movement now should be the establishment of twenty sectoral study centres, jointly financed by existing national unions. They should comprise only a small core staff (maximum five, including support staff). They would establish short-term working groups on particular firms, which would draw in national trade union researchers, academics, and others from the industry. These groups – which might normally last for three months at a time – should seek to involve local trade unionists through local and national meetings, and they would present their reports both to the research board of the associated unions, and through multilingual newspapers. The annual cost of the twenty centres would be £8 million.

In each study the aim would be to consider not only the particular firm's strategy of restructuring, but what alternatives there are. The value of such sectoral plans would not be confined to the trade unions in their national and international negotiations. They would also fill a large hole in the work of the European Commission. Over the past fifteen years, employer pressure has led to a rundown of sectoral work in the Commission, so that the few sectoral specialists who remain are now forced to concentrate on establishing the internal market and bringing European businesses together. Those I have talked to are not doing sustained strategic research. The European trade union movement could take the lead in providing such research for, as a number of national unions have pointed out, strategic direction is becoming one of the key elements in capitalist competition. If this is the case for capital, it should be equally so for labour; indeed, it may be more important to devote trade union resources to strategic research and to focus collective bargaining on strategic alternatives than on more immediate conjunctural issues. I have recently been working on a number of public sector industries in this country, and have been dismayed at the lack of such strategic research being done in the trade union movement (and in the case of the Post Office and the airlines, anywhere else).

Second, Kodak raised the problem of language. Is there not a case for drawing on the funds promised by the Commission under the Lingua translation programme to fund language teaching for trade unionists? This could be taken a stage further by the establishment of a European Trade Union Education College, on the lines of the Northern College or Ruskin, to be supplemented by exchange plans at existing trade union colleges within the EEC. For any successful sustained European trade unionism, there must develop a wide group of people able to speak the community languages and be part of the wider European culture. There are already European colleges which have these aims on behalf of civil servants and professionals. There are commercial courses to service international capital. Should not the trade union movement do likewise?

Third, there is the question of training. In the UK there is grossly inadequate training, in many fields, at the national level. Some unions have responded to this by developing their own training schools. With the free movement of labour, and the Channel Tunnel in prospect, the French have begun training workers to meet English certification standards. Is the provision of training and support for skilled workers wishing to find work in the many parts of the EEC labour market an area in which an early initiative could be taken?

These are three indicative ideas. The further steps of consolidating a structure capable of collective bargaining at a European level may be best left until more modest steps are achieved. Certainly the GLC/Val de Marne experience suggested a little full-time support went a long way.

What should be the aim of the collective bargaining? In the case of Kodak it was the meeting of the seven demands. In the case of Ford, the report of the GLC's public enquiry suggested that the company should be made to accept an agreed production code. Such a code would not only specify employment levels, it would cover wages, working hours, health and safety, the intensity of work, and equal opportunities. Side by side with it should be a code of use, which would include provisions for lead-free petrol, minimum safety standards and noise control. The report suggested a public sector purchasing code and an information code as well. No car would be allowed to be produced or sold in Britain which did not conform to these four responsibility codes.

These examples suggest a further point. That in building a means for exerting social control over the transnationals, a coalition of interests is necessary. There should be a pluralism of countervailing power. This is the importance of a strategic plan, for the process of planning as well as its final form has proved to be an excellent means for building coalitions. Such coalitions should include – in addition to trade unions – local authorities, user groups, community organisations, as well as national and EEC government to support policies which cannot be realised in other ways. Worked at in this way, information about companies is not a major problem. The more broadly based the planning, the wider the sources of information, often from quite unexpected sources. Indeed this suggests that the battle of Vredeling may have had greater symbolic than substantive importance. Far more important would be to get the Commission to part-fund the twenty sectoral research centres.

I have argued that it will need a more powerful and consolidated European labour movement to shift the Commission towards a more adequate approach to the transnationals. It will also need a strengthened European Parliament. At that point it would become relevant to consider measures which would require national and European state support: a European Enterprise Board, able to intervene in support of sector strategies; sectoral development banks which would take a public stake in companies that received R&D and other aid from the EEC; a new code for European enterprise plans to strengthen the collective bargaining procedures we have mentioned above; and provisions to end state-to-state competition, by putting a floor on wages and social provisions, and limits on the extent to which firms can be attracted through fiscal and other financial incentives. As with firms themselves, the aim should be to shift competition away from the financial and the regulatory to the promotion of innovation and quality. These issues, which should be the subject matter of the forthcoming European elections, require the preconditions of a strengthened Parliament and a consolidated trade union movement.

National governments should give their support to these directions. They should minimally open their books – so that Vredeling might, in part, be achieved through particular national windows. They should use their powers of public purchasing (in spite of the EEC's codes) of grant aid, of trade and competition policy and of publicity to add to the weight of the trade unions in the course of their bargaining. They should strengthen their monitoring units of the multinational's flows of trade and finances – the units, both in customs and the Inland Revenue, were weak at the end of the 1970s, and certainly much less effective than those in the US Treasury

Department. They should also consider imposing a closure tax on any firm closing a branch plant, the proceeds of which would be used to provide new investment and employment in the locality affected. Finally, national anti-trust policy should be undertaken within the framework of the international and not merely national economy. There are frequent anomalies in the way the MMC continues to treat competition as though it were ringfenced within national boundaries.

The problem, however, with all such national initiatives is that if sustained they are likely to be countered by transnationals shifting out. This is why international action is so central which, for the UK in the 1990s, means first and foremost Europe.

If, in Britain at least, much of the weight of extending social control over the multinationals in the 1990s rests with the unions, within the trade union movement itself, MSF has a history and perspective which is already pointing the way. Vic Godfrey, from all I have heard about him, played a central part in building a countervailing power in one of the European transnationals. What I have said is dedicated to his memory.

Waste and Recycling

6

Creating wealth from waste

This is an edited extract from the open-access book of the same name published by Demos in 1999. The extract is published with permission. The full text of Creating Wealth from Waste *by Robin Murray is available here: https://www.demos.co.uk/files/Creatingwealthfromwaste.pdf*

This book is the result of joint work on a project on the employment potential of the new waste economy during the mid to late 1990s. The project came about as the result of a request from the London Planning Advisory Committee to consider their long-term waste strategy in the light of recycling experience elsewhere. They were interested in the extent to which recycling could deliver on a number of aspects of their planning policies on sustainability, particularly in terms of air quality, CO_2 reduction, resource saving and the re-industrialisation of run-down areas of London, as well as the creation of jobs. This work overlapped with the Demos Working Cities project, whose aim was to develop a new approach to job creation through influencing the way changes take place in 'productive systems'. Waste was an example of a productive system, spanning households, councils, governments and a range of industrial and service sectors, and was on the point of a major change. This book develops themes emerging from the work that ensued in London on recycling planning, and parallel work in Essex, in relation to wider national issues.

Beyond the dustbin

Waste has always been the shadow side of the economy. In production and consumption, it is that which is rejected as useless and barren. Whatever the word – garbage, rubbish, refuse, waste – and whichever the language, the meaning is similar. The social task of waste management has been to get rid of it. Today's waste is carried away through sewers and dustbins, dispatched in the air through burning, dumped in disused quarries or the oceans, onto middens or fly-tipped in gutters or behind hedges.

In the UK alone, 435 million tonnes of waste is disposed of every year. The household dustbin accounts for only six per cent of the total. Eight per cent is sewage sludge, 36 per cent comes from the commercial and industrial sectors, and half is produced by primary industries like mining, quarrying, dredging and farming. In the words of the anthropologist Mary Douglas, it represents matter in the wrong place. Farms and quarries use waste as a resource. Farmers spread muck on their fields. Quarriers use rubble to landscape the land they have blasted. But for most industries and households, waste has to be collected, transported and tipped. This has been the basis for waste as a sector of the economy.

Where there has been muck, there has always been money. In the waste heaps and streets of nineteenth century and twentieth century London, as in those of the third world today, it has been a sector of scavengers, of Steptoes and their sons, of car breakers' yards and scrap merchants. The steel mills have provided a steady outlet for scrap. Rags have been the basis for factories making reconstituted cloth and felting. Even food scraps found a use. Until the early 1970s much of the organic waste from London was used to feed pigs in East Anglia. Tottenham became famous for its recycled sausages. That which could not be recycled was largely landfilled. By the early 1990s there were 4,077 registered landfill sites in Britain, accounting for over 90 per cent of unrecycled waste. Landfill was primarily a small firm business (like its sister industry, the funeral sector) made up of local operators with empty holes to sell.

This can hardly be called an industry. It is a low technology, labour intensive service, marginalised by the nature of its trade and traditions, working at the margins of health regulations and below the radar line of the stock-market. In local government, waste management has been a low status occupation, not a career path for aspiring chief executives or aspiring politicians. Waste only hits the headlines when things go wrong. Economically and politically, as the Latin origin (*vastus*) of its name implies, waste is a desert.

The new economy of waste

All of this is now changing. Three basic drivers of change are turning waste and waste management into a dynamic, fast-changing, international economic sector. This transformation presents new choices and opportunities, and provides lessons and pointers for industrial, social and environmental policy in the new post-industrial landscape. The drivers of a change are growing concern about the hazards of waste disposal, broader environmental concerns, especially global warming and resource depletion, and the economic opportunities created by new waste regulations and technological innovation.

In the UK, officially designated hazardous waste has increased by 50 per cent over the past decade to 4.5 million tonnes a year (this does not include nuclear waste). Awareness of the dangers of 'non-hazardous' waste has also grown. Landfill sites for example, because of their methane emissions, are a significant cause of global warming and a source of ground water pollution.

Incinerators also produce hazards. Their emissions of acid gases, mercury, dioxins and furans have led to widespread protests in North America, Japan and continental Europe, forcing the closure of plants and the abandonment of plans for new ones.1 Several North American states and provinces have now banned new incinerators.

In Japan, a 1997 stockbroker's survey found that only eight of the 1,500 operating incinerators met international dioxin standards, with one of them emitting 10,000 times the concentrations allowed elsewhere. In Germany, one million people signed petitions against incinerators. In France, a government survey of incinerator emissions in 1998 led to the closure of twenty incinerators and probation for others. Concern was further heightened by high dioxin levels in milk produced near an incinerator north of Paris and, in another case, by radioactive materials in incinerator waste. In the UK, recent epidemiological studies found abnormal rates of cancer for people living near incinerators and, most recently in Derbyshire, near landfills. Such studies have awakened awareness of the hazards of waste.

This is partly a new awareness of old dangers, for example of methane from organic waste. But it also reflects the increased toxicity of materials in the modern waste stream. Paints, batteries, motor oil, aerosols, solvents, fridges with their CFCs, are all potential pollutants. Many of the new materials become toxic when incinerated. Burning releases dioxins from plastics and toxic flame retardants from TVs, computers and textiles. Waste scares, like food scares, are generating a new environmental politics.

In the nineteenth century a new sanitary order was established because of the threat of disease. Today, waste has re-emerged as a political issue because of the threat of toxicity.

Earth and air

The second driver of change is concern about global warming and resource depletion. In 1900 the US consumed 200 million tonnes of materials. By 1945 this rose to 600 million tonnes, and by the late 1980s to 2,600 million tonnes, out of world consumption of 16 billion tonnes. There is now widespread recognition that this level of consumption, along with the energy required and the greenhouse gases produced by it, is unsustainable.

The effort to reduce consumption of primary materials and the energy needed to produce them has focused on five industries – paper, steel, aluminium, plastics and container glass – which account for 31 per cent of manufacturing energy use in the United States. The US Environmental Protection Agency recently estimated that a 1 per cent increase in recycling in the US would reduce carbon dioxide emissions by an amount equivalent to taking 1.2 million cars off the road. By 1998 the US recycling rate had reached 31.5 per cent, compared with eight per cent in 1990. This is the equivalent of a reduction of 28 million cars.

As environmental concerns came to the fore in the 1990s, all roads led to waste. From centuries of obscurity, the waste industry found itself at the hub of environmental argument. The main response by governments was to strengthen environmental and waste regulation. The Germans passed an ordinance to reduce packaging and increase taxes in 1991. Denmark put taxes on waste disposal. The EU tightened up on incinerator emissions, negotiated agreement to a radical reduction in landfill and introduced a community-wide directive to cut packaging waste in 1995. While the international trend in economic policy was to reduce regulations and cut taxes, waste has been subjected to ever tighter regulations and higher taxes.

Waste and the economy

The third driver of change is economic. New opportunities were created by regulatory change – in waste management, in recycling and in the use of the recycled materials. The world of municipal collection, small firm disposal and the rag-and-bone man suddenly came into contact with a wider economy.

Multinationals are taking an increasing interest in waste. Privatisation has opened up new markets in collection. The new standards of treatment and the industrialisation of waste management require resources beyond the means of small and medium-sized firms. A 420,000 tonnes incinerator now requires an investment of £125 million. A typical waste incineration contract over 25 years costs £1 billion, once recycling, composting, residual landfilling and the return on investment are taken into account. This is big money, which requires big firms.

As a result, there has been a wave of takeovers and expansion. In Britain there were 420 recorded takeovers of waste firms between 1990 and 1998. UK waste management is now dominated by seven majors: three American, two French, one Australian and one British. Four of the top five are owned by water companies. Other large firms are being attracted into the recycling sector, some of them are processors looking for materials, others are applying recognition and sorting technologies to recycling.

The opportunities for waste processors are particularly significant. Faced with diminishing primary resources and tighter regulation of energy use, major industrial sectors have been shifting their sources of supply from virgin to secondary materials.

A typical example is paper. Global consumption of paper and board has risen from 46 million tonnes in 1950 to 253 million tonnes in 1993. The Food and Agriculture Organisation (FAO) forecasts that it will rise to 479 million tonnes by 2010, a tenfold increase in 60 years. This has already led to the destruction of natural forests and to the growth of plantation forestry, which creates problems for biodiversity, acidification, erosion and water supply. The FAO estimates that no more than two-fifths of the growth in paper consumption can be accommodated from virgin wood. Even this will mean increased transport distances, new hydro-electric schemes and further pressure on natural forests. For the remaining 60 per cent, the FAO sees recycling as the only option.

In the past ten years the paper industry has been transformed by these necessities. Improvements in de-inking technology have cut costs so that, in Germany, France and Britain, it is now 35 per cent cheaper to produce newsprint from recycled paper than from virgin pulp. Germany recycles the greatest amount of paper – 71 per cent – while Europe as a whole has reached 50 per cent. In North America the proportion of old paper and board recycled has risen from a third to a half during the 1990s. Overall, there has been a dramatic shift from mills located near virgin forests (in Scandinavia and Northern Canada) to those near concentrations of used paper in major cities and towns.

This story is being repeated in other industries. Foundries for aluminium auto parts are using recycled cans, and new can recycling plants are appearing each year. Glass factories can now use up to 90 per cent recycled inputs and new technologies are emerging for recycling electronics and plastics.

In short, the environmental movement has created a new economic interest in waste and recycling. This interest, combined with the opportunities created by technological innovation, is extending down through the supply chain.

A new competition between nations

These changes offer a new basis for international competitiveness in the global economy. Rather than seeing resource constraints and tighter regulation as a brake on economic growth, governments are beginning to recognise that the emerging 'secondary materials' economy and 'eco-efficiency' offer opportunities to stimulate innovation and create new sources of wealth and jobs.

The pioneers of advanced national environmental regimes will generate technologies that can be exported, especially once the new regulatory regimes are adopted internationally. But where governments have traditionally sought to promote and protect individual technologies and companies, it is now whole systems of regulation and production that matter most.

This strategy is an explicit goal of German economic policy. The federal government has introduced strong, and often high cost, environmental legislation, which gave its recycling, packaging, chemical and processing industries a competitive edge when the same regulatory standards came to be extended throughout the EU.

The US government has also recognised this opportunity. Warren Christopher, Secretary of State during the early 1990s, promoted a strategy to use 'environmental initiatives to promote larger strategic and economic goals ... helping our environmental sector capture a larger share of a $400 billion global market'. Canada has also realised that it needs to shift from its historical role as a primary material producer to a specialist second materials economy, In 1990 Japan produced a 100-year plan for developing high technology solutions to the sustainability challenge, which was reflected in its strategic programme for the waste industry.

Waste and the economy are now bound together, as in a double helix. Waste should no longer be seen as a cost and an economic drain on productive resources. It has become a source of innovation. Like energy, it is contributing to a profound restructuring of the international economy.

In managing this process, public policy has a central place. Whereas previous waves of innovation have been generated from within the economy, the environmental redirection of the economy

– because it deals with costs external to the market – is driven by politics and government.

Social and economic opportunities are created during economic transitions. Waste is at a historical turning point, but this does not mean that its path of development is fixed in advance. Transitions can take place in different forms and follow different courses. A function of public policy in this context is not just to facilitate the transition but to shape it in a way that meets wider policy goals.

Financing the local

Increasing the rate of municipal recycling should be one of the main priorities for policy over the next five years. Municipal waste is contributing to many of the problems in landfills and is now being targeted for incineration. Leaving aside construction and demolition waste, municipal waste comprises nearly 40 per cent of controlled waste: one of the largest untapped segments of waste as a resource.

The initial national targets should be those set by the Essex local authorities: 40 per cent recycling by 2004 and 60 per cent by 2007. Increases of this order, even in short time scales, are being achieved in North America. But meeting them here will depend on making a transition to a new system of waste disposal and secondary material conversion. How can this be financed?

Funding is needed to cover the transition costs of establishing an integrated four stream system of municipal waste management. On the basis of the Essex studies, we estimate that the investment costs of 'smart' intensive municipal recycling throughout the UK would be £1.1 billion. Start-up operating costs would amount to £200 million a year. The overall cost could be met by a combination of private sector investment and public revenues supplied by the increases in landfill tax over the next four years. The question is not the overall level of finance but how it is deployed.

A successful recycling and composting programme is marked by its diversity and a capacity to involve communities and small local enterprises in the economics of the programme. A financial package must provide for diversity *and* stability. The first problem is that the UK financial system favours large, underwritten capital-intensive projects over decentralised alternatives. Just as governments and the centres of large organisations have difficulty in dealing with diversity, the same is true of banks. It is significant that the small and medium enterprise (SME) success stories in the industrial districts of continental Europe had their own sources of flexible finance. Both middle Italy and Germany had strong traditions of local and regional banks, whose personnel built up detailed knowledge of local areas and people. These sources of finance were complemented by financial consortia formed by the SMEs themselves, including very effective mutual guarantee schemes.

The UK does not have this tradition of flexible finance. Its banking system has become even more centralised and de-localised over the past two decades. This contributes to the bias towards large-scale waste treatment methods at the expense of the new style labour-intensive ones. Incinerators (and other large capital-intensive options) are financed on the basis of long-term contracts with disposal authorities, covering 70 to 80 per cent of waste throughput at a given price. They also have access to three other sources of revenue: medium to long- term contracts and spot market sales of electricity at commercial rates; and subsidies as the result of NFFO (non-fossil fuel obligation) and the PRN (Packaging Recovery Notes) arrangements. For financing large capital investment, this contractual structure provides a measure of stability, through the underwriting by the waste disposal authorities of most of the project.

An intensive recycling system, however, has much smaller and more fragmented capital needs. It is composed of many small investments by a large number of local authorities and is subject to greater levels of uncertainty. The range of investment projects and the need for local variation and for flexibility have meant that it has been considered inappropriate for local authorities to engage a single private contractor who might be able to fund a scheme of this kind. The mismatch between the flexible financial needs of an intensive recycling system and the kinds of large capital investment on offer has been a major blockage in creating a new, more efficient system.

A financial package would have to ensure stability and diverse investment. It would also have to enable local authorities to realise the potential cost savings of intensive diversion. The package should have two main elements: capital and operating budget. Capital could come from equipment leasing (covering 50 per cent of the capital required); private investors for particular projects, notably composting, and a share in MRFs (material recovery facilities); development agency loans to small and medium joint venture partners as part of a long-term investment package; top-up capital grants from existing public programmes (SRB, EU) and from the packaging recovery scheme; existing capital allocations for waste management in district and county budgets: and local schemes could also be encouraged to make contributions in kind, in the form of existing land and buildings and use of equipment, that would be credited in any joint financial package.

Operating budget

This is the critical constraint for local authorities in developing intensive recycling. The start-up costs include the recruitment and training of new staff to develop schemes; the provision for door-to-door recycling and composting advisory services; investment in new management information systems; and the establishment of enhanced four-stream collection systems. During the initial years, these costs will have to be borne while some existing contracts are still in force. There are five sources of finance for gross operating costs.

Firstly, transfers from the local authority disposal budgets. Disposing of waste through composting, re-use or recycling provides large savings to local authority waste disposal budgets. Part of the operating budget for developing intensive recycling comes from recycling credits paid by the disposal authorities. But such transfers require the savings from waste diversion to be audited and this in turn encourages the centralisation of facilities to simplify the audit trail. A few centralised compost sites are easy to audit (but have higher environmental costs) and receive credits. Home composting is difficult to audit and gets no credits. The needs and techniques of surveillance determine the institutions. A more effective way of dealing with the issue in non-unitary authorities is simply to charge them for disposal on a tonnage basis rather than through a precept based on council tax property value.

Second, the costs of disposal have put increasing strain on county and waste disposal authority budgets. Intensive recycling strategies should aim to reduce these costs on behalf of the disposal function, both by the quantities of waste diverted and also through cutting the net costs of CA (civic amenity) sites. Currently, waste managed through CA sites may constitute 40 to 50 per cent of a county council's disposal budget because they are paying for CA site management as well as disposal. Re-orienting CA sites towards intensive recycling would substantially reduce these costs and help offset the steep rises forecast for residual waste.

Third, through smart savings there is scope for making existing budgets go a long way to cover the costs of transition. Although much of the waste service has been cut to the bone, there are nevertheless ways of improving the budgeting of waste in a council, rationalising some services across departments, redeploying assets and raising non-sales revenue. All these will help to reduce the incremental costs of the four-stream system. For example, some councils still do not cross-charge non-waste departments for their handling of waste; once they do this it encourages reduction in institutional waste, particularly if supported by an advisory service. Waste reduction in municipal offices has a payback period of less than two years. There are many best practice examples of cutting organic waste in parks, schools and municipal markets, and recycling highways and housing maintenance waste. Intensive recycling on high-rise estates helps cut the high costs of waste on housing department budgets.

Other examples include using existing vehicles and assets more intensively for recycling by using them in off-peak hours, cutting back-up vehicles through changed maintenance arrangements, reorganising works depots in relation to recycling and composting, and using non-waste department assets for recycling and composting (schools, housing, parks). Further options include expanding recycling facilities for trade waste and sharing gains with the traders; rationalising special collections in conjunction with CA sites to reduce costs and increase revenues.

The details are not important except that they are details, and they grow ever more visible the nearer you are to the ground. Every waste manager and dustman will give many such examples: how consumer durables in good working order are regularly thrown out in well-off districts and then landfilled because there is no system for reclaiming them; how after Christmas there are many new presents in waste bins that are landfilled or burnt; how landfills close early so that collection time is restricted and so on. Every intensive recycling programme should aim for a 20 per cent component of smart savings.

One of the main factors paralysing municipal recycling is the problem, or more accurately the nightmare, of markets. There are two issues: the uncertainty of material revenues and their level. The uncertainty is at odds with local government budgets and their financing, and only adds to the fear of expanded recycling flooding the market. Along with financial limitations, this is the major giant blocking the path in the minds of members and officers in local authorities. It has got to the point, locally and nationally, where the fact that the giant may be friendly and going in the same direction is obscured. Moving from under eight per cent recycling to 60 per cent in eight years can be seen in terms either of the need for an eightfold expansion of markets, or of an eightfold expansion of employment. The question is how to bridge the gap in time and uncertainty between the two.

The problem of markets is financial not physical. Existing capacity can take all the aluminium and steel that households can deliver. Paper can be exported as can textiles and glass. If compost is of the right quality, then there is a wide range of uses for it. It is a problem of quality, rather than one of finding outlets. If there is too much green glass it can be stockpiled in landfill voids until new uses have been established.

For the above reasons, we do not need to fear the idea of mountainous stockpiles of secondary materials appearing. The question is the price and how it affects the financing package of an individual authority's business plan. Much depends on the steps taken now to expand reprocessing capacity in line with increased supplies of recycled materials. The prevailing pattern elsewhere has been to expand supply and trigger new investment as a result. The UK, as a latecomer to municipal recycling, has the chance to mini-mise the gap between establishing the supply line and expanding re-processor capacity. Simultaneous investment in increasing the supply of secondary materials and in reprocessing will reduce the costs of transition.

However, for local authorities the initial shortfall in the level of material prices needs to be made up by funding support. This is better provided as revenue support than capital grants because it will encourage investment in the software rather than the hard-ware of recycling schemes. The finance should come from PRN and landfill tax revenue, through channels that also address the second problem, that of fluctuations. In order to expand recycling, revenue uncertainty should be removed from the system. Income should be stabilised through an underwriting mechanism. Local authorities and small collection enterprises need access to the same kind of financial reserves that large materials companies use to manage commodity price fluctuations.

The alternatives

Long-term contracts with a private sales intermediary that would guar-antee the value of a package of recycled materials. Such a contract is often negotiated in conjunction with the operation of a sorting facility (MRF) so that the MRF 'gate fee' is lower than it other-wise might be because the contractor can keep the materials sales revenue. The problem here is that waste contractors themselves have difficulties with market fluctuations. They are waste manage-ment companies rather than materials traders and, unless they lay off the risk in turn, they are likely to estimate sales at relatively safe levels and treat upward price movements as a bonus. Any council taking this route should look for bonus sharing.

Negotiating long-term floor and ceiling price contracts with proces-sors. The most critical material is paper. On the continent there have been moves to make long-term contracts of this kind between large newsprint mills and municipal suppliers. It suits both parties, providing security of supply for large capital investments and stable prices at levels that cover collection costs. In the UK, floor price contracts are being signed but at floor prices that are below the costs of collection and transport, and considerably less than the long-term price level at which recycled newsprint is economic. Any public financial support for new investment by processors should encourage long-term supply contracts with floor and ceiling prices as part of the investment package.

Developing marketing expertise and facilities that allow a flexible response to price fluctuations. It is usually necessary to establish an independent sales consortium of collection enterprises and/or districts/boroughs. The Community Recycling Network (CRN) runs such a consortium, as do local authorities in the UK, the US, Canada and Holland. In Holland a grouping of 200 local authorities negotiated a successful long-term contract for their newsprint, having hired an industry specialist to act for them. In Ontario, the consortium negotiates material prices and offers them to its members. The advantage of the consortium approach is that it allows local councils and small firms to develop specialised market expertise, working in close co-ordination with the collection schemes and MRFs over the quality and category of materials, and being in a position to benefit from the long-term improvement in material prices.

The underwriting of a revenue stream by a packaging compliance scheme. This is the arrangement made between Bath and North East Somerset and Recycle UK. Recycle UK commit to provide a revenue stream to the council in return for the right to the PRNs. Alternatively, the PRN scheme could make up the difference between sales prices and an agreed benchmark price on the Dutch and Manitoba model.

A consortium revenue guarantee scheme. This combines the consortium advantages with the stability of under-written prices. An independent not-for-distributed-profit (NFDP) consortium would sign long-term contracts with collection enterprises and councils, guaranteeing a minimum price for a package of materials. The price should be settled, as in Canada, on the basis of best practice costs. Any profits above this price would be shared according to a formula that would build up the consortium's reserves. The guarantee would need backing, essentially insurance against the fall of the price below a minimum. This could either be provided commercially or, more appropriately, through support from a packaging compliance scheme or landfill trust.

Landfill tax offsets have already been used in a similar way to bear the risk of soil remediation in circumstances where commercial return is uncertain. Guarantees could be paid in the budget year following any claim, which would avoid large sums having to be held as security and would meet local authority needs for secure payments. In terms of available recycling support funds, the advantage of the guarantee is that it would limit support to what was necessary to cover shortfalls, rather than funding the total recycling scheme.

Summing up

Whatever the instrument, the kind of package required is clear. It should be advanced against an integrated business plan for the development of four stream intensive recycling to include local and community enterprises on a partnership basis. The financial package should provide capital and stable revenue funding during the build-up period; give long-run price stability for the major materials; comprise a portfolio of finance from different sources, including financial and in-kind resources from the local authorities themselves.

Until now, local authorities have born much of the risk of recycling. This has been a prime reason why recycling has remained marginal in the UK. The difficulty that councils and SMEs have in raising capital to finance the build-up phase of intensive recycling is one reason why capital-intensive disposal and recycling options continue to be built, even though properly managed labour-intensive recycling schemes promise much higher long-run returns. New arrangements of the kind we propose would provide a major stimulus for extending recycling in Britain. Local authorities cannot bear the risk because of financial and regulatory constraints. The private sector could do so – though at significant cost because of the innovative nature of the programme.

Most appropriately, the risk can be taken by bodies established to promote recycling because of its environmental benefits. This is why the first responsibility should rest with compliance schemes and landfill trust offsets. Reducing the risk will both limit the size of revenue subsidy required and remove one of the main constraints that has been blocking municipal recycling.

A Zero Waste Agency

Any profound change needs an entrepreneurial force to drive it. This has conventionally been seen as the preserve of the market. But recently attention has turned to social entrepreneurship and entrepreneurialism within public institutions. They, too, have a key role to play. In the case of waste, it is striking that the one large waste firm that has made a point of working with the community sector to promote intensive recycling has strong links through its parent company to the 'new gold rush' of the Californian recycling industry. The private and community entrepreneurs representing eco-modernisation are, by the nature of this new economy, usually smaller and weaker. The sector has not offered the returns for re-investment enjoyed by some sectors of the knowledge economy. Nor do the eco-entrepreneurs yet have the social and organisational capital built up over time by small and medium-size firms in the industrial districts of Europe.

In other countries where recycling has taken off, there has been a mixture of private and public drivers. Strong political leadership has always been important. At the economic level, the drive has sometimes come from new market entrants from the non-waste large firm sector, either those which have knowledge that can be adapted to the multi-stream household oriented systems, or which have a particular interest in promoting recycling. It may be paper companies establishing their own kerbside collection systems, or soft drink companies concerned to avoid any take-back legislation. In Ontario the soft drink firms played this animating role, providing advice and financial security for newly established recycling schemes. Many worked through community and municipal organisations. When they did it directly, as in Germany, the results have been more 'industrialised' and costly.

High recycling areas of Canada tended towards a partnership

model. Manitoba is a case in point. There the producer responsibility requirements led to a Product Stewardship Corporation, an arms-length quasi-public agency run by a board drawn from the main firms involved in packaging, with government, recycling industry and public interest representatives. Its task was to 'animate' a waste reduction and prevention programme, provide for the economical waste management of specified materials and administer industry levies (the equivalent of the UK PRNs). It advised and financed municipalities in the development of recycling and supported market development and research.

In many instances it is municipal administrations and non-profit organisations that have provided the main impetus. But at this point the particular organisations need not concern us: the important fact is that there are some core institutions pushing change forward. They have developed the new expertise, acted as the go-betweens and given financial support to make recycling happen. In Britain, that role has yet to be filled. The compliance schemes could have provided the leadership but, with the exception of Recycle UK, have failed to do so. The community sector has played this role in an increasingly fruitful way but its resources and influence are limited. No hands-on consultancy profession has yet developed to diffuse the knowledge of the new economy. Municipal recycling officers are greatly overworked and have had to plough their own furrow.

All this again reflects the trading approach that runs as a strong undercurrent in the history of British economic policy (as against the German orientation to production, with its emphasis on skill and technology). If the markets can be got right, they will deliver. But this does not hold true with complex systems and complex processes of change. There needs to be a much denser weave of co-operation between the sectors, comprising players in each sector who can provide leadership in making that change. For the transition to waste reduction and recycling, the market has only partially delivered. The material processors have often taken the lead in establishing capacity. What has not happened is a similar dynamic on the side of supply.

We now need a new body to animate the change. Its task would be catalytic and developmental. Its form would not be a closed structure: it would work with and through others. Funded from the redirected landfill and disposal tax, it would have the resources and clout to restore confidence among those active in recycling. It could appropriately be called the Zero Waste Agency: 'zero-waste' as an indication of its purpose; 'agency' as an indication of its bent for action.

It should not be structured according to the regulative tradition, burdened with procedures, classifications and rules of allocation. Instead, it should be created to achieve a set of outcomes and be judged by the success with which it does so. This means that it needs to be shaped as a developmental institution, working in the quasi-public sphere. What is required is an extension of the idea of social entrepreneurialism to the change in systems. The Zero Waste Agency should see itself as a 'system entrepreneur'. Its imagery should be drawn from energy rather than construction, from cultivation rather than engineering.

There are a number of guidelines that can been drawn from successful initiatives of this sort.

They seek to change systems not through the introduction of universal, pre-designed alternatives but through the generation of multiple initiatives, through encouraging pluralism and creating networks among the innovators to act as a focus for expansion.

Their primary roles are to provide a shared strategic focus, manage cross-boundary relations, support and advise frontline operators and set in place systems for training, information flow and assessment. They seek immediate ways to form coalitions in practice around particular issues that have been already studied and agreed. They favour flow over stock, working through temporary, goal-oriented full-time task forces and project teams rather than fixed positional institutions. They are not dependent on regulative change but take advantage of regulatory amendments that are in process, or work through special orders and the many levers of administrative influence within a given regulatory framework. Rather than pre-planning and detailed targets imposed by the centre, they work within a broad strategy that is elaborated and readjusted through feedback from practice. They need to be staffed by people experienced in the frontline rather than the back room.

Outcomes

In terms of outcomes, the agency would be charged with delivering on two immediate targets for municipal waste: 40 per cent recycling and reduction by 2004 and 60 per cent by 2007. There would be similar targets for the commercial and industrial sector, and for construction and demolition waste, following the completion of the current Environment Agency survey into these categories of waste.

Functions

A Zero Waste Agency would establish and/or operate the following seven prime functions.

i)   A zero-waste tendering programme. The zero-waste programme would aim to bring forward and provide finance and advisory support to entrepreneurs from any or all sectors that had schemes to promote recycling and waste minimisation.

ii) A 'waste academy' charged with developing the new trades and professions required by waste minimisation. It would have its own premises but would also be expected to work with existing institutions, using distance learning, technical colleges and universities.

iii) A recycling price guarantee programme, which would underwrite material revenues for approved municipally based or local enterprise-based projects and be run in conjunction with a recycling advisory service.

iv) A PRN brokerage, which would negotiate sales of PRNs on a consortium basis for recycling collectors. The brokerage would seek to promote long-term relationships between the 'obligated' packagers and the new wave of recyclers, encouraging the underwriting of revenues on the Dutch model.

v)   A new secondary material industries and technologies initiative comprising a small staff of industry specialists drawn from the relevant industrial sectors to act as animators and links between the expanded recycling programmes and new industry. It would work alongside the regional development agencies, through a secondary materials task force. It would sponsor an international competition for technical innovations on waste minimisation as part of an international search for relevant systems and technologies in the UK.

vi) Waste minimisation advisory services and development finance. The task would be to promote ecological production through support for zero-waste advisory services, provided both through individual consultancy and sectoral working groups (as in the construction and demolition sector). There would also be the provision of development finance for a range of waste minimisation initiatives and new enterprises.

vii) The environmental body support programme currently regulated by Entrust and run by the landfill companies.

The Zero Waste Fund

This would be a primary initial focus of the agency's work because it would be the principle means of tapping into and helping to resource collective intelligence around the problem of waste and its reduction. The past ten years have seen many innovations in the field that seek to use competitions and open-ended bidding to draw in ideas and people to carry them through. One recent example is the Architecture Foundation's Car-Free London competition, which drew entries from over 200 groups – schools, colleges, consultancy practices, environmental groups – all around the theme of reducing cars in a city. Entrants were given access to a resource centre with articles and videos on international experiences. A shortlist was given £5,000 each to work up their projects and all the entries were displayed in a major exhibition. What the process recognised was that new strategies involve work and knowledge as well as inspiration, and the process was structured so that all three were encouraged. The Zero Waste Fund could immediately sponsor such exercises on waste free towns and cities.

Another example is the New Opportunities Fund, which has been created to encourage the establishment of healthy living centres and study support centres. These are initiatives to promote preventative health and out-of-school learning in ways that are open to the applicant partners to determine. These bidding systems, when managed properly, have turned out to be creative innovations in administering social and economic policy. The Zero Waste Fund would promote 'preventative waste' in this way. The bidding process would have the following features:

- a clear outline of the broad rationale and goals of zero-waste
- an encouragement of partnerships between those who would be involved in the realisation of any programme
- professional promotion of the programme to potential bidders
- the availability of specialist support to bidders in preparing their bid
- a two stage process: i) an outline bid for which partners can apply for pre-feasibility funds of say £10,000, and ii) a detailed bid for which partners can apply for a 50:50 contribution to a full feasibility bid; this pump priming finance would be complemented by a time budget of specialist advice for both the first and second stages
- no restriction on who can bid
- where multiple bids from any town or industry are entered at the first stage, the bidders can be brought together to determine some division of labour between them or bring in other partners
- particular support can be given to areas of high need where project development and delivery capacity is weak
- projects should in general involve counterpart funding; the assessment of a bidder's counterpart resources would take into account the relative financial strength of the bidders in question and contributions in kind
- each bid should contain proposed means of assessment in addition to the basic assessment required by the

programme; assessment for all parties involved should be seen as a central part of the programme and encouragement given to imaginative forms of assessment.

- the bids should not be treated as sealed bids - the aim in all cases is to ensure that a bid is as good as it can be, and this may involve consultative work after the bid is received (for example on the size of budgets and what can be done with given sums of finance).
- the panels assessing the bids would have lay members who may reflect the specialist knowledge and the social constituencies involved in the bid.

Multi-dimensional policy

One of the aims of the agency would be to encourage the delivery of a number of different government policies through the expansion of recycling and waste minimisation. To encourage cross-departmental working within central government, a fund of £50 million a year financed from the landfill and disposal tax should be made available for bids by partnerships of departments and the Zero Waste Agency to carry through multi-faceted programmes. These could include special programmes for environmental task force placements, traffic minimisation and sustainable means of transporting waste, hazard reduction and residential/occupational health, urban and rural policies, the development of innovative environmental technologies, a multi-purpose programme of environmental home visits.

Staffing

The key role would be played by recycling, waste minimisation and industrial animators. They would be recruited from those with hands-on experience, including those involved with intensive recycling overseas. The core staff of animators would be complemented by approved consultants working on a part time basis. Over the period of the first phase (up to 2004) one of the goals would be to develop a new group of Green technical advisers trained up with the animators and consultants.

Governance

The agency would initially be established for the eight-year period up to 2007, with a review in 2004. It would be overseen by a board drawn from all stakeholder groups with an interest in promoting recycling and zero-waste, or with skills necessary for the programme's success. It would look, for example, to the retail and information technology sectors, to organisational specialists and applied scientists.

Conclusion

An organisation of this kind would marry the drive of the private sector with the multiple policy goals of the state, working with and complementing both. As well as delivering change and working flexibly in pursuit of outcomes rather than according to fixed structures, it would be a source of knowledge creation. It should be a catalyst of innovation and a promoter of wider debate and the sharing of good practice. It would help set the model for a new kind of public agency, as well as playing a central part in creating a new economy of waste.

Finally, alongside the practices and regulations necessary for a zero-waste programme to take shape, we need to develop a new way of managing risk in relation to waste. The politics of waste exemplifies the problems of risk management that governments face in a growing range of policy fields. Scientific knowledge, for various reasons, no longer commands the legitimacy to determine policies that will win public support. Governments are finding it increasingly difficult to arbitrate and regulate in ways that spread risk in the right ways. The most graphic illustration of this is food and its growing domination of the policy agenda in the UK. A new waste regime would be an important opportunity for government to create and test a new approach to risk management.

One tension at the heart of the waste debate in the UK is the opposing views on the hazards of incineration. The industry argues that the latest generation of incinerators are safe and have eliminated excess emissions through improved technology. They appeal to science to determine what is and is not safe, and what is and is not environmentally preferable. This is how it was put by Malcolm Chilton, Chairman of the Energy from Waste Association, to the House of Commons Select Committee in March 1998:

> Any decision about which is the best option, recycling or energy from waste, should be based in sound science. I think we should have a strategy that leaves that decision open to science, open to changes in our understanding as time goes on ... public perception itself should be driven partially by a reasonable understanding of the science.

But public perception remains critical: despite the reassurances about modern incinerators, there are still strong residual fears among people living near proposed incinerator sites. It is not just the older generation of incinerators that provoked a decade of protest in North America, continental Europe and Japan: the new generation has continued to do so.

So far, waste scares have been relatively localised. The banning of cow's milk on the continent because of dioxins emitted from incinerators never reached the level of the BSE scares. But the most recent case – the dioxin crisis in Belgian food, which was traced to waste oil from transformers that found its way into animal feed – is the first to cause a European government to fall on a waste issue and also resulted in the banning of all European food exports to the US. Despite new technology, incinerators are a generator of dioxins. As with BSE, GM crops and Monsanto's genetically modified hormone in milk (BST), there is a deepening gap between scientific assurances and public anxiety.

The German sociologist Ulrich Beck has argued that this tension is the defining characteristic of our age (he calls it 'the age of risk') and that what we see happening in waste is part of a much wider development in 'late modernity'. In his view there has been a shift in Western society from the problem of scarcity to one of how to limit and distribute a new category of 'latent side effects': the hazards caused by the success of science and technology in meeting material needs. He argues that the distribution of risk is replacing the distribution of wealth at the centre of late modern politics.

As part of this process, science itself is drawn into politics. It can no longer stand aside. In developing responses to old risks, science creates new ones. He calls this 'manufactured uncertainty'. Operating as it does with probabilities, the worst case – of environmental or human catastrophe – cannot be excluded, nor can science determine what is acceptable. It can no longer act as the final authority, as Malcolm Chilton still wishes it could. In part, science has lost its position as arbiter because its effects can never be fully charted. The US National Academy of Sciences reports that there is insufficient information to make even partial health assessments of 95 per cent of chemicals in the environment, let alone their interaction with each other. In this sense, we are dealing with an economy of ignorance. Even if we can chart them, by the time effects are observed, the technology may itself have moved on.

The growing economic importance of science raises the economic and political stakes of publicising what knowledge there is. In the US, only 7 per cent of known information on toxic materials is made public. When it does come out, its effects can be far reaching. The statement of a single scientist can now affect a product, or whole sec- tor, more violently than any parliament. Given the uncertainties, and the high stakes, it is not surprising that hazards are a subject of scientific controversy and have given rise to a new politics of risk – of knowledge about it, its acceptability, the responsibility for its creation and of its distribution.

Beck's analysis provides a way of understanding what is happening in the waste sector. The epidemiological studies linking incineration with toxins and disease have by their nature taken so long to produce that the technology has moved on, and the results are dismissed. But then new facts are discovered and fought over – most recently the highly toxic emissions from the incineration of TVs and computers, highlighted by the World Health Organisation and downplayed by the UK. There is growing suspicion that the 'clean incinerator' technologies reduce toxins leaving the chimney, but redirect them to the ash, and that in any case what works out on paper is always different in the reality of production. Politics even influences the way that environmental effects are researched and analysed. We need to look no further than the US EPA waste studies, whose 1997 draft, despite its academic standing, was subject to heavy pressure by the incineration industry in the US.

So if science cannot settle the question of waste hazards and the costs and benefits associated with their risk, what is the political process that can? A centralist response is to try and force through what is regarded as a solution, with the way smoothed by investment in 'education'. This worked in Lewisham for the construction of its incinerator, and in Cleveland. But in an increasing number of cases it is running into profound difficulties. The incinerator industry itself feels uneasy at pushing their projects through against public opposition. This is Malcolm Chilton again:

> I believe in democracy, so I think we should involve the public, yes. One thing we will not do in my view, having tried it on many occasions, is convince people living in the immediate neighbourhood of a plant that this is a good thing and get them to vote democratically in favour of it. That is quite difficult at a very local level and that is why I think that if these plants are required, then there has to be some form of compensation for living nearby. I cannot see any other alternative to it.

This shows an industry intensely aware of its major problem, one that has halted the expansion of incineration in the US and caused most US manufacturers to leave the industry. It recognises that industry can argue its case before local people, it can offer some form of compensation, but that in the end building new facilities will depend on securing public agreement.

This is one of the emerging principles for modern waste planning: that it must start from those at risk and work backwards. With mobile phones, individuals can make the choice about risk given adequate information. With waste treatment plants, like nuclear installations or electric power lines, there is a collective risk that is subject to individual choice only by moving out of an area. There must accordingly be collective ways of dealing with that risk, of allowing communities to make choices about how particular problems are solved, with what risk and at what price. This is what I mean by the democratisation of risk.

One field in which this issue has clearly begun to emerge is law. There has been a clear change in planning law during the 1990s, in the weight given to 'public perception' and 'public concern' in planning applications. Most notably, in the case of the Browning Ferris hazardous waste treatment plant in Newport, the court of appeal ruled that public anxiety could be the sole material reason for turning down a planning application even if this anxiety was not well founded. In Beck's terms, the individual perception of risk has become a material factor in what should and should not be allowed.

There has been a significant increase during the 1990s in the number of judicial review cases about the environmental impact of industrial development, including many waste treatment facilities, that are increasingly bringing to bear human rights principles (and are embodied in the Human Rights Act 1998). This parallels the link established in the US between the environmental impact of waste facilities and civil rights. What is emerging is a new body of law on the distribution of risk.

Public concern, and therefore consent, is thus becoming ever more important. The redirection of French policy towards waste reduction and valorisation' sets out, as the third axis of its new policy, 'restaurer la confiance des citoyens et des contribuables'. To restore confidence of citizens and taxpayers. This is a good starting point. What follows it as applied to the planning and management of waste?

First, decisions on waste planning should be made at levels that are local and that can implement alternatives. This goes against the trend. Decision making is becoming progressively centralised. The DETR's draft waste planning guidance proposes that regional planning bodies establish regional technical advisory boards for waste, with a membership dominated by the old waste order, and even further removed from those affected by waste facilities. The movement needs to go the other way – to the districts. If districts were responsible for their own disposal they would have to weigh up the options for themselves, negotiate on an equal basis with neighbouring districts where they had no local facilities and decide for themselves what risk and what costs they would be willing to take on. We would move away from a position where counties seek to impose incinerators on unwilling local communities, to one where districts are made responsible for their own waste according to the proximity principle. The argument for centralising responsibility for waste disposal in the counties was based on 1960s principles of economies of scale. The 1990s proximity principle argues the case for returning the responsibility to a more local level.

Secondly, we need a new economy of information for planning and managing risk. Risk turns on knowledge and how it (or the lack of it) is perceived. The problem is that science is a particular kind of codified knowledge. Beck points out that critiques of science therefore have to come from within the scientific community, from other scientists. The expert creates the counter-expert. Democratising risk requires that those who are invited to bear it should have access to their own scientific advisers, civil society's own 'civil service'.

Accordingly, as part of any planning application for waste facilities the applicant should be asked to provide, along with their application fee, a sum of, say, £10,000 for bona fide community groups to assess the company's environmental statement. For operating facilities, the licence fee should have added to it another £10,000, for those living in the neighbourhood to undertake their own monitoring and analysis of the company's and the Environment Agency's monitoring. In all planning matters where the economic stakes are high, giving due weight to civil society means creating the financial means to take independent advice on the existence and significance of hazards.

This is linked to a greater openness required on information. Environmental hazards need their own freedom of information act. Agencies set up to protect the public often end up closer to the industry they are regulating than to the people they are meant to protect. Regulative capture is a well-established feature of environmental regulation. Scientists move between the agency and the industry. Agencies take on the problems of the industry and try and solve them. The high stakes involved in hazards information encourage a culture of secrecy and a nervousness about public interest. As I argued above, these are structural rather than personal issues: they stem from the ways in which institutional structure influences culture, and the influence of culture on organisational behaviour.

We need a new culture that turns the regulatory agents outwards. Public hearings, local authority select committees, rights of access to facilities and independent monitoring are all needed if confidence is to be restored. The flow of information and its processing must be reversed. Instead of it coming from the operators and being fed through by professionalised PR or managed public 'liaison groups', the public interest must have its own assessors, analysts and consultative 'spaces'.

One example of a different kind of information culture is the incinerator in Vienna, where the results of the continuous emissions monitoring are displayed on the street, side by side with the regulatory limits. This symbolises the turning outwards that is necessary for operators and agents.

Effective monitoring depends on six things: the knowledge of regulations; the design of operations to make infringement difficult; surveillance and inspection; the capture of infringers; their trial and punishment. In minimising environmental risk from waste, prevention will always come first, the design of products and handling waste that minimises hazards. But after that, we also need regulations that instil confidence, regular independent inspection and, where necessary, inspection of the inspectors and finally, strong penalties for infringement and compensation for those affected.

These are all elements in a strategy of restoring trust. Again, we have lessons to learn from the French: their redirection of strategy began with an independent review of emissions from existing incinerators, punishment of the many who were not confirming to regulations and tightening of the emission limits against which future operations would be judged. The principles proposed here should be applied to all waste operations – to recycling and composting as well as incineration and landfill. The principle must be openness and transparency, not just to build public trust, but because they lead to improved practices. I have already argued that the new waste economy is information intensive. It also matters who produces this information, who has access to it, and who is able to read it and make it comprehensible.

The choice about risk must be returned to those who are asked to bear it. They are able to choose the balance to be struck between technology and life. They should bear the cost in deciding the direction. A new waste strategy based on expanding incineration, with increasingly centralised control of decisions, runs right against this tide of environmental decision making and will run into the same kinds of problems that it has faced elsewhere. Centralising environmental decisions generates its own risks, political and administrative, and its own unproductive costs. For this reason, waste strategy must be built from the ground up. The government's task is to ensure that localities take responsibility for their own waste. That is the point of district waste plans. They should ensure that there is full and open information and the resources to interpret it. And there should be a regulatory regime that is seen to turn outwards to those it is intended to protect, not inwards to those who are being regulated. Along with a revised tax structure, new financing mechanisms and an 'animating' agency, decentralising decisions on waste will give the fourth major boost to the expansion of recycling in Britain.

Political Economy

7

The new political economy
of public life

This article appeared in Soundings, *Issue 27, 'Public Life', Summer 2004.*
The journal is available here: https://www.lwbooks.co.uk/soundings

The question of how the state – or more properly the public
sphere – should be organised remains at the heart of the crisis
of social democracy and socialism; it is an issue on which little progress has been made since 1989.

Much of the debate on the left has been conducted in terms of the
issue of the commoditisation of public life, and has focused on such
questions as the extension of markets and quasi-markets, the introduction of vouchers and tradable permits, and the application of
market accounting (liberalisation). Bound up with this problematic
of exchange is that of consumption (choice, the individualisation
of consumption, personalisation) and that of distribution (who
should have access to public goods, on what terms, and how this
relates to distribution via the market). In a theoretical sense these
could all be described as problems of circulation. They have been
posed by the right in a sustained campaign over the last forty years,
and this has repeatedly pushed the left onto the back foot. But in
the left's resistance to commoditisation, and the asset-stripping of
the public sphere, the over-riding questions has persisted: if not
this way, how?

The movements of the 1970s and 1980s soon clarified the point
that the old form of the state was itself suffused with problems: it so
often reflected the organisational models of Taylorism and Fordism
– which were facing a gathering crisis in the private sphere. The

term 'in and against the state', coined by a group of socialist economists and state workers in the late 1970s, captured the point. But in
so doing it necessarily asked 'what are we for?'

I want to suggest that the starting point for an answer to this
question should not be issues of circulation but of production,
and specifically of the labour and consumption processes around
which production in the public sphere is organised. It was the
experience and analysis of public labour processes that underpinned the critiques of groups like 'In and Against the State', and
in posing the issue in this way they pointed to issues on which
the right were silent, and which offered alternative ways forward.
Faced with the onslaught of neo-liberalism, much of the old
Fordist public order has collapsed – most notably the centrally
planned economies of the East and South. The latter have in some
ways left the deepest scar.

Liberation movements which militarily and politically overcame
the mightiest world powers in the 1970s (there were nine socialist
revolutions in the South during that decade) have subsequently
succumbed almost completely to those world powers economically. The left lacked models which were the economic equivalents
of nailey boards and guerrilla strategies in the military field.

At the same time, the severity of the neo-liberal onslaught, not
least in the UK, has sparked a great range of alternative experiments in the organisation of public life from which a pattern is
emerging. Partly this has come from within the state itself – from
local authorities like Harlow or the GLC. But it has also come from
outside the state through civil society movements. Those around
food, health, transport, and the environment have been particularly important in suggesting alternative models. They have moved
the debate beyond the issue of public/private boundaries and the
transformation of micro processes of production, to questions of
the ways in which whole systems of producing certain general
needs are organised.

Take food as an example. For the most part, in social democratic
countries, the state does not produce food directly. But it massively
influences what is grown and where. Its instruments are subsidy
and regulation. The critique of the food movement is of state policy
captured by the leading agricultural, food processing and retailing

interests, at the expense of the environment, small farmers (both in the UK and in the developing world) small shopkeepers and the consumer.

Over twenty years, this movement has developed an alternative both in theory and practice – agricultural production which is more benign environmentally (and to agricultural workers), alternative distribution systems, and a quite different mode of consumption.

Much of this has been put into practice by the civil economy, with little if any support from government. The sphere of the state most open to the innovations has been local government – not all but some – which has used its purchasing power, and in rare cases its authority over school meals, to encourage healthier eating and farmers markets; or has resisted the impact of supermarkets on local food distribution.

And once the question is posed as one of productive systems, the food movement in the UK found that there were areas of the world in the North as well as the South where such systems were well established. Emilia Romagna, for example, has a remarkable network of co-operatives – of farmers, food processors, retailers – which has not only resisted the Fordist food economy locally, but has expanded internationally (Parmesan cheese is produced by a consortium for more than 900 small cheese producers in the Parma region, Parma ham by a similar co-operative of over 100 local pig farmers).

In the case of co-operative-centred food systems, the starting point has either been from that of primary producers (as in Emilia) or from consumers (as in nineteenth–century Britain). In contemporary Britain, the food movement has funnelled into the food system from both directions, that of alternative farming methods (driven by environmental and health concerns) on the one hand and from consumption on the other. But in this case, the consumption problematic is very different from that of neo-liberalism's pre-occupation with markets and choice. It is rather with a material mode of consumption, which is then connected directly with production and with politics as part of what in conceptual terms is a labour process analysis of the food system.

Take another example, energy. The pioneers of new electricity systems in the early twentieth century were municipal and regional governments. Power stations and local distribution systems were established as part of 'gas and water' socialism. These were later consolidated by the central state, and connected via a national grid, until they were all privatised, like other utilities, over the past two decades.

What privatisation has meant is not a change in system – this is still centred round large power stations and distribution via the grid – but modifications within the system about which power stations come on stream when, or how consumers are charged and how much.

The environmental imperative to reduce greenhouse gases, and the movement against the dangers of nuclear power, have now opened-up quite different ways of meeting the demand for heat, light and cooling.

New technology has cut the cost of small generators, and when these generators are linked into piped heating and cooling systems (so called tri-generation), the reduction in energy losses in comparison with traditional centralised power stations, and from the national grid, are such as to outweigh the scale diseconomies of generating electricity from smaller plants. The net cost advantages captured as surpluses in public hands can be used to reduce prices for those in fuel poverty, and/or to fund renewable energy production, which in straight market terms is for the time being more expensive than conventional power sources.

This form of distributed energy system has often gone hand in hand with action to reduce energy consumption, through a whole range of measures in industry, commerce, and the home. The so-called fourth energy source (reduction) has turned out to be the cheapest way of meeting power demand, but it requires quite different types of labour process, organisation and culture in order to deliver it.

New informational and production technologies have re-opened spaces for municipal enterprises and small-scale producers and their collective organisations. Eighty per cent of wind power in Denmark is co-operatively owned. In North Rhine Westphalia, now the leading wind power producer in Western Europe, it is the regional government which has taken the lead. In Manitoba, Canada's last social democratic state government, which has just been returned to power on a radical environmental ticket, a new public hydro project (in which the native people have a one-third share), and a local system of wind power (distributed to farms and owned by farmers and local co-operatives) has set Manitoba at the forefront of all jurisdictions in reducing CO^2 emissions. What's more, it has used energy production as an instrument of regional policy and income redistribution.

In the UK, the local council in Woking has become a leader in the introduction of distributed energy systems internationally. They have established sixty generators distributed over 'private' wires (in fact municipal wires), using gas, solar, hydrogen fuel cells, and geo-thermal energy production, coupled with combined heat and power (CHP). Woking now accounts for 10 per cent of all CHP and solar energy in the UK. This shows the way for a new era of municipal enterprise.

Finally, let me take an example of an area which has remained a municipal responsibility: the collection and disposal of waste. Here the traditional regime was established in the late nineteenth century. It was focused on the dustbin, which in Britain was collected weekly. For a century, until the late 1990s, the service remained much the same. Collection vehicles got larger and were fitted with compactors. Mixed waste was taken to landfills or burnt in incinerators. It was a labour-intensive service, using unskilled labour, and it expanded in line with the growth of the economy.

Widely based social movement protesting at the dangers of landfills and incinerators, coupled with growing concerns about climate change, are forcing this old model to change. Throughout North America and Western Europe, public policy is now trying to decouple waste from economic growth. Reduction, re-use and recycling have become the watchwords at the beginning of all local and national waste strategies.

Some regions and countries have been remarkably successful in changing their waste services over the past decade. Germany, Holland, Switzerland, Nova Scotia and a handful of American states all now recycle 40 per cent or more of their municipal waste. In place of a single mixed waste stream, they have introduced systems based on the collection of distinct streams, some separated at source, like organic waste or dry recyclables, others using various mechanical separation systems. Mass waste is being reconceived as multiple secondary materials.

The production problem is similar to that faced by mass manufacturers from the 1970s onwards, but in reverse. For the manufacturers, the challenge was to move from the single product flow principles established by Henry Ford to multi-product flow as developed by Taiichi Ohno for Toyota in Japan. (Kiichiro Toyoda, the founder of Toyota, was inspired by visiting an American supermarket in 1937, and retailers have been leaders in developing the multiple flow practices that characterise the new industrial paradigm.)

Recycling is retailing in reverse. The remnants of the mixed bag of commodities are separated out and returned as secondary materials (sometimes via the retailer) to the manufacturing cycle. Some countries have responded to the challenge of recycling by using old collection technologies in parallel to collect the separate streams. German households, for example, may have four different bins (for packaging, organics, paper and residual waste), collected by four separate large waste collection vehicles. Some recyclers use a traditional waste vehicle divided into separate compartments, into which the waste is sorted at source. The result of this approach has been an escalation of costs. The cost of German packaging waste collection and sorting is some £260 per tonne, compared to mixed waste collection and disposal in the UK of £50 a tonne. The problem is that there has been a replication of traditional methods of waste handling. The work process, technologies and forms of organisation remain similar.

But there are some regions and municipalities which have introduced quite different systems. There are over 1000 municipalities in Italy which have 'deconstructed' the traditional dustbin, firstly by introducing separate food waste collections. Residents are given small buckets in which they place bio-degradable plastic bags containing the food waste. The buckets are collected by one person with a small truck costing less than a tenth of a normal refuse vehicle and transferred to a closed vessel compost plant. With food waste out of the way, and garden waste composted at home or collected occasionally at weekends, the remainder of the dustbin no longer has to be collected so regularly. Paper, glass and tins are removed, and the residual may be 'gleaned' with a mechanical sorter, to get other recyclables out and to neutralise any remaining organics.

The key technologies here are not complex waste treatment systems, but the biodegradable plastic bag. The bag keeps in the odours and allows quality control by the collectors. Waste is no longer hidden in black plastics sacks or dustbins but made visible through transparent bags and open.

The single giant compacting lorry can now be replaced by vehicles designed for the particular materials – local authorities in the UK have pioneered a small electric recycling barrow which carries up to a tonne and goes on the pavement. When income from the sale of materials is taken into account, the result – in the case of the Italian system – is high recycling (nearly half of municipalities in the Milan region now recycle over 50 per cent of their waste, with some exceeding 70 per cent), and a reduction in overall municipal waste costs, in spite of the multiple streams of collection.

An emerging pattern in each of these cases, social and environmental movements have taken the lead in developing alternative models of productive system. Here we are not restricting the definition of productive system to a narrowly defined view of production; we are extending it to include forms of distribution, modes of consumption, the types of labour and professional skill required, and adequate forms of allocation and ownership.

Although each of the examples I have discussed are very different, there are common patterns emerging – a new paradigm of social production. And this can be found to apply to many other spheres – water, transport, health, schools and prisons.

We can identify six features of this new paradigm: a move away from addressing symptoms and towards looking for cures; production avoidance (looking for ways to rethink old, often wasteful practices); shifting from mass delivery to user-centred services; a trend towards flexible service production; new built forms; and new forms of finance.

Each of these applies to the emerging models I have discussed.

Symptom prevention and production avoidance

Whether in transport, health, or the utilities, the rise in costs is leading to renewed interest in the prevention of problems. The food movement is currently celebrating a breakthrough in public policy in favour of disease prevention through a healthier diet; this has happened not because of a change of course in the agricultural section of DEFRA, or even the Department of Health, but through the influence of the Treasury, who recognise that only radical changes in the food system will stem the spiralling costs of treating the consequences of obesity (or smoking).

Similarly, the debate on waste has now moved to seeing waste as a symptom of bad design, and policy is being directed at shifting the responsibility for waste from the state to producers (and to a lesser extent consumers), as a way of introducing a dynamic for waste reduction. In energy, the issue is how first to reduce the need for energy, not just through switching off lights, but more significantly through designing buildings so that they use minimum energy (and in some instances even act as mini power stations, exporting energy from solar production).

The user is now recognised as a co-producer, as an intrinsic part of the chain of production. There is a new interest in the informed consumer (in food), in the efficiency of consumption (of energy or water), in the importance of the provider/user relation for the effectiveness of the service (in health or education), and in the part that users play on their own account in meeting the goals of the service. There is also a growing interest in the way users experience services and the built environment emotionally, and in the nature of 'emotional labour' of frontline workers.

One result is a new focus on the relationship between frontline workers and the users. There has been an expansion of advisory services and home visitors – energy efficiency advisers, 'compost doctors', post-operation action teams and district nurses, probation officers. Local councils now provide one-stop shops, and information services. Most public services now have websites and service guides. New responsibilities are being given to caseworkers. Front line delivery staff are now being re-trained to provide advice and support, and, like the Toyota workers, to take greater responsibility for the analysis of service information and for improving quality. Teaching is being redefined as facilitation.

The user is no longer a passive consumer, or a citizen with rights of access to a universal service. Instead, meeting the goals to which the service is directed depends critically on him or her. This is clearly the case for waste and recycling but is also true for education, and health (exemplified in the latter's explosion of support groups, specialist advice lines, and healthy living centres).

Flexible and adaptive production systems are at the core of the new emerging social productive systems. Mass customisation in manufacturing rested on a shift from dedicated equipment towards general purpose machines, which enabled a rapid switching of production from one product to another. Similarly, flexible infrastructure and equipment is a feature of the new public service paradigm. The demands for flexibility are of two kinds: short-term and long-term.

In the short term, infrastructure has to be able to respond to different levels of demand, different service mixes, and different kinds of use. Roads and pavements, for example, are general purpose infrastructures that can be used flexibly. Their use can be switched in time and space: for example, the direction of flow in road lanes can be reversed to match the rush hour. Pedestrians and bikes can take over on Sundays. Re-allocating road space can be done quickly and cheaply.

Schools are now being designed with multiple uses in mind. Currently schools in the UK are only used thirteen per cent of the time. But their facilities could be opened up to local communities as learning and leisure centres. They could be booked for conferences and events. The same goes for other public buildings – colleges, parks, museums, and even waste transfer stations (the waste site in Phoenix, Arizona was designed with the help of artists and is now a community centre, museum and educational facility).

In transport the principle of flexible equipment can be seen in road-rail buses, in lorries that can rapidly switch their loads from road to rail and back again, in containerisation more generally, including the standardised containerisation of personal luggage, the use of adaptable vehicles (like the recycling vehicles with cages and bags rather than fixed compartments), and of buses and trains that can have flexible capacity according to demand (the Singapore metro system varies the length of its trains according to real time feedback on passenger numbers).

These are all examples of short-term flexibility.

Equally important is long-term adaptability, the capacity of a system to respond to changes in the external environment. With the mass production paradigm, the emphasis was on scale, including large-scale finance, and a reduction or displacement of risk. Major plants – whether they were nuclear power stations, new reservoirs, incinerators, motorways, or airports – had long lead times, became the focus of local and environmental opposition, and were subject to expensive retrofitting. They tended to freeze technologies. They were open to serious capacity problems if demand fell below forecast or rose above it.

The new systems are built to be adaptable; faster to plan and build; to have shorter economic lives; and to be more open to technological adaptation or replacement. They are smaller, cheaper, and more distributed, therefore more easily absorbed into any locality. Modern windmills, for example, can be planned and built in six months. Nuclear stations take nine to fifteen years.

Intensive recycling systems can handle sixty per cent of waste within as little as three years, while incinerators take a minimum of eight years to come on stream. Traffic management schemes based on converting a network of streets to bus-only roads, or raising a separated lane for cyclists, can be introduced in a fraction of the time and at a fraction of the costs that it takes to build a major new metro line or urban motorway. New water purification and delivery systems are being developed which do not rely on large-scale infrastructure. Micro closed-vessel composters based on microbiology have now been developed which match the costs of large-scale plants, and can be fitted into parks, or school grounds, high rise estates or car parks. With smaller scale equipment and modular buildings, economies come from volume production of standardised designs.

In all these examples it is not just a question of scale, or that small is beautiful. Rather it is a question of how large systems are constructed and maintained – whether they are centralised round large flagships, or distributed with small, locally adapted plants and equipment, supported by system-wide communication and information systems, and specialised know how. It is the model of the Third Italy as against Turin.

These new technologies have organisational implications. The hierarchical, Taylorist model of public sector management is seen as inadequate not only by critiques of traditional service systems but by many public service managers themselves. There have been numerous attempts to introduce organisational arrangements which are flatter and networked and give greater autonomy to the operating units. There has been a thinning out of middle level supervision, which has been counterbalanced by experiments in strengthening user groups (parents for example), by imposing targets (often reminiscent of Soviet-type planning), and by extending internal and external contracting and widening the remit of inspectors and auditing bodies. There has also been an emphasis on strengthening horizontal links via partnerships, and new cross-institutional bodies (such as primary health care trusts).

These experiments are at the core of public sector reform. In some sectors re-organisation has followed re-organisation, as errors are recognised and new routes are tried. Some of the more successful (such as the New Deal for Communities) have involved pooling central government resources for inner urban areas, and giving authority over the spending and contracting to newly elected small area partnership bodies in which residents form a majority. This is a first notable attempt to reverse the thirty-year trend in the UK to centralising hierarchically organised municipal government on grounds of economies of scale. The broad goal of these organisational reforms is in line with the new paradigm, to give greater autonomy for operating units, so that they can run themselves on a day-to-day basis, and can innovate and allocate resources, while at the same time remaining accountable to users and funders of the services. The new forms of public finance are not confined to the prison service. For the social economy, the form of finance is as important as is the market for neo-liberals. The structure of finance provides the skeleton of an organisation. The centralisation of public finance and the form of the budget, established by the late nineteenth century in Britain after a century of institutional struggle, have underpinned the centralisation of government and the vertical fracturing by department.

Flatter, networked and more directly publicly accountable organisation require a parallel innovation in public finance. The old model of direct taxation gathered into a central Treasury and dispensed in ever more complex and non-transparent ways through levels of government and hierarchical layers, has lost its legitimacy. Throughout Europe and North America anti-tax parties have gained ground. The problem has been made worse by the shift in the relative incidence of tax, away from internationally mobile companies and individuals and towards the immobile.

There has been a wide range of public finance reforms in response to these problems:

- a shift from direct to indirect and property taxes to secure a greater tax take from the mobile
- the introduction of hypothecation between particular taxes and expenditures
- the financing of new investments by public bonds (which may themselves be subject to referenda)
- the increasing use of tax and differential charging as an economic instrument (providing rebates for 'goods' and higher charges for 'bads')
- tithes to be paid by private developers for hypothecated uses (for the arts, or low cost housing, or environmental improvements)
- more generally the use of ownership, property tax or the sale of permissions to gain a share in betterment that results from public investments.
- the introduction of tradable permits or tax contributions linked to the achievement of targets
- the encouragement of not for profit companies and co-operatives to provide services in which users and local residents can invest (this has been the secret of the spread of co-operatively owned wind power in Denmark)
- the use of challenge funds involving bidding by public and partnership bodies, as an element of partnership funding (this has been used within central government as a means of encouraging cross departmental working)
- the provision of area budgets to be allocated by partnerships responsible for services within an area

These measures make more permeable the boundary between a public sector funded by direct tax and the spheres of the household and the market as they relate to the state. A number of them are aimed at making a closer link between tax and service (other than through direct charging). In some cases (such as the bond or a discretionary tax subject to voting) they provide a measure of the public acceptability of the proposed investment. Those arguing for the investment have to win a majority. As the flow of funds to finance public services becomes less centralised so it provides the material basis for organisational decentralisation and a wider range of service accountability.

There have also been elements of Schumpeterian taxation, with rewards of lower tax, or more funding, or revenue from the sale of permits for successful innovators. The incidence of the economic instruments is specified over the long term. There has also been a growing use of not for profit bodies charged with promoting restructuring in public and private sectors, which are used as intermediaries for the provision of public funds by the central exchequer.

These are just some of the avenues opened up by the productive systems critiques and alternatives developed by the social and environmental movements, and by innovations from within branches of the state. But here I want to return to a more general argument: that by re-entering the economic and political debate about the state not through the neo-liberal problematics of circulation but through a material critique of productive systems, the left can once again be on the front foot in the questions it poses as well as the ways in which it answers them.

The examples discussed here suggest that there is a new production paradigm, which is applicable to the social and economic infrastructure that was formerly the responsibility of the state.

But it is an open question as to whether or not this paradigm can become generalised, as the mass public service paradigm was in the previous wave. In those countries where the old paradigm is strongest, there is a coalition of interests – bureaucratic, professional, and private – for whom the future is seen to lie not in the new paradigm, but in an intensification of the old. Privatisation and other aspects of recent public service reform have served to belatedly introduce into the public sphere key elements of Fordism – deskilling labour, concentrating power into the hands of managers, increasing the scale of plants and service centres, standardising services, and making them more rigid (through the details of long-term service contracts for instance). And new technologies have facilitated this centralisation of control. The globalisation of infrastructural services (in the utilities, and in services such as prisons, leisure facilities, construction, freight transport, and the running of schools) is likely to intensify this trend, since few of the global corporations are (so far) offering the new generation of services.

What is needed is a coalition for the new paradigm, which will include elements of the state services, progressive trade unions, younger professionals, not for profit and environmental groups, and a number of SMEs and major corporations who have adopted the new production and environmental paradigms. The difficulty is that the cost savings promised by the new systems depend on volume production of means of production and construction, and this pre-supposes wide-scale adoption of the new system internationally. Governments play a critical role here, in funding the initial stages of the new paradigm services until a sufficient critical mass is reached. (There is also the strong possibility that new systems of production can decouple the demand for many services from the rate of growth, as has been the case for energy.)

But developments along this path cannot be confined to the fortress that marks the old state boundaries. The critical issue now is the determination of wider productive systems, which necessarily involve private, public, the household and the not-for-profit sector. The task of the state is to provide a structure of incentives, and ensure an institutional framework, which will allow productive systems to develop along the lines of the new paradigm rather than reproduce the old. To do so, the state will have to reconstitute itself (in Britain at least); it needs to move away from the subaltern status it has been driven into by the politics of the last two decades, and restore its specialist knowledge and public identity, so that it can partner with the new interests on whose support and capacities any substantive post-Fordist state will depend.

Social Economy

8

Danger and opportunity:
Crisis and the new social economy

Edited extract from Robin Murray's report Danger and Opportunity: Crisis and the New Social Economy, *the Young Foundation with NESTA, September 2009. The full text of the report is available on the Young Foundation website. Reproduced with permission.*

The argument

The early years of the twenty-first century are witnessing the emergence of a new kind of economy that has profound implications for the future of public services, as well as for the daily life of citizens. This emerging economy can be seen in many fields, including the environment, care, education, welfare, food and energy. It combines some old elements and many new ones. I describe it as a 'social economy' because it melds features which are very different from economies based on the production and consumption of commodities. Its key features include:

- The intensive use of distributed networks to sustain and manage relationships, helped by broadband, mobile and other means of communication.
- Blurred boundaries between production and consumption.
- An emphasis on collaboration and on repeated interactions, care and maintenance rather than one-off consumption.
- A strong role for values and missions.

This economy can be found in parts of the public sector, the non-profit world as well as commercial markets, though it thrives most in the spaces where the sectors overlap. It is already helping to address some of the most intractable problems facing modern societies, including adaptation to climate change, ageing, inequality and spreading learning.

However, this emerging economy still lacks adequate capital, methods and skills. There are major gaps on the side of demand, as the great majority of public and private money is still locked up in older models, providing services to essentially passive consumers.

There are, too, major gaps on the side of supply. Although there are thousands of promising initiatives, few have grown to scale, and there is a dearth of support to turn good ideas into big impacts.

The current economic crisis, like that of the 1930s, is the hinge between an old world and a new. Such crises, as the Austrian economist Joseph Schumpeter pointed out, are periods of creation and destruction. In these circumstances, monetary and fiscal measures are unlikely to restore growth by themselves. What is needed is a programme of more profound structural change, of a radical transformation of infrastructures and institutions that will be the precondition for a new, qualitatively different period of growth. Anything less is an appeasement of the past.

In this transformation, environmental and social innovation will have a central place. There is an economy of social innovation which has been expanding rapidly. In the UK it looked at first as if the crisis might marginalise this movement. Instead, conditions are emerging that require its acceleration. In many cases it will require systemic innovation – changing the way in which whole systems of production and service are conceived and delivered or the need for them avoided. Many of these changes do not require new resources, but rather radical new ways in which existing resources are used, regulations are framed and incentives provided. Where support is required is in seed funding this innovation, inside and outside the public sphere.

The context of crisis

The first great economic crisis of the twenty-first century has been met with the economic theory and instruments of the twentieth century. The crisis has been analysed largely in terms of problems in the financial system – of complex, unregulated financial instruments, of bankers' bonuses and irresponsible borrowing. There has been broad agreement about the tasks. Governments must help the banks to get back on their feet. They need to revive demand; regulations need to be tightened to guard against some of the abuses of the past.

This framework is inadequate to understanding the crisis and to resolving it. There are deeper structural issues which lie behind the storms of the financial markets, and which require a more far-reaching economic programme to address them.

My starting point is not the financial world of monetary aggregates but the material world of production and distribution, of Cisco and Microsoft, Tesco and the oil wells of the Middle East. It is a world of technical revolutions and seismic social and political shifts, shortage and plenty, destruction and creation. And it is in understanding the dynamics of this real economy, and its connection to finance, that Schumpeter is a more compelling guide than Keynes.

Schumpeter, as an Austrian, had witnessed first-hand the hyper-inflation of the early 1920s, the expansion of large-scale German industry, and the full economic and political consequences of the Great Depression. He analysed the way in which bursts of technological change connected to business cycles, and this analysis has been deepened and extended into theories of long waves of economic activity.

Long waves and sharp crises

Carlota Perez is one of the few economists to have foreseen the course of the financial bubble and its crash in the current decade.[1] She argues that such moments are critical turning points in technological revolutions. They come after twenty to thirty years of the installation of a new technological and organisational paradigm, first through its initial period of irruption, followed by a finance-led frenzy. Prior to the frenzy, financial capital faces declining yields from the mature industries of the previous paradigm. The emerging paradigm offers fresh, extravagant hope, and finance rushes to back the prospects and infrastructures of the new. This period of financial frenzy invariably ends in a bubble and a crash.

The crash leads to a brief period of capital devaluation, and institutional re-composition that opens up the possibilities of a golden age. Perez refers to these post-crash years as the period of deployment – when the emergent technology, and the new forms of organisation and regulation that allow the technology to flourish, spread to all industries, activities and institutions. Finance is bruised but available. It is a period of intense private and social innovation.

Whether these possibilities are fully realised depends on whether the powerful industries and organisations of the previous paradigm use the new technologies to re-enforce their entrenched position, or whether the new forces can reshape the institutions, spread the gains from the new technologies more widely and reach a new social settlement.

The current crisis

The roots of the current crisis are in the loss of dynamism of the mass-production paradigm in the early 1970s, which was reflected in a marked fall in profitability. This was offset by three factors:

- International liberalisation that opened up new markets and exposed old ones.
- The diffusion of flexible production systems linked to just-in-time retailing that refreshed Ford's industrial model.
- A long-term shift in the functional distribution of income from wages to profits, both nationally and internationally as the mass-production industries moved to areas of low-cost labour. In the OECD countries, the share of earnings in national income fell from three-quarters in the mid 1970s to two-thirds in 2005, with the decline being notably severe in the US.

These factors extended the life of the mass-production paradigm without resolving its limitations. In particular, the falling share of wages created a problem of final demand, exacerbated in those countries, such as the US and UK, where there were increasing inequalities of pay and bonuses among wage earners. The consequences of the resulting structural imbalance between demand and supply were deferred by consumer credit, which corporations and banks were only too ready to extend and which consumers were only too ready to receive.

Set against this picture of a faltering mass-production model was an emergent new paradigm centred on information and communication technology. Starting in the 1970s, and gathering pace in the 1980s, it offered the promise of a major upsurge of profitability, and was the basis of the financial frenzy of the 1990s, where hope ran ahead of itself, and ended when the bubble burst in 2000. On this occasion the IT crash did not develop into a generalised depression because finance, helped by low interest rates in the US, tracked back to create a new bubble in housing and consumer credit. Whereas the bursting of the IT bubble deferred the future, the eventual bursting of the consumer bubble in 2007-08 was a reckoning of the past.

On this reading, a systemic crash is the hinge between the period of financial frenzy and the period of deployment. It is a moment of uncertainty, when the key question is how to refashion institutions and reach new social settlements which will allow the new paradigm to become generalised. There is a sense that there is no going back to the old order, and that major change is required.

The emerging economic landscape

Distributed systems

To chart the contours of a future deployment period, Perez encourages us to look to the leading sectors and regions of the new technologies. Currently this means the information and communication sectors. It means Silicon Valley rather than Detroit; Cambridge, England rather than Dagenham; Finland rather than Poland. From that vantage point we can see the break-up of the old model of centralised command-and-control that developed in the period of mass production and in its place the emergence of distributed organisation, in which initiative and innovation are widely dispersed, and connected by networks. It is a model of small units and large systems.

Peer-to-peer, disintermediation, wikis, platforms, collaboratives, open source, indeed open everything – this is the new lexicon of distributed systems.

This is one territory for expansion in a post-crash period – extending the movement of distributed production to sectors that have become ever-more centralised, like energy, or finance, or the commanding heights of food.

A green industrial revolution

A second related area is the emerging green industrial revolution. Every long wave of industrial development brings its own innovations in materials and energy. Scientific advance has led to new composite and 'designed' materials. The chemical industry is re-orienting itself from oil-based to plant-based plastics. Wind, solar, wave and geothermal all promise to be major new sources of power.

But what is striking about the current period is that the pressure is for less not more. Climate change has added a new and over-riding imperative to the course of the current technological revolution. As far as materials and energy are concerned, the goal is to dematerialise and detoxify, to cut energy use, and to conserve what is used through recycling and re-use. It is to avoid production rather than expand it, throwing the resource-expansive impulses of the economy into reverse.

This calls for transformation in every part of the economy, from design and processing to distribution and consumption. It involves innovation not just in how we retrofit old buildings, but how we build new ones; not just in how we deal with our waste, but what materials and processes we use in the first place. In many of these areas the prototypes are now up and running. The necessary technological innovations are advancing at pace. The issue is how to accelerate one of the deep structural changes that will be central to a future period of growth.

A new social economy

There is a third frontier for change, closely related to the first two, that has received less attention, and which is the subject here. It is a transformation in the significance and organisation of the social economy. By social economy I mean all those areas of the economy which are not geared to private profitability. It includes the state but also a 'civil economy' of a philanthropic third sector, social enterprises and co-operatives operating in the market, and the many strands of the reciprocal household economy – households themselves, social networks, informal associations, as well as social movements.

This 'associative' civil economy was strong in the second half of the nineteenth century, but the expansion of the state in the twentieth century relegated it to a back-seat role. In the past thirty years, the trend has reversed and there has been a resurgence of the 'civil economy', for three main reasons.

1. The user as producer

First, digital technology, the core of the new technological paradigm, has provided the infrastructure – or more accurately the inter-structure – that has transformed the relations of consumers to markets and of citizens among themselves. In many sectors there is a gradual incorporation of users into the process of production. Householders are becoming producers of their own products using programmable machinery (printing, music and video have been pioneering sectors here). Consumers are being drawn into design. Production is no longer a linear process with the consumer as the end point. Rather it is reorganised around the consumer in the manner of the machine shop rather than the flow line. This is as profound a change as Ford's development of mass production.

In this reconfiguration of the economic process, the consumer morphs into the producer-consumer, or 'prosumer' in Toffler's phrase.[2] What becomes critical for the prosumer is an array of support to help him or her carry out the task rather than being a passive recipient of generalised services or commodities. The support economy takes over from the commodity economy as the organising principle.

The institutional implications are profound. Systems are being reconfigured around households, connected in a multiplicity of new forms – virtual and real – rather than being concentrated in centralised institutions. The spread of mutual interest and support groups has been a feature of the past thirty years – connected via the web, or meeting at events and weekend schools. Groups are forming to take over micro-breweries, pubs, farms and even – in the remarkable case of Ebbsfleet United in Kent – combining via the web to buy and run a professional football club.

This is a long way from the passive consumer and deskilled worker of the 20th century. It repositions households individually and collaboratively as 'living centres' in distributed systems. It raises a wide range of questions about the conditions that permit households to take part, questions of digital access and house design, of skills and working time, of credit and tax relief, and so on. It is incompatible with a wage regime of long hours and low pay, and an educational system that is not geared to imparting life skills.

2. Increasing social imperatives

Second, there have been increasing pressures on state services delivered on the basis of a producer-driven, mass-service model of provision.

One set of pressures comes from the sheer scale and growth of the demands on these services. In the UK, as in other industrial countries, there are dramatic upward trends in obesity, chronic disease and demographic ageing, each of which has been described as a time bomb waiting to go off. In terms of ageing, the ratio of those of working age to those over 65 is set to fall from four to one to two to one in OECD countries within forty years (in the UK, within twenty-five years), posing a radical challenge to two of the principal strands of the 20th century welfare settlement, pensions and care for the elderly. If the thirty-year trend of increasing inequality is not reversed, it will exacerbate these problems, given the close correlation that has now been established between inequality and ill health.

These trends pose a double challenge to existing structures. First, there is a growing mismatch between traditional services and new needs. Second, it has proved difficult to offset the growth in service need by equivalent reductions in cost. Schools, prisons, care homes and hospitals have cost structures with heavy overheads that are difficult to offset in labour- intensive services. As a result, these sectors command an ever-growing share of national resources. In the UK, care is already approaching 4 to 5 per cent of GDP, education is edging up to 10 per cent. On current trajectories, the biggest sectors (both by value and employment) of Western economies in 2020 and beyond will not be cars, ships, steel, computer manufacturing or personal finance but rather health, education and care.

The still-predominant policy approach has been to promote technical solutions that upgrade old models of production. In health, for example, industrial methods once associated with Henry Ford have been adapted to improve the flow of patients through hospitals. Costs have been cut through outsourcing, and repeated efficiency drives. Prices have been applied to what was once free, and quasi-markets established to inject a market discipline. But the pressures have continued to rise inexorably. With health, as with other social and environmental issues, the most effective policies are preventative, but these have been notoriously hard to establish through states and markets as they stand.

Both professions and politicians have become only too well aware of the evident disconnect between established social institutions and many of the concerns and needs of the users as producers. They recognise that active households are central to many of the major social issues. For those with chronic diseases, householders and their networks of support are self-evidently the primary producers of services. In diabetes, for example, 98 per cent of care is provided in the household. Much the same can be said of the care of young children and of the sick and elderly.

In these cases, citizens are active agents not passive consumers, who need resources and skills and a whole range of support and connections that existing services are not geared to provide. This and the pressure on costs are the factors behind experiments in co-designed public services, and the recognition of the role of third-sector organisations as innovators in the shaping of new services.

While governments have tried to engage citizens, citizens themselves have radically changed their views. The postmodern citizen – consumer, producer, traveller – is concerned with identity, meaning and self-improvement rather than the consumption of standardised products.

Post-Fordist production was in part a response to these changes. An industrial revolution in itself, it enabled firms to manage multiple complex supply chains that allowed them to respond to widely differentiated and unpredictable demand. By the end of the century, the postmodern consumer had got used to an economy of variety, of consumer-oriented production, of fast food and fast fashion.

This shift marks a change from an economy dominated by commodities to one centred on services, information and communication – what has come to be referred to as 'cognitive capitalism'. The move to personalise public services is also a reflection of these trends, as is the shift in cultural policy from the delivery of cultural objects to the enabling of expressive lives. But there is another, marked collaborative feature. The disjunction between the contemporary sensibility of the active citizen and the institutions formed in a previous age – corporations, public bureaucracies, mass parties and the church – has led to the multiplication of social movements and of citizens taking matters into their own hands.

The last thirty years has seen the emergence of a social and economic re-formation, one in which individuals, singly and together, are taking social and political responsibility into their own hands. It is a movement from passive to active. And out of this has come a wave of value-based economic initiatives, many in the social sectors, but others finding their own space in the market. This wave has developed its own forms of networked organisation, mixture of paid and unpaid labour, and its own culture. It is the source of an extraordinary range of social innovation centred on those very issues which the state and the private market have found themselves ill-equipped to adequately address.

The social economy is pivotal to these innovations and to the services and active relationships that develop from them. The social economy, including the redesigning of the systemic role of the state, is the critical player in the extension of the new paradigm to a section of the economy which has been remarkably insulated from it.

3. The social economy and the green industrial revolution

The environmental movement exemplifies the practices and new organisational forms of the new social movements and has been a prime example of the resurgent social economy. Those involved have set a twenty-first century agenda – on energy, food, waste, transport and the whole issue of well-being and lifestyle. In each of these areas, citizens' networks have developed their own political economies of protest, production and consumption. They have created a great wave of alternative technologies, new forms of consumption and distribution, which now constitutes its own international micro economy. In some places it has already become a leading part of the mainstream economy:

- The growth of wind energy in Denmark was the result of a movement of resistance to nuclear power and the emergence of a large network of decentralised wind turbines, two-thirds of them owned by co-ops and small farmers.
- Progressive transport coalitions have provided the inspiration and influence to build cycle ways and walkways, re-allocate road space, and the impetus for the introduction of municipal systems of bike and electric car hire.
- The new waste economy – of reduction, re-use and recycling – grew out of the community sector and has advanced most at the state level in federal states where protests against incineration and landfill gained sufficient political traction to transform policy and produce citizen-centred innovation.
- In mid-Italy, there is an integrated chain of food co-ops from farm to table which is not only a central part of the regional economies, but a leading exporter (Parmesan cheese, for example, is produced by a network of 980 small farmer co-ops in Emilia Romagna).

Many of these innovations are now being taken up and amplified within the market and public economies. The utilities and the major corporations of the old order, as well as traditional public administrations, have found it difficult to graft distributed micro systems on to their structures. But new firms enter the field from outside, often with an electronics or materials background. It is distributed systems, based on micro, semi-autonomous units or networks (some domestic, others local or regional) that are emerging as key to a low-carbon future. And that means the social economy will remain an active player – as operators of micro utilities, or domestic recyclers and gardeners, or as local authorities developing low-carbon systems for the energy and mobility of their towns.

The social economy is not in itself a solution but it is a necessary part of one because of the remorseless growth of the social and environmental issues which neither the state nor the market in their current forms are able to stem. These issues reach back into the way production is organised in the market, and the way production and consumption take place in the home.

The shift to a networked paradigm has the potential to transform the relationship between organisational centres and peripheries. Its distributed systems handle complexity not by standardisation and simplification imposed from the centre, but by distributing complexity to the margins – to households and service users, and in the workplace to local managers and workers. Those at the margins have what those at the centre can never have – a knowledge of detail – the specificity of time, of place, of particular events, and in the consumer's and citizen's case, of need and desire. But to realise this potential requires new terms of engagement with users, new relations at work, new terms of employment and compensation.

This holds for those operating in the private market. It has even greater significance for those managing the state. At the moment the social economy is split between a hierarchical and centralised state and a multitude of small organisations and informal associations (including households). Yet the new techno-economic paradigm coupled with the emerging social movements allow us to think about this divide in a new way – one that is able to combine the energy and complexity of distributed responsibility with the integrative capacities of modern system economies, thereby healing the split.

Substantial structural reform and institutional changes will be needed for a social economy of this kind to work effectively. It will require new infrastructures, tools, platforms and means for distributing resources, new forms of organisation, new ways of linking the formal and informal economies. This amounts to a far-reaching programme of social innovation on a scale not witnessed since the second half of the nineteenth century. The current crisis provides the opportunity for social innovation – for so long marginalised – to take its place on a par with private innovation at the centre of the economic stage.

Can the new social economy respond?

There is then the opportunity. But is the social economy in a position to respond? It has been a pioneer of new approaches to many social and environmental problems, but its potential role goes beyond this, and it will have to step up several gears and re-orient itself if it is to fully play its part. There will need to be new tax and pension provisions and other rights for different types of paid and voluntary work, new types of property, and new institutions, particularly in the field of finance and 'formation' – the French term for the creation of skills and culture.

The task of re-orienting the social economy has been hampered by the fact that there is too little analysis of how it works as an economy. It is made up of four quite different sub-economies: the market, the state, the grant economy and the household. Each has its own means of obtaining resources, structures of control and allocation, rules and customs for the distribution of its outputs, and principles of reciprocity.

What is common to these different spheres is that they are driven by social values as a primary imperative rather than private financial appropriation. They are bound together by ethics (a moral economy) with multiple threads of reciprocity (a gift economy), and their production ranges from the micro scale of domestic care in the household to the macro services of a nation state. It includes

social enterprises engaging in the market, as well as some of the
activities of private companies that have social rather than financial goals.

There is a distinction between these four sub-economies and the
institutions that operate within them. They have a primary base in
one of the four sub-economies, but also operate across its boundaries. In the market, private firms receive grants from the state,
for example, and social enterprises attract all sorts of voluntary
support. But for both private and social enterprises the primary
discipline is the market. Similarly, charities and other grant-based
organisations run their own shops and other market enterprises,
and many contract services to the state. Yet organisations like
Oxfam and Age Concern are still primarily shaped by the grant
economy in how they raise their money, distribute their services,
and in their forms of accountability.

Social innovation

The idea that the social economy as a source of innovation and
production could stand on an equal footing with the private
market economy goes against prevailing assumptions. The public
sector remains a major player in services which are difficult to
commodify, but even here it has been in retreat as quasi-market
mechanisms have been introduced into public services.

As for third-sector organisations, they are seen as the economic
herbivores, providing services for casualties of the market and the
state, the disadvantaged, the sick and the dispossessed. This is a
different economic realm from the carnivore world of the mainstream market.

There have been many who have wished the social economy to
play a more central role. But while there are innumerable examples of small-scale projects that embody these values, only a few
have made it into the mainstream.

There is the co-operative movement, for example, which
remains strong in some European regions. But for the most part,
the twentieth-century consensus holds sway – that production
should be left to the market, while the state (or its social partners)

focuses on redistribution and those social needs which the market has failed to address. In this reading, innovation and economic growth will come from the market, and the social economy will ensure society's cohesion.

Looked at dynamically, the market is held to have the mechanisms and incentives that drive innovation. In Joseph Schumpeter's formulation, it has the power of 'creative destruction',[3] destroying the old in order to open the way for the new.

Neither the state nor the grant economy have the structure or incentive to innovate in this way. Their economic calculus is based on costs, and it is argued they lack the mechanisms that allow the best to flourish and the less effective to wither away. The household on the other hand – that most distributed of economic systems – generates ideas but on its own lacks the capital, surplus time and organisational capacity to develop and embed them.

The argument of the previous section suggests two main reasons why this Schumpeterian view may no longer hold. First the new social and information technologies provide scope for social collaboration. Small units in the social economy can be wired together to become big systems, capable of competing with the market economy both as innovators and providers. Second, what have been regarded as subordinate areas have now become central – health, education, care and a whole range of environmental services, in all of which the social economy has been the primary innovator.

Yet whether the social economy can respond to the possibilities that are now emerging remains an open question.

Public innovation

There are many structural features of government that inhibit risk-taking and innovation. There are major barriers (from cost-based budgeting and departmental structures, to audit and accountability processes, as well as a lack of career rewards) and few enabling conditions, such as the dedicated budgets, teams and processes found in business or science. Yet if we look at the UK state, and given its structures and reputation, it is remarkable how much innovation there has been. State pensions, the BBC, the National Health Service, the Open University – these are only a fraction of the twentieth-century public innovations that shape culture and society in the UK today.

In the past twenty-five years, the pace of UK public innovation has quickened. It could be said that there has been too much innovation, too many turns, twists and reversals rather than too little. And this leaves a paradox – a public sector structured against innovation, which in recent decades has engaged in hyper-innovation. How do we explain this? And what kind of innovation has been taking place?

The answer is threefold. First, public innovation is institutionalised in the political process. It is the politicians who are expected to come up with new ideas, embody them in election manifestos, and then oversee their realisation through the civil service. The process of formulating the proposed innovations usually draws on multiple sources of ideas – think tanks, policy advisers, particular interests, experiences in local government, the media – and is then fed into the civil service to consider how best they can be implemented. It is a linear top-down model, with final accountability through the ballot box.

Innovations of this kind have advantages, as with all changes introduced by large organisations. There may be economies of scale. The changes can become system-wide rapidly and have both the political and administrative backing to overcome resistances – if the leadership is strong.

But they have the disadvantages of all large organisations. How can they handle high levels of complexity without recourse to simplification and standardisation? The new post-industrial paradigm that has developed on the back of the information revolution and environmental pressures offers new ways of embracing this complexity through distributed systems, but these are in tension with the centralised institutions of the mass-production age.

Second, many of the radical innovations of the past twenty-five years have not been to the material way in which public services are delivered, but rather to re-drawing the boundaries of the state – delegating responsibility for operations and innovation to private capital or the third sector, establishing agencies with greater autonomy, or encouraging collaborative working between different sections and levels of government. The underlying institutional principles of the public economy have remained largely intact.

Third, where innovation has taken place, it has too often been working against the grain of these deeper structures. There are innovators. But they innovate often in spite of rather than with the support of the machinery of government.

Innovative local councils complain about being criticised by the Audit Commission for innovating beyond the terms specified by central government. They plead for 'safe places' where they can try out new ways of providing a service. When initiatives from the heart of government to promote innovation are put into practice, the innovations are too often restricted in their scope. Where centrally driven service innovations are introduced, such as the Sure Start programme, their operations are folded back into the iron cage of public finance and accountability.

It is not, therefore, the lack of innovation in government that is the issue, but the centralised and episodic nature of its innovation process, together with the structural limitations on distributed innovation at the service level. The state has the potential to be a generative force of distributed social innovation, but if it is to be fully realised, then there are profound structural issues that need to be addressed around how the state raises and allocates its funds, and how it is accountable for them.

The grant economy

The grant economy in the UK is tiny compared to that of the state. In 2006-7 the expenditure of general charities was £31 billion compared to public expenditure of £550 billion. Yet it has been a significant source of social innovation. In almost every social field, third-sector organisations have not only provided new kinds of services but have been strong advocates of change within the public sector. Age Concern and Help the Aged are examples in the field of elder care. The hospice movement has transformed end-of-life care. In some cases, mental health for example, successful services are adopted by the state. Greenpeace and Friends of the Earth have had a massive impact on public policy.

Looked at as an economy, there is ease of access – a new organisation only needs to convince one of the multiplicity of grant funders to back it. The problem is growth and the reliability of funding sources. In spite of widespread individual contributions to charity, such finance accounts for less than 40 per cent of UK charity income. The bulk of funding is institutional.

Institutional funding has its own risks and limitations. As donors, institutions tend to avoid long-term commitments, and prefer funding start-ups. Grants are cost-based, and do not allow for the generation of internal surpluses that can finance growth. Many grant programmes have a preference for projects and programmes and are reluctant to provide core funding. Grant-aided organisations are often the first to suffer in state budget cuts and economic recessions. Grant programmes throughout the developed world complain of a lack of sustainable grant funding.

One trend for grant-based organisations has been to rely increasingly on earned income, principally via service contracting with the government (over 50 per cent of voluntary sector funding in the UK now comes from earned income). Another has been for a growth in venture philanthropy, which is the application of venture capital approaches to the voluntary sector. Private donors have sought to avoid some of the limitations of traditional grant funding by treating grants more like equity with project involvement, technical support, continuous funding and the coverage of core costs.

The grant economy is therefore a seed bed of innovation. Studies of its impact on social services suggest that the fact that voluntary organisations are mission-driven means that in addition to delivering contracted services, they seek to expand the coverage (frontiers) of the service, develop new service systems, and become advocates for those with under- recognised needs.

But their economic base remains fragile. Grant-based organisations survive on the strength of their proposition and some evidence of their capability. Yet donors' experience of the impact of their donation is indirect and quantitative assessment is usually difficult. Instead of the immediacy of the commodity (as in the market economy), this sector strives for the immediacy of the need.

Instead of the tangibility of the balance sheet it seeks the tangibility of the outcome.

From this perspective the web offers new horizons, in reducing costs and widening connections. Internet donor sites like First Giving dramatically reduce the cost of fundraising (estimated at between 15 per cent and 33 per cent of funds raised in the US). Blogs, video connections and forums will encourage continuing connections between funders and the funded, a form of grant-based Facebook. This is promising new territory for the gift economy, because these experiments in 'crowd funding' potentially enrich the gift relationship and democratise the sector's source of finance.

There is a close relation between the grant economy and social enterprises operating in the market. Just as many grant-based organisations increasingly supplement their income through commercial sales and tendering for public sector contracts, so social enterprises have supplemented their sales income with grants. Many also share the grant-based sector's central preoccupation of how to validate the effects of their work to consumers – how to make these effects tangible.

Unlike charities, social enterprises are structured to earn surpluses and accumulate. They are 'for-profit' but their growth is focused on their social goals. In the case of companies limited by guarantee, there are no shareholders, so all profits become reserves for re-investment. With community interest companies (CICs) there are shareholders but a cap on dividends, and a requirement that the enterprise be oriented towards its social 'beneficiaries'. A significant number of social enterprises are ordinary limited companies, with shareholdings held by other social enterprises, ethical funds and the enterprise's beneficiaries (Divine Chocolate and Liberation Foods for example). Whatever their particular form, all have the structure and incentives that traditional theory suggests makes the private market a driver of innovation.

In respect to innovation, there is one primary difference between private and social enterprise. Social enterprises are concerned with innovation that will support their social and environmental goals. This may be the development of disruptive environmental technologies or alternative food systems for example. Or it may be an innovation in ownership and the management of the enterprises (as with co-ops), or changing the distribution of the company's gains (through profit-sharing). It may transform the relations and terms of business of a supply chain (as with fair trade) or employ those facing discrimination in the market.

The challenge for social enterprises is how to maintain their commercial position in the market, given their social goals and non-proprietary approach to innovation. The bulk of social enterprises remain tiny. Where their innovations are successful, larger commercial organisations will tend to enter their markets and swamp them (as has been the case with organics, fair trade and recycling). Yet there are many examples where social enterprises have established themselves successfully in the mainstream.

The Grameen group is particularly relevant to the argument. The rural villages of Bangladesh, where its work is centred, could hardly be further from Silicon Valley, yet Grameen has many of the characteristics of the new paradigm. Its bank, which has 7.34 million borrowers, is a highly distributed credit network in 39,000 villages, by far the most extensive in the country. It has developed a method for personalising loans and easing their repayment, and a support structure based on networks of women. As a social enterprise, it is majority owned and governed by its borrowers, 98 per cent of them women. Significantly, it calls its lending 'micro' credit and it has grown both by the spread of its model internationally, and through its own diversification in Bangladesh into mobile communications, internet services, education, fish farming, weaving, housing and, most recently, yoghurt manufacture.

Grameen operates in the market with the same freedoms and disciplines as a private company, but with a social goal – improvement of the incomes and well-being of the poorest – coupled with social ownership and a social distribution and re-investment of profits. Muhammad Yunus, its founder, argues that his project is to socialise the market rather than replace it.[4]

There are now an estimated 55,000 social enterprises in the UK, accounting for 1 per cent of GDP. Some are well established, notably the large retail co-ops, mutuals and housing associations – who now have a combined turnover of £42 billion. But by and large this is a small-firm phenomenon, where the structures of mutual support and inter-firm co-operation are rudimentary.

What is important is that there is now an increasing body of experience and successful business models. There are new organisational forms (like community interest companies and limited liability partnerships),[5] supportive public policy and new funding streams. As social innovators their influence extends well beyond their own size. Social and environmental marks and brands (such as those of the Fairtrade Foundation, Soil Association or the Forestry Stewardship Council) are prompting mainstream firms to change their practices, and have encouraged the growth of co-ops and farmers' mutuals in their respective supply chains. These ethical market developments have challenged mainstream businesses on their social and environmental impacts, and many have responded through triple bottom line policies, environmental initiatives and the adoption of codes of corporate social responsibility.

But for social enterprises the issue remains of how to move to the next level and find a distinct way for managing and developing their growth which is in tune with their values.

The household

Mass production has automated and commoditised some traditional domestic tasks, and those responsible for them – primarily women – have moved from the informal to the formal economies. But much domestic production remains and is being expanded. Learning, shopping, convalescence, music-making, working and the management of chronic disease, are all examples of the trend to redistribute activities that were previously concentrated in the external economy back into the home. The ways in which these are carried out are potentially central to a new wave of social innovation.

Households are already responding dramatically, using the internet to connect to institutions of the old in new ways – shopping online, for example. But the more profound innovation is the way in which householders are collaborating directly, reconfiguring institutions and inventing new ones.

The iconic example is open-source software, developed voluntarily and distributed freely. There are few parts of the industrialised world that do not rely on some form of free software. Such forms of collaboration are already extending much more widely – to mutual learning, group formation and discussion around health, the growing of food and its preparation and consumption, around childbirth and bereavement, as well as contributing to the solution of particular problems (as in science) or to the management of public spaces (like parks and streets).

The questions raised for the household economy by this extraordinary historical development are twofold:

- What institutional forms are developing to enable these new kinds of collaboration to function effectively and economically?
- What are the conditions that allow households to fully engage in this economy?

On the first, those organisations providing the platforms, the protocols and tools that enable the new systems to work are having to develop innovative business models to cover the costs involved. Some are charged for, but many are free, raising their funding from fees for premium services, or from advertising, or are financed by local government or employers who provide the service as a perk to their employees. For householders, there is a shift in their relationship to all parts of the social and private economies from one based primarily on the receipt of content to one which provides the means and spaces for collaboration.

This kind of collaboration raises all sorts of issues about how such an economy can work – questions of trust and reliability, confidentiality and acknowledgement, and in some cases of language. We can already see institutional contours emerging – protocols and codes of conduct, and formulations about the terms on which the uncommodified information can be used.

This is not a purely virtual economy. It is linked to meetings and conferences; some of it leads back into the market and some to the state; it leads to greater volunteering – of time and money.

What does it take for households to participate fully in this new world? There are a number of dimensions – time, resources, skills, physical space, access to information networks, and to support and facilities. For those with time, and with resources and skills, and who are connected to the high-speed internet, this is less of an issue.

But to spread the benefits of the social economy, we will need to rethink many of the ways in which the household economy relates to the two main sources of finance – the market and the state. Issues such as the distribution of working time, the valorisation of voluntary labour, the content and channels of life-skills learning, the role of many of the social and educational services, the arrangements for retirement and unemployment, the size and location of public service centres such as schools and hospitals, and the organisation of public safety – all these will need radical changes.

Circuits and interfaces

Although these sub-economies have different economic structures and sets of relationships, they are at the same time intimately related. Money and ideas flow between them. Civil organisations have their feet in many camps.

Yet at times it seems as though there are deep moats between them. With four sub-economies there are six interfaces and there is distance and mutual suspicion along each. State versus market. The third sector as unaccountable and a threat to the solidarities of the state. Markets structurally separated from charity. Volunteering as undercutting labour in the formal economy. Personal tax seen as an alien imposition by households. But if there are moats there are also bridges and it is important for this next phase that innovation has a free flow across the divides, and that the divides themselves are softened.

Relations between governments and third-sector organisations, for example, seem at times like oil and water. They have different cultures, horizons, accountabilities and sensitivities to risk. The transaction costs and skills demanded by public-contracting procedures favour the large over the small supplier, as do the requirements for track records of experience and the size of contracts. Governments are grappling with how better to procure and contract from the third sector, and third-sector organisations in their turn are engaging consultants to support them to meet the requirements of that interface. But there are structural forces which make it difficult for the two to mesh.

Governments are also grappling with their relationship to households – should they allow or encourage volunteering for people on benefits; should they tax exchange through time banks? In the reverse direction, there is the question of how the flow of household funds to the state can gain greater public legitimation, through earmarking and making their use tangible.

The terms on which finance criss-crosses the boundaries between the state, the third sector and households, these too need to be redesigned to reduce the tensions between them.

The answer to the question of whether the social economy is able to be the innovative force required by the next wave of economic development is twofold. First, there is the need for structural changes in the conditions for innovation in each of the component economies, and second, for a new institutional architecture that allows the distributed points of innovation to be wired together to develop and sustain their innovations in practice.

The primary challenge for the first of these is the reconstitution of the state. The state has to find ways of opening up its iron cage, finding new structures which have their own force field for innovation and which are able to work fruitfully with other parts of the social economy.

The challenge for the second is to learn from the successful productive networks – both virtual collaborative networks that have developed the human genome and open source software and the established co-operative or Grameen-type networks – to provide the connections between the multiplicity of micro initiatives.

There is a third task for all those working in this economy. It is to understand the process of innovation more fully, from its generation to its generalisation. Parts of this process are similar to the process of private-market innovation, but much is distinct.

In many ways we are still at the foothills of applying the ideas and innovations of the new paradigm to services in the social economy. But new connections are being made. The issue now is how to ensure that the resolution of the current economic crisis is undertaken in a way which hastens these changes rather than undercuts them.

Social innovation and the crisis of policy

After the collapse of Lehman Brothers in September 2008, the predominant policy approach has been a blend of monetary and fiscal policy – in the spirit of Keynes to restore the level of demand – as well as the recapitalisation of the banks and measures to restore the flow of credit. This was the policy initially pursued by the UK, France and Spain, but has since been taken up to a greater or lesser degree by other countries (including China). Since then, however, individual governments have been under heavy pressure from the money markets to limit their public debt. The political debate has come to revolve round the timing and amount of cuts in public expenditure rather than its counter-cyclical expansion.

There are three main problems with this traditional macroeconomic approach. First there is the problem of restoring the level of demand. The discussion has been oriented towards the restoration of consumer demand, when the first priority is investment in the infrastructure for the diffusion of the new paradigm. Another problem is that of the insufficiency of mass consumer demand as the result of increases in the inequality of income. Few governments of deficit countries have sought to address this internally. Rather, the pressure has been on the surplus-exporting countries, particularly Germany, Japan and China, to raise their level of internal demand, if necessary, through structural changes.

Encouraging luxury consumption runs into the headwind of the environmental imperative that requires a greater modesty in what we consume and a change in how we consume it. Economic policy has to ask what kind of consumption it should promote rather than treating it as the undifferentiated aggregate that was suited to the era of mass production. It needs to provide incentives for the 'new demand' that will drive the transition to a low-carbon economy as much as the push of incentivised supply.

One element of this 'new demand' is part of contemporary household consumption that is properly considered as investment

– expenditure on the tools of a 'prosumer' and the infrastructure of a distributed economy. Some are the traditional tools of the household – from spades, drills and food blenders, to bicycles and cars. Others form part of complex infrastructural systems. Smart domestic energy and water systems, for example, require investment both in the structure of a home and its pipes, and in the control systems that regulate them.

This is the hardware of domestic investment. There is also the software – the investment in individual and collaborative skills. Some of these skills are technical, such as those needed to make full use of digital technology, but many are soft social and organisational skills – for the care of the elderly for example, or for the organisation of social activities, like sports or after-school clubs, or mutual support groups. Consumer spending on education, going to college and evening classes or health clubs and keeping fit should all be seen as forms of investment. We need a new category of presumption to be distinguished from consumption, reflecting the fact that in a distributed model of the economy a significant part of investment is itself distributed (to both the home and the workplace).

A recovery policy needs to prioritise the new paradigm's infrastructural investment, dampen the consumer culture of excess in favour of presumptive investment and 'resource lite' consumption, and reverse the trends of income inequality to ensure that these new trends in consumption are inclusive.

Government spending

Government spending too, needs to be directed towards 'transitional investment'– including putting in place the new digital, transport and energy infrastructures, the promotion of green commercial and domestic investment, the speeding up of the design and introduction of 'open' public services, and the consolidation and upgrading of government back-office services.

The main danger currently is that premature public budget cuts will fall first on these necessary innovations, even though it is these which will secure the long-term health of the economy. This is why it is important for governments to set out an integrated 'transition' programme as the determining framework of their recovery programmes.

A set of tests should be applied to every recovery programme and every response to the recession. Is it oriented to the future? Is it promoting innovation in the new services, products, businesses and public services that will be needed as the recovery takes shape? Or, in the case of infrastructure, will it freeze old technologies and service models as the result of inflexible, large-scale capital investment?

While some of the necessary infrastructure and transformations will take longer to implement, others could be achieved far more quickly, such as the conversion of empty shops to fast colleges, or fast commissioning. In a distributed economy there is distributed investment, some of it in households, and this can be turned on rapidly.

For example, the move to electric and plug-in hybrid vehicles requires an infrastructure of plug-in points and charging and battery change stations. London is at the foothills of the project, with 250 charging points being installed. This programme could be rapidly speeded up, bringing with it the jobs in the laying of the grid, releasing demand for a new generation of electric and hybrid vehicles.

Similar arguments apply to the smart electricity grid capable of handling multiple sources of supply, to local combined heat and power systems, to an infrastructure for digesting and composting food waste, and for high-speed broadband, and wind power. Much can be accomplished therefore in a government-led three-to-five year recovery window.

A policy aesthetic

These are 10 principles of a new policy aesthetic that apply to any of the major spheres of the new social economy:

1. *The parish principle* of distributed geography. In some cases the distribution is to households, in others it is to localities. Existing structures such as parish councils (10,000 in the UK) or new ones, like transition towns, could serve as centres of initiative to invest in low-carbon or health-gener-

ating projects, and to the social mapping of needs, land use and potential.

2. *The Grameen principle.* The Grameen bank adopted the policy of lending tiny amounts of money to the poorest (initially rural women and later 100,000 urban beggars), increasing the size of the loans based on the borrowers' reliability. The record of reliability together with the support of their lending circle became the borrowers' effective collateral. A similar approach could be adopted in public policy, with small grants and loans advanced to parishes and their equivalent, with peer assessment and group support, and amounts rising on the basis of performance.

3. *The Park Wood principle.* Public policy has found it difficult to connect with small-scale self-organising groups that sit between the individual household and the formal collective. These self-organising groups are key cells for the social economy. There is scope for encouragement of such groups. For example, incentives for home retrofitting could be substantially increased for groups who agree a common programme of measures (and cut costs as a result). On the Park Wood council estate in Maidstone, the Design Council developed a prototype with residents and local frontline service providers for self-organising groups to increase exercise.

4. *The church spire principle.* The success of Comic Relief illustrates the significance of ambitious collective projects, which can be sub-divided into innumerable pockets of activity that are united by purpose. Thus schools, and shops and offices each had their own ways of 'being funny for money' and together with individual donors and a supportive media raised £80 million for Comic Relief in March 2009. Like raising money for repairing the church spire, organising such common endeavours is a creative art in itself. Such campaigns can be sub-divided by municipality, locality, workplace or school using common metrics and a central resource of advice and information.

5. *The support principle.* The role of the tutor, coach and personal adviser is central to the new economy, as is the support of volunteers. In the UK, health coaching has been growing rapidly in the market economy (and in private health insurance schemes like BUPA) and more slowly in the NHS itself. This will be a key new profession in the future health economy (as in environmental services, and those sectors with a support tradition, such as lifelong education and home care).

6. *The zero-waste principle.* Reducing the use of energy and non-renewable resources implies among other things the reduction of waste – in the production process, consumption, and the decommissioning and disposal of products, as well as in the use of land. Recycling and reuse are only one segment of an emerging industrial model involving the extension of product life, lowering repair costs through the modularisation of design, the re-skinning of old products, disassembly and the re-use of parts, re-refining of oils, re-sterilisation (of plastic tubing in hospitals) re-treading of tyres (with higher quality treads), the move to leasing. These principles can be applied to many areas of the social economy.

7. *The intensity principle.* The intensive use of urban land is one of the principles behind the concept of the compact city and is informing much contemporary urban policy. It involves the redevelopment of brownfield sites, the refurbishment of existing buildings, the use of wasted space – both public and private – and finding multiple uses for existing spaces. There is already an Empty Homes Agency in the UK – an independent charity seeking to reduce the 780,000 currently empty homes – and a rapidly developing movement of 'guerrilla gardeners' replanting wasteland, expanding allotments, and borrowing garden space for food production.

8. *The social property principle.* Legal theorists have argued for a more differentiated concept of property extending from private to public. They argue that those owning property have some social obligations, that they are to an extent

stewards and the terms of ownership should reflect this. Unused or derelict land could be transferred to public or social use. Unused space could be leased to groups offering to use it for the common good. In areas of regeneration, community land trusts in which local communities invest time or money would ensure that the appreciation of property value returns in part to those communities.

9. *The Wörgl principle.* Wörgl was an Austrian town which, at the height of the Great Depression in the 1930s, established employment projects paid for by a town currency which the municipal council agreed to accept in payment of its fees and taxes. The result was a remarkable expansion of the town's economic activity. To promote the informal and formal economies, there is scope to issue quasi-monies (such as Green tokens) to be paid to volunteers on environmental projects and which a town council as the issuing authority would agree to accept for a percentage of debts due to it. This would greatly extend schemes like Time Banks and LETS already in existence within the informal economy.

10. *The OurSpace principle.* One of the over-riding features of the new system is that an aggregation of micros makes a macro not just in consumption, as in the age of mass production, but in production also. The question is how they are connected. It is platforms that are now the new social infrastructure – the village squares of the virtual economy. The social networking sites are the early prototypes of such platforms, but they are now multiplying in almost every field, driven both commercially (as with MySpace and Facebook) and socially (as with the Open University). This is a post-industrial revolution in itself and has transformed the landscape of the social economy.

Prospects of advance

The environmental imperative is set to drive a major reorientation of the economy. There is now a dominant consensus about the

problem, developed over forty years by the environmental movement. It is reflected in the direction of public policy, in widespread
citizen action like the Transition Towns, and is being taken on
board by an increasing number of corporations.

The legacy of the previous industrial order has meant that the
UK has been a regressive force in the development of EU environmental policy, and has focused on low-cost measures to comply
with Directives rather than large carrots and sticks to shock industries into change (as happens in the market economy).

While the primary driver of innovation in environmental policy
comes from the pressure of climate change, in social services the
principal driver is likely to be a crisis in public finance in the face
of expanding and changing social needs. We have already seen
an unprecedented period of innovation in health services, education and care. But, it has been more concerned with shifting the
boundaries of ownership and with channels of delivery rather than
with the transformation of the services themselves. Over the next
decade, however, the possibilities opened up by the new methods
of distributed organisation will potentially lead to major changes
in these sectors, with the new social economy – including a transformed state sector – playing a central role.

Conclusions

The successful diffusion of the emergent techno-economic paradigm does not, of course, depend on the social economy alone.
There are many areas of the private market economy where the
new systems have still to take hold. My argument, however, is that
during the next phase of the long wave, the state and the rest of the
new social economy will need to play a leading role if solutions are
to be found to the intractable problems exposed by their impervi-
ousness to commodity solutions. To play this role, all parts of the
social economy must transform themselves institutionally, and in
their human and technological capacities.

The lesson of Schumpeter and Perez is that massive institutional innovation accompanies the shifts of direction that follow
economic crises. Currently the UK lacks the institutions able to

adequately support the different stages of social innovation, let alone to orchestrate systemic innovation. Some of these institutional reconfigurations are needed within public sectors. Some need to be part of the public sector, but sufficiently arm's length to take risks. And some of the tasks of support need to be taken by wholly independent bodies, such as trusts and foundations.

Beyond these there are major institutional gaps. There are a handful of intermediaries to link promising ideas to uses in the social field, but nothing comparable to what exists in the mainstream market economy. The institutions seeking to accelerate global learning survive with very modest resources. There is, above all, a need for institutions that wire together the myriad of small social enterprises so that they can benefit from being part of large systems.

The forms of support also have to adapt. Governments and foundations are used to funding specific projects, programmes or organisations. But some of the most exciting innovations are platforms: neighbourhood web media; finance models like In Control; or moderated health platforms like healthtalkonline.org.

There is finally the need for intensive work to improve the capacity and skills of social innovation. A starting point is a greater awareness of the hundreds of methods already being used to generate social innovation.

There is an urgency to the task. The public sector and all those depending on it need to prepare for a sharp squeeze in public spending. There is a serious risk that such a squeeze will side-line creativity and innovation. Public bureaucracies will be tempted to impose salami-slice cuts. Yet, more than ever, public agencies will need radical innovations that can deliver improved outcomes with 10-20 per cent fewer resources.

The challenges described here are not unique to the UK. But the social economy in the UK has made a distinctive and powerful response. It is imperative that the momentum is stepped up – not merely to counter the recession, but, at this particular moment of transition and in the spirit of Carlota Perez, to engage radically in the shaping of the social and economic history of the next two or three decades.

Notes

1 Carlota Perez, *Technological Revolutions and Financial Capital*, Edward Elgar: Cheltenham, 2002; see also her article on the economic downturn of 2008-09, 'After the crisis – creative construction', Open Democracy, 5 March 2009, https://www.opendemocracy.net/en/how-to-make-economic-crisis-creative

2 Alvin Toffler, *The Third Wave*, London: Collins, 1980.

3 Joseph Schumpeter, *Capitalism, Socialism and Democracy*, London: Unwin, 1943, p83. He wrote this in the middle of the second world war, after a decade of economic depression, when economies were being planned on a war footing, and the Soviet model appeared an advantageous economic alternative.

4 Muhammad Yunus's economic memoir, *Banker to the Poor*, London: Aurum Press, 2003, has been an inspiration to the new social economy movement.

5 Limited liability partnerships were originally introduced for professional service firms like accountants, but they have been used experimentally for environmental and social ventures because of their flexibility and scope for stakeholder involvement.

9

Global civil society and the rise of the civil economy

First published as Robin Murray, 'Global civil society and the rise of the civil economy', in M. Kaldor, H.L. Moore, S. Selchow (eds), Global Civil Society 2012: Ten Years of Critical Reflection, *Global Civil Society Yearbook series, Basingstoke: Palgrave Macmillan, 2012, pp144-64. This edited extract reproduced with permission from Springer.*

A new millennium

Ten years is a long time in economics. The decade opened with the Nasdaq crash and finished with a world financial crisis, which hit first the banks, then national governments, and is now calling at the doors of the international financial institutions. The world's mass production continued its move to the East, with the result that by the end of the decade China alone had doubled its share of world GDP (gross domestic product – from 7 per cent to 13 per cent in relative purchasing power) and had become the world's largest manufacturer, its largest exporter and, by 2011, its second largest economy. That growth has darkened further another shadow: climate change. The past decade has witnessed the highest average temperatures on record, with the Arctic ice cap melting to an all-time low.

At the same time over these ten years, the web economy has taken off. Google was only two years old at the start of the millennium. At that point it had developed an infrastructure of 6,000 web servers and indexed 1.3 billion webpages. It now runs one million servers in data centres globally, has an index of 46 billion web pages and processes one billion searches a day. And this is just one marker of the growth of a new economy of the ether, one that operates in cyberspace and makes its connections by airwaves and spectrums rather than roads and railways.

This is a discordant symphony, with its powerful global contra-flows of creation, crisis and destruction. Yet it had its counterpart in the continuing and ever-expanding response to globalisation from civil society – part-political, part-cultural, part-economic. From time to time this response has made the headlines, but for the most part it has spread through a multitude of initiatives that, taken together, may shape the nature and direction of the world's economic future.

Global civil society

Ten years ago, in the launch volume of the *Global Civil Society* year-book, the editors defined civil society as:

> the sphere of ideas, values, institutions, organisations, networks and individuals located between the family, the state and the market and operating beyond the confines of national societies, polities and economies.[1]

It was autonomous and interstitial and challenged both the state and the multinational corporate economy.

In its twentieth-century conceptual origins and in the studies that the yearbooks have contained, the notion of civil society is first and foremost a political one. Developed within the context of dictatorial states, and in what was increasingly experienced as an absolutist global market economy, civil society created both spaces of survival and platforms for contesting the existing order. How this contest has developed since the first yearbook is one strand of the story of the past decade.

The economy is a central theme of that story. The chapters in the yearbooks have discussed the various positions taken by civil society movements in relation to the great contemporary economic issues: international money and trade, aid and the environment, and the many global dimensions of labour – wages, trade unions, the insistent surge of international migration. On these issues, and in specific sectors like water and food, or the media and sport, the movements have mounted a political challenge to the policies and practices of states and the corporate global market. They have contested how others run the economy.

This chapter is about another side to the story, a second strand closely linked to but distinct from the first. It is about the innumerable cases all over the world where people have taken matters into their own hands and set up for themselves. It is a kind of productive democracy, and as such is part of a long-term shift. For much of the twentieth century, the main alternative economic projects were state-driven national ones; however, since 1989 and the fall of the Berlin Wall, there has been a surge in these micro-economic initiatives. It is as if the energy that had been focused on creating alternative national economies has been redirected towards creating new versions of the economy from below.

In some cases these initiatives have been a matter of economic survival. In others, their creators aim to show that another way is possible; a kind of propaganda of practice. There are a growing number of areas where neither the private market nor the state are providing adequate services, and where social initiatives are proliferating as a result. All of these different types have intensified in the past decade and been further extended by developments in the internet. Taken together, they amount to another form of economy: one that is driven by social and environmental rather than financial imperatives and is fuelled by a mixture of necessity and enthusiasm. I refer to this as the civil economy.

The civil economy

One of the issues in civil society theory is whether or not the concept includes the civil economy. For the civic humanists of the Italian Quattrocento, as for Adam Smith and his Neapolitan contemporary Antonio Genovese, the civil economy was a central element in civil society. It was considered a market economy with autonomy from the state but embedded within social norms and marked by the principles of trust and reciprocity. For these authors

the market was both subordinate to society and helped to reproduce it. As a means of connecting small scale producers it had not
yet been coupled to the imperative of capital accumulation, nor the
tendency to erode social ties rather than strengthen them.

Once industrial capitalism took off and the market economy
was seen more in Hobbesian than in civic terms, a civil society that
encompassed the market economy came to be thought of either as
grounds for a state that represented the general interest (Hegel), or,
later, when the state was clearly imbricated with private capital, as
a cultural and political space separate from the economy (Gramsci).
It is this latter view which has remained predominant in contemporary analyses of civil society.[2]

The experience of the past twenty years suggests that we need
to revise these approaches. First, the civil economy as it has developed is both a cultural and a political space. It is not just an idea
or a demand, but an alternative realised in practice. As such it
carries political and cultural weight whether or not it is part of a
wider social movement. Second, while it may engage both with
the market and the state, it is an autonomous productive force, a
'sphere of ideas, values, institutions, organisations, networks and
individuals' applied directly to economic production and circulation. It is a significant element in the concept of civil society where
the civil economy exists as a subset of a hybrid social economy.
The key distinction is not between the market, the state, and some
notional third sector, but between those parts of the economy that
are driven by social goals (the social economy) and those which are
subject to the imperatives of capital accumulation. I see this as the
major distinction in contemporary political economy.

The social economy encompasses four sub-economies each of
which is distinct in terms of how they are financed, who has access
to their outputs and on what terms, what social relations they entail,
how any surplus is distributed, and what forms of economic discipline are exercised over them. We can describe them as governed
by reciprocity (the household), the gift (the grant economy), the
exchange of equivalents (the market), and the combination of
levies and bounties (the state). They are not separate economies,
but rather represent distinct, semi-autonomous but inter-related
economic force fields.

In some cases the state may be functionally integrated into the requirements of capital accumulation, just as the grant economy may act as a subaltern to private corporations or to an incorporated state. But there is nothing intrinsic within the nature of the state, the grant, or the household economies that drives them towards capital accumulation. As economies they are oriented to their own social goals; each can operate in the market in pursuit of their goals without being drawn into the vortex of accumulation.

The grant economy is included in the social economy since nominally it is defined as serving social goals. So is a minor segment of the market representing social enterprises, co-operatives and petty producers, such as those small farmers and artisans who operate according to the model of the civic humanists. Some parts of the state are excluded (such as the military), while from the household economy I include all those activities that involve inter-household collaboration, whether of mutual support, common projects, or the voluntary economic activities of social movements.

The civil economy is a subset of this wider social economy. In some countries and in certain periods, the distinction is minor: there is a close relationship between the state and the other parts of the social economy; they share goals and pool resources. But in other cases – and notably in the global arena – the distinction is significant, particularly where the state or states have been subordinated to the requirements of accumulation. We then have the kind of turbulence that results when two currents run against each other.

Importantly the civil economy is far from homogeneous. It includes enterprises established by professional associations and by intentional communities; inspired by environmentalism or social exclusion. There are charities and foundations, civic associations and numerous other forms of formal and informal cooperation. Many institutions, whether religious organisations, guerrilla movements, prisons, or schools, have their own internal economies. The goals of these diverse organisations may be different, but what is shared is that they are driven by top-line social or institutional goals rather than bottom-line financial ones.

The re-emergence of the civil economy

The mass production paradigm that dominated twentieth century economies had little space for the civil economy. The role of the household was to provide labour on the one hand, and a demand for commodities on the other. The home, whose associated daily tasks were themselves revolutionised by the new mass-produced goods, was redefined as a site of passive consumption rather than active production. Wider social provision – from social insurance to health, education and housing – which in the nineteenth century was provided by the civil economy or the private market, was now supplied on a mass basis by the state.

But side by side with the process of globalisation, there is evidence of a surge in new civil economic activity. The expansion of NGOs picks up pace from the mid 1970s and by 2005 the Johns Hopkins Project estimated that the non-profit sector of its forty sample countries had an operating expenditure of $2.2 trillion and accounted for an average of 6 per cent of the workforce. Historical data for five of the countries showed non-profit institutions growing at twice the rate of national GDP.[3] There has been a parallel expansion of philanthropic funding: the number of US foundations more than trebled between 1980 and 2009 (from 22,000 to 77,000), with grant-giving rising by nearly a third in real terms from 2000 to reach $45.7 billion in 2010.

These data reflect the US emphasis on the non-profit element of the civil economy. There is an even larger sphere of civil 'for profit' enterprises. One sizeable group are co-operatives, which are estimated to have a worldwide turnover of $3 trillion. Both nationally and sectorally they have been expanding. The number of credit unions, a specific type of financial co-op, went up from 37,000 to 53,000 between 2000 and 2010, their membership grew by two thirds to 188 million, and their total savings more than doubled to $1.2 trillion.

While in Europe there is a strong tradition of industrial and consumer co-ops, in the developing world it is agricultural co-ops that have been in the forefront of the movement. In Latin America they were promoted by governments in the early 1980s, then contracted as a result of neoliberal policies. Over the past decade they have revived and expanded not least because of the growth of another recent civil economic movement, fair trade. Fair trade global sales trebled between 2005 and 2009 to 3.4 billion Euros, with the UK accounting for over £1 billion. Three quarters of fair trade is sourced from co-ops, and this has helped to expand and establish new farmer co-ops not only in Central and Latin America, but in Africa and Asia.

There are many social enterprises that are not co-ops. The data have not kept pace with the experience of their growth, social enterprise being only recognised as a category in the early 1990s. An official estimate put their number in the UK in 2010 at 62,000, of which only 8 per cent were co-ops, and evidence from continental Europe suggests that there is a similarly large body of social enterprises in addition to formal co-ops.

These data do not cover many of the less formal associations, nor the informal collaborations whose growth has been one of the most striking features of the past decade. But they bear out the general proposition of growth of the civil economy and help explain the recognition that is now being given to it as a source of human-centred production, employment, and social innovation.

In 2006 the Labour government in the UK established an Office of the Third Sector – now the Office of Civil Society. The Obama administration created an Office of Social Innovation in 2009 and the European Union followed suit by launching Social Innovation Europe from its Enterprise and Industry Secretariat in 2011. The United Nations meanwhile has declared 2012 the International Year of Co-operatives. Having been marginalised and at times attacked during the twentieth century, the civil economy is now being officially promoted on the public stage.

Causes of the expansion

What accounts for this striking upsurge? In this chapter I want to identify three forces that I believe have particular relevance:

The counter movement of the marginalised

If we understand the period of globalisation as one of intense creative destruction in the Schumpeterian sense, the counter movement can be framed in a Polanyian one. Karl Polanyi argued that market liberalism was an unsustainable and utopian project, because it threatened to destroy the social and environmental conditions necessary for a market society to flourish.[4] State-led attempts to impose unregulated liberalism by treating labour, land and money as commodities would provoke a counter movement for the 'self-protection of society' led by those suffering at market liberalism's hands. Drawing on the first instance of such an uninhibited liberal project, the 1830s in industrialising Britain, he cites as the counter movement the political campaign of the Chartists, the economic alternative of Owenism and the remarkable growth of co-operation from the 1840s onwards.

There is such a counter movement to global neoliberalism now taking place. La Via Campesina is in many ways a contemporary parallel to the Chartists. It was formed by peasant movements in 1993 and has grown and strengthened in the past decade, its members now representing 500 million peasants and family farmers from both the developing world and North America, Europe and Japan. Their platform has strong echoes of Polanyi. 'We do not own nature – it is not a commodity'.[5] They demand domestic food sovereignty as a means of protecting a peasant life based on reciprocity and rural ecology against the unregulated and unequal power of international markets. It is a political movement on a global scale. It is also an economic one, the rural equivalent of Owenism. It has involved the strengthening of peasant co-operatives and of ecological farming practices and the expansion of control by these co-operatives of the food chain nationally and internationally (through fair trade).

Many similar responses are found in towns and communities, all over the world, hit by structural adjustment and liberal trade policies. In the south, Argentina – hit by the default crisis of 2001-02 – exemplifies the growth of civil economic initiatives provoked by crisis. They range from the development of local currencies to the takeover of 200 abandoned industrial plants (the *fabricas recuperadas*) by worker co-operatives, all but four of which are still operating.

In the north, a flourishing movement for community economic development sprung up in Canada. It was concentrated in those places hit by industrial decline after the introduction of the North American Free Trade Agreement in 1990, as well as among marginalised areas such as declining fishing communities or people from the First Nations. In Europe, a strong current in the expansion of the civil economy has been the so-called 'work integration social enterprises' that are geared towards creating jobs for those excluded from the labour market.

What runs through these counter movements is a spirit of self-reliance, a strong sense of human (and in many cases ecological) well-being as the starting point for any economy, and an opposition to neoliberalism. In the words of the Landless Workers Movement (the MST) in Brazil, 'the enemy is the model'.

Economic alternatives

Although counter movements have traditionally sprung from the marginalised, what is striking in the current era is that there is a second counter movement that is lodged at the heart of the mainstream. It argues for alternatives not just for those people and places abandoned by the market, but for the core structures of the mainstream itself. The alternatives that it promotes are not, as in the 1930s, about national models of economic management – more or less central planning – but about the very models of production and consumption that prevail in the world economy, whether private or public, planned or unplanned.

The leading challenge to the status quo has come from the environmental movement, not only in the field of resources – energy, water, waste, forests and farming – but also against the oil-based, resource-intensive and hazardous character of the economy as a whole. The challenge has been at the same time particular and universal, directed at both the policies of governments and the practices of corporations. In each case successful campaigners have recognised that they first needed to develop their own alternatives. Some have established laboratories to show that products could be made without the use of hazardous chemicals; others started solar companies and local wind co-ops. Many countries saw the growth of community recycling networks, and social companies have built zero-energy housing. In Brazil there were remarkable social innovations in low-powered rural electrification. A recent catalogue listed 110,000 environmental initiatives of this kind.

Similar stories are increasingly common in other fields: in the media there are leading newspapers owned by trusts (like the *Guardian*) and a growing number of community cable channels; in the field of finance, there has been the widespread growth of credit unions and socially-driven micro credit enterprises. Football fans are not only fighting the finance-driven ownership of football but are starting their own clubs or taking over ones in difficulty; Real Madrid, Barcelona and Benfica are all co-operatives. Campaigns against industrial food chains have generated a remarkable alternative food economy, from organic farming and local processing to consumer food co-operatives; in Japan, for example, the latter have twelve million members. In health and personal services there has been a flowering of campaigns and development of alternative services, from birthing to education and on through each stage of life, to the care of the aged and to dying and mourning.

This remarkable growth of civil alternatives can, at least in part, be seen as a Polanyian counter movement to the commodification of labour, nature and money. He no doubt would have felt his propositions confirmed by the rise and strength of opposition to the industrial destruction of nature and to the inequalities to which that gives rise, as he would by the growth of alternative finance. But many of these alternatives go beyond Polanyi's categories. They concern alternative forms of consumption, of ways of living and caring, of being human in the widest sense. And they are also a counter not only to the impact of a disembedded market, but also to the limitations of a particular model of the administration of the state.

The ICT revolution

It is one thing to develop counter movements and civil alternatives; quite another for them to have more than marginal significance or to shift the structure of economic control. It is striking that some of the civil innovations are taken up by private corporations (zero-energy housing for example, or fair trade) or adopted by the state (the hospice movement in palliative care, for example); one way in which the civil economy and its significance is now being viewed is as a source of social innovation for the private market and the state.

What this reflects is the emergence of problems for which neither the market nor the state, in their current forms, has persuasive answers. Multiple environmental issues are such an example; the twenty-first-century epidemics of diabetes and obesity, another. Chronic disease more generally, together with issues of funding and caring for an ageing population, are described as time bombs for health care and public budgets. Then there is the incessant widening of the gap between rich and poor, exacerbated by the crisis of private and public finance. The civil economy has been a laboratory for alternatives on all these issues.

The question is whether these alternatives can be incorporated into the forms of the private market and the state as they stand, or whether there will have to be a change in those forms. Does the civil economy have a long-term place in the next economic phase, rather than being merely a pressure valve, a provider of first aid, and a source of innovative prototypes?

The answers may be found partly in the counter movements and the extent to which they can reshape the mainstream. But there are also significant forces that are expanding the civil economy that have arisen from within the womb of the mainstream itself. This is a departure from Polanyi, because these forces are less about the 'self-protection of society' from erosion by the market, than the creation of new productive relations from within capitalism itself. Put schematically, the last decade has shown, in outline, how the ICT revolution is opening a space for the civil economy to play an active and in some cases a leading role in production.

I want to consider three aspects of this revolution:

1. *The return of the micro.* The ICT revolution underpinned a paradoxical feature of globalisation. On the one hand, it has allowed corporations to manage complex systems on a much wider scale. Retailers, who along with banking and the military, were pioneers in the use of the new technology, are now managing up to 80,000 product supply chains to as many as 10,000 stores world-

wide with the aid of modern information systems. Such a capacity has been a major factor in corporate global expansion from the 1980s onwards.

On the other, the technology has led to the return of the micro. At the heart of ICT is micro-electronics. Its characteristic capital good is not the large 'satanic mill' of the industrial revolution but the micro-computer, so small that it has now become available to any consumer who can afford a 'smart' phone. In energy generation, solar panels, heat pumps and mini combined heat-and-power boilers turn the home into a power station. The latest machinery used for industrial production can be sized to fit into a garage. Mini-mills have sprung up for the production of steel and for paper. Small is being rendered not just beautiful but economic. Some of these micro-technologies realise the Gandhian dream of a technology that is open to local control. In brewing, for example, the consumer movement that campaigned against mass-industrialised beer has been able to start up numerous micro-breweries, some owned by their consumers.

In other cases, these micro-capital goods are part of larger systems: locally generated domestic energy, for example, may be connected to other micro-suppliers via smart grids; local convenience stores are linked together through retail networks. This model of distributed systems potentially increases the autonomy of those on the front line as workers, users and communities, by distributing complexity to the margins. It also involves profound institutional and technical changes, calling into question the role of the old, administration-heavy, central institutions (whether corporations and central states or utilities, hypermarkets and hospitals). In many areas it is these 'systems economies' that are more important than 'scale economies', with power and control passing to so-called 'system integrators'.

The key question then becomes who controls the design and management of the systems. In many parts of the private economy, giant corporations have designed their systems to increase control from the centre. While this allows for a degree of outsourcing, the micro-producers are merely part of a modern, often global, putting out system. But as often it is the micro-producers who have formed and control the systems, enabling them to combine the benefits of autonomy – creativity, flexibility, and motivation – with the advantages of scale, which are provided in this case by inter-firm federations and consortia, and by local intermediary institutions such as banks, colleges, and specialist research centres. This explains the continued resilience of the Italian and Spanish co-operative industrial districts, the food and livelihood co-ops in Japan, and the small-scale shoe-producers in Brazil; the dominance of the credit unions in Quebec, and the success of the Mittelstand in Germany. Up until the 1980s these were regarded as relics of the past. Within twenty years they have been taken up as a model for the future. The civil economy is at the heart of these systems, involving the household and the local state along with co-operative and family firms, and bound together by strong social bonds – or 'social capital', as it has come to be called. It is a model being adopted in other fields, by energy co-ops, in social care and among networks of co-operative schools, providing an alternative way of governing complex systems.

2. *The new consumer.* The passive consumer of the mass production age is now being recognised as an active producer – or 'prosumer' – in the present one. Of course this has long been the case; it is just that domestic work has not been acknowledged within a market economic model. But now the work of the market is crossing the domestic threshold. One factor is the availability of the microcapital goods mentioned above. The home is becoming not just a power station but the new workshop: an office, a print works, even a recording studio.

Another factor is the incorporation of consumers into industrial and service production. New flexible production systems are involving consumers in co-design and co-production. Toyota have been a pioneer of these new forms of mass customisation. As a purchaser of a Toyota house – and the company produces 10,000 houses a year – you can spend a weekend with an architect, designer and a whole park of model houses, parts and visualisations, deciding on everything from your new home's shape and size to its decoration and fittings. This becomes an I-house, just as a Dell computer is an I-computer. Lego even helps its consumers to design their own models.

Much of this relates to individual households being drawn into the world of private market production. But this type of active consumption cannot be contained. Clubs form. Home workers attach themselves to hubs. A social market arises for training, support, advice, and troubleshooting – the things that are required for anyone involved in production.

These trends of prosumption apply even more in services. In expanding environmental services, like recycling, or household energy and water management, the householder plays a key part in the productive cycle. The same is true of relational services, such as health, education, and in many aspects of social care in which the 'user' is both the subject and object of production.

Relational services have three characteristics: first, relationship and trust are central to the efficacy of the service; second, there are limits to the extent that labour can be substituted by machinery, since it is the human relationship that remains central; third, each involves not only the user but the voluntary help of those around them. They have been called 'I-services', with packages of support assembled around the particular requirements of the user.

Both the private and public sectors have provided such services, and have sought to adapt to the relational requirements of, say, elder care or higher education. One strand of public sector reform, for example, has been to try and incorporate those involved in the decision-making process. Health and social services have been 'co-created' and 'co-produced'. Greater weight has been given to users, both individually, through personal budgets, or collectively, through feedback websites such as Patient Opinion (http://www.patientopinion.org.uk).

It is no accident that these services are the ones that have seen a rapid growth in the civil economy. Social services and early years education have formed the majority of social enterprises in many European countries. In Italy, there are over 7,000 social care co-ops. In the UK there has been a sudden upsurge of co-operative schools. In North America there are long established health co-operatives, and in Japan the food co-operatives have diversified into livelihood co-operatives that include social and elder care.

This new wave of social and educational co-operatives is multi-stakeholder in governance, involving both the users and those providing the service. A typical UK co-operative school, for example, will have members drawn from parents, staff, pupils, a local further education college, the local authority providing the funding, and so on. In this case, as with the Italian and Canadian social co-ops, the civil economy is not separate from and rival to public provision, but rather provides a structure that allows the state to participate, through funding and engagement, alongside the many other civil parties involved.

Multi-stakeholder co-operatives of this kind are emerging as the adequate organisational structure for relational services and they are set to expand. For it is these services which are threatening to overwhelm public budgets; in a number of post-industrial countries, spending on relational services is approaching 25 per cent of GDP and is forecast to increase further. It is the civil economy, not the state, that is expanding in response.

3. *Information.* The ICT revolution has, above all, enabled people to collaborate, both as 'prosumers' and citizens. The big change came in 2003, when Silicon Valley realised that the future was less in content than in platforms. As the newspaper industry realises only too well, content is costly. Platforms, on the other hand, create a space for the content of others. These platforms can be 'enclosed' and administered as if they were property; the issue for such web platform companies as Facebook or YouTube has been that of any landlord: how to maximise the usage of resources, and then raise a rent on the basis of that usage. With the rise of web-based platforms, capitalism has shifted its axis: from the capturing of profit through control of production to the generation of rent from its informational property. Battles become ones over intellectual property as much as distributional struggles between profit and wages.

That is one way of looking at it. From another perspective, capitalism has provided the infrastructure for a massive increase in the civil economy. The most striking example is the production of knowledge itself. This can no longer be constrained within the traditional structures of property; households are collaborating directly in a new economy of sharing that is treating creativity and knowledge as a social resource, voluntarily developed and freely distributed. New legal structures have been developed to ensure that this resource is treated as a commons and not a commodity. The Creative Commons licences are one such example; launched in 2001, they now cover over 400 million works of art. Similar protection applies to open-source software, a creation of volunteer collaborators that now accounts for two-thirds of the world's basic software.

The primary principle at work is one of openness: open involvement, open access, open source, open knowledge. This has extended the civil economy far beyond the formal structures of NGOs and co-operatives, into a world of informal cooperation. As an idea, it has exploded over the past decade seemingly into every corner of social collaboration. For example:

- Common projects (Letsdoit, Mars Mapping and Wikipedia, founded in 2001 and whose 3.7 million entries greatly outstrip the *Encyclopaedia Britannica*)

- giving away (Freecycle, Kiva, Landshare, Jumo)

- sharing (Limeware)

- hosting (roomrama, couchsurfing)

- recommending (Grubhub, Foursquare launched in 2009 with now 6.5 million users worldwide)

- connecting (Diaspora, Gaydar, Netmums, Meetup)

- co-consuming (Netflix, Zipcar)

- co-renting (Zilok, the hirehub, Erento)

- swapping (Thredup, big wardrobe, swapstyle, Swap.com)

- exchanging (eBay and Craigslist)

- bartering (u-exchange.com, planetgreen)

- financing (Zopa, Quackle, Profounder, Kickstarter)

- news producing (Reddit)

One of Marx's central theses was that capitalism developed the 'socialisation of labour'. By this he meant the direct organisation of labour within the sphere of production, which he held to be the result of the development of technology. The rise of the web has seen a remarkable shift into the direct organisation of citizens; in part political, but also increasingly economic. It is a socialisation of civic life, extending the socialisation based on physical proximity to the open medium of cyberspace.

The civil economy and globalisation

How far is this expanding civil economy global? Some of its elements are clearly so, as is the case with fair trade. There has been a steep rise in the number of international NGOs from 1989 (from 5,000 to 27,000 in 1999 and to around 55,000 in 2010), and NGOs now administer an estimated 15 per cent of all overseas aid. Some projects extend overseas through social franchising, as is the case with Freecycle, an Arizona-based project to promote the re-use of products by a form of eBay without payment. Within ten years they have developed 4,000 local chapters in eight-five countries with eight million members. Another example is Habitat for Humanity, with its franchised system for both financing and building low-cost housing.

In contrast, the responses of those marginalised by neoliberal globalisation have been framed in direct opposition to it. Whereas in the 1930s the effects of depression led to demands for more autarchic national economies, the recent post-globalisation crises have sought to develop self-reliant local economies. They emphasise the local against the global. They argue for an economy driven by values rather than value. And they see their projects in terms of an extension of economic democracy that is best realised at a local, micro, level.

There has been a similar emphasis in the environmental and food movements, dissolving the global into innumerable locals, as a means of reducing transport, increasing resilience, and redirecting the appetite for cheap globally-produced commodities towards a richer form of civic life. They have championed everything local: local energy systems, local closed loop recycling, local sourcing and locally integrated food chains. The remarkable growth of the transition towns movement (www.transitionnetwork. org) which seeks to support each member town or neighbourhood in developing its own self-reliant low-carbon economy embodies this approach. Globalisation of the mainstream economy and the tensions to which it has given rise has in this way provoked its opposite, an intensely local, self-governing, socially embedded alternative.

It is, however, only one side of the story. For while material production may be local, the networks and communications that connect them are uninhibitedly global. The internet has allowed global communities of practice to mushroom. Networks like Zero Waste International (http://www.zwia.org) compare experiences, share information, form research consortia, and develop common curricula and training materials. They mutually diffuse know-how not through cross-licensing or corporate expansion, but through the free circulation of people and information, with a regular round of conferences, workshops, visits, speaking tours, exchanges, and assignments.

Some have developed international advisory networks that act as a 'civil civil service' for projects in the social economy. A striking example is Healthcare Without Harm, an initiative started in the US in the mid-1990s to make hospitals less hazardous to health – initially by closing down incinerators, but then expanding into finding alternatives to the use of PVC medical apparatus, mercury thermometers, and so on. It is now an international network of over 500 social organisations sharing a common goal and a network that identifies relevant innovations globally and gives advice on how they can best be applied.

In many fields, civil projects and their networks have become a principal channel for the local generation and global diffusion of social and environmental innovation. A good example is the Bio Regional environmental group. One of its projects has been to produce local recycled office paper with an input of straw or hemp, but in starting the project the group encountered a global problem: black liquor effluent is produced by this process. Bio Regional has spent fourteen years researching a solution and is now prototyping a mini-mill with the aim of making the technology available worldwide, thus preventing the closure of similar recycling projects in India and China. As with its parallel development, a now iconic model of zero-carbon housing in South London. Most recently, the group posted detailed building information and blueprints about its zero-carbon housing on the internet.

The idea of the civil economy as global information applies even more so to the cyber economy. Linux is produced through global collaboration. So is Wikipedia and all the growing number of projects that are based on the 'crowd-sourcing' of ideas. Medical websites for those with common medical conditions are global. Universities are placing their course content and even their recorded lectures on the internet, free to download. Around 20 per cent of the 250,000 students enrolled at the British-based Open University are from overseas, with their own support systems of local tutors and study groups, coupled with virtual conferences, chatrooms and lectures. As improving language translation programmes remove the barrier of language, we can see these as examples of hyper-globalisation.

The internet has swept away the geographical and property frontiers of information. We now have not just Medecins sans Frontieres and 'Engineering sans Frontieres', but *information sans frontieres* taken to a new level. The traditional environmental slogan 'think globally and act locally' can be rephrased as 'click globally and produce locally'.

The first decade of the twenty-first century has witnessed a historically unprecedented expansion of a civil global information and knowledge economy, side by side with a multiplicity of initiatives that, seen from within, are experienced as local and self-reliant in character, but viewed from without comprise a highly distributed network of material and service production. They are not bound by the chains of ownership or by being a small cog in an interdependent global wheel, but rather connected together through the movement of people and the free circulation of ideas. Because significant parts of this civil economy have developed in opposition to the mainstream and are democratically rooted, these scattered initiatives can be seen as examples of globalisation from below. But we might equally describe it as a globalism of the head and the heart, rather than the hand.

Conclusion

The civil economy is commonly regarded as an economy of small things, marginal to the main action in the economy of the large ones. It is the lamb next to the lion. Yet over the past decade, as the lion has run into difficulties the lamb has grown, and now plays an ever more significant role in the global economy. This is partly due to its distinctive relational and motivational quality, and to its reintegration of the social and the personal with the economic. It is also because of the freedom from the constrictions of property intrinsic to an economy based at least partially on information.

I have described it as a hybrid of force fields rather than as a distinct 'third' sector, with clear boundaries and legal forms. In practice the interfaces between the different spheres of the hybrid are in constant movement, particularly that between the civil economy and the state. One opinion holds that the civil economy is an alternative to the state, another that it is a staging post to privatisation. Neither is inherent. Both the state and the civil spheres are part of a social economy, often in pursuit of common aims but subject to different structural political forces.

Which leads us to one of the major challenges to be met as the social economy grows: how to reintegrate the state and the civil spheres. Some of the projects that I have described in this chapter suggest possible answers: new forms of public-social partnerships, and the closer involvement of civil society in the shaping of the public economy. Here, it is movements in the global South that have been pioneers, from planning and literacy campaigns in Kerala to participatory budgeting in Brazil. Such initiatives have now spread to Latin America more generally, and are now showing, through their practice, how to heal that conceptual split introduced by nineteenth-century liberal theory – the forced separation of the economic and the political.

Notes

1 Helmut Anheier, Marlies Glasius and Mary Kaldor (eds), *Global Civil Society*, Oxford: Oxford University Press, 2001, Introduction.
2 See Luigino Brunio and Stefano Zamagni, *Civil Economy*, Bern: Peter

Lang, 2007. The authors have sought to reintroduce the tradition of civic humanism into the contemporary concept of civil society. They argue that the market economy needs to re-internalise the principles of equity and reciprocity alongside equivalence and efficiency, and re-orient itself from the production of goods to the strengthening of relationships.

3   Lester M. Salamon, S. Wojciech Sokolowski and Associates *et al.*, *Global Civil Society: Dimensions of the Nonprofit Sector*, Kumarian Press: Greenwich, CN, 3rd edn, 2010, pp187, 201; Salamon, 'Putting the civil society sector on the economic map of the world', *Annals of Public and Co-operative Economics*, Vol. 81, No. 2, 2010, pp167-210.

4   Karl Polanyi, *The Great Transformation*, Beacon Press: Boston, 1957.

5   La Via Campesina: http://viacampesina.org/en/

Fair Trade

10

Raising the bar or
redirecting the flood

First published as Chapter 13 of John Bowes (ed.), The Fair Trade
Revolution, *Pluto Press: London, 2010. This edited extract reproduced
with permission.*

From economic experiment to social movement

There is scarcely a corner of Britain which does not have an active
presence in fair trade. In Keswick there are regular morning
breakfasts of fair traders. On the borders you find fair-trade goods
in outby farmhouses. Co-op delivery wagons travel the motorways
with 'Fair trade' emblazoned in great letters on their sides. Schools,
universities and local government offices have become promoters
of fair trade. In Lewisham Borough Council the staff canteen has
become fair trade, with pictures of farmers and their statements
covering the walls. In less than a decade, fair trade has changed
from a practical experiment into a social movement.

What explains this extraordinary phenomenon, and how can
this dynamic be sustained? In part it reflects a new kind of politics, one in which people are looking for ways to change things in
practice and not merely express their views through conventional
political channels. It represents a new social pragmatism. We know
and engage with the world through small actions, but which have
meaning because they are part of a much larger whole.

Just as the women's movement, in declaring that the personal is
political, started the change in the household and everyday relationships, and in doing so created a new cultural and social ethic, so

fair trade is creating an ethic about how trade should be conducted, and providing a means for citizens in the northern hemisphere to relate tangibly to those marginalised by the world economy.

Initially it was seen as a micro-economic project, a way of paying small farmers a better price for their product. It was a modest means of redistribution from the global north to the south. But with the growth of fair-trade towns, of fair-trade schools and universities, it has become a movement with wider claims. For some, like Britain's pioneer fair-trade town, Garstang in Lancashire, it is nothing less than a movement to end the 'second slavery' that an unequally structured global market imposes on the poor.

The Quakers, whose networks underpinned the campaign against the 'first slavery', led a boycott of sugar to strike at the economic interests of the slave trade. Fair trade has inverted this, replacing boycotts with buycotts. In a world now saturated by the media it has highlighted the negative by promoting the positive. In an economy of attention, a Kitemark can be as potent as a strike.

The early fair-trade companies and those running stalls after church or in village markets found their message amplified in the media and further widened by the promotion of the initially fair-traded products. Consumer awareness of fair trade grew remarkably; those commercial companies closest to the consumer – supermarkets and coffee shops – were the first to seek the 'halo effect' of stocking fair-trade goods, and their displays further widened awareness. Now even the mainstream brands are converting one or two of their products to fair trade, or in the case of the sugar giant Tate and Lyle, all their cane sugar. Sugar has re-entered the story, this time not in the shadow but in the light.

Mark to market

An expanded economy is also a more complex one. The pioneer brands – Cafédirect, Divine, Agrofair, Equal Exchange, Traidcraft and Liberation – surfed the wave of expansion. But in the past five years they have faced the challenge of all first movers. Competitors began to try to copy them, adopting the Fairtrade mark and seeking out supplies from approved producers. The supermarkets developed their 'own-brand' fair-trade lines. Now high street names like Cadbury, Nestle and Starbucks are promoting fair trade in ways that mimic the pioneers. The song of the nightingale is getting lost in the noise of the dawn chorus.

The very success of fair trade now threatens these firms and their model of fair trade. They have always sought to operate a 'fair trade plus' model that goes well beyond FLOCERT's [the global certification body for fair trade]. They have all taken on a large measure of the risks of trade rather than pushing them back down to the primary producers. They have strengthened the position of primary producers in the supply chain, supporting them in developing their own warehousing and exporting capacity so they can sidestep the previously powerful local merchants. Producers are joint owners of many of the fair-trade companies in the north, participating in their governance, and taking a share of the profits. For them, fair trade – in the spirit of Garstang (see above) – has been a question of power and capacity as well as price. These fair-trade companies now find themselves undercut by fair-trade products that do not carry the costs of producer support, of participatory governance and the redistribution of risk.

The Fairtrade mark faces similar pressures. It has been at the heart of the expansion of fair trade in the past decade. But it has its own competitors. Manufacturers and retailers who were unwilling to pay the price guarantees and credit conditions of the Fairtrade mark have supported a growing number of alternative marks – notably Rainforest Alliance and Utz Certified – or promoted their own ethical schemes. In Britain the vitality of the Fairtrade Foundation has meant the Fairtrade mark still predominates. But on the continent there are many countries where sister labels now take second place to those which have lowered their standards to extend their coverage. Even in Britain potential new adopters of the mark press the Fairtrade Foundation to soften its standards. A kind of Gresham's Law ['bad money drives out good'] threatens the economy of marks. There is always pressure for the bad marks to drive out the good. In such a situation, the first task is maintaining the bar as the basis for raising and widening it.

The retailers

A key role in the future of fair trade is played by the retailer. There are two courses they can adopt. On the one hand, they can play a conventional market role. They can treat fair-trade products like any others, requiring key money to get on the shelves, and taking on the burden of high retailer margins to keep their place on them. They can encourage their buyers to source fair-trade goods from anyone who conforms (or claims to conform) to the fair-trade standards, treating its supply chains at arm's length without contracts or commitments. This approach will strengthen the downward pressure on standards and the mark. It will also maintain the current main anomaly of the fair-trade supply chain, where retailers have margins of 35-60 per cent, dwarfing the proportion paid to the farmers.

The other course is to enter into developmental partnerships with producers and their associated companies in the north, using a retailer's pivotal position between consumers and producers to connect the two, to strengthen the supply chain by technical assistance, and ensure that there is a fair distribution of margins between producers and retailers.

One example of such collaboration is the Food Retail Industry Challenge Fund (FRICH) programme financed by the UK's Department for International Development. The programme part-funds partnerships between producers, importers and retailers that develop primary producer capacity in Africa. Such guaranteed access – once adequate quality and cost levels have been reached – provides some insulation from the normal day-to-day pressure on the retail buyers to drive down costs and maximise turnover.

The supermarket chain Sainsbury's have shown their commitment to this second course by their decision to source all their bananas from fair-trade sources. They have worked closely with Windward Island producers, providing a secure market (via a three-year contract) in the face of low-cost plantation competition from the three main banana multinationals in Latin America. They followed this up by fair-trade sourcing 100 per cent of other own-label products – cane sugar, tea, roast and ground coffee, and Kenyan roses – as well as establishing a £1 million Fair Development Fund administered by Comic Relief to promote supplier development.

Then there is the Co-operative. The Co-op is the natural fit for fair trade. Just as in Italy there are regional co-operative supply chains selling through co-operative retailers, so in fair-trade, retail co-ops are the final stage of a global co-operative supply chain. And the Co-operative Group has historically played a central role in the development of British fair trade. It was the first supermarket to convert its own lines to 100 per cent fair trade. It has been a long-time supporter of a fair-trade banana farm in Ghana, a banana co-operative in Costa Rica and most recently a Panamanian banana co-operative which has been impoverished by a 'second slavery'-style long-term contract with Chiquita.

The Co-op Group is only part of a larger archipelago of independent co-op retail societies, the top ten of which have a combined turnover of £3.3 billion. Most are members of the Co-op Retail Trading Group (CRTG), which although centralised allows independent co-ops to develop their own local or ethical sources which are then traded through the CRTG. All these co-ops could extend the number of 'twinned' partnerships with producers' groups in the south. The partnerships should be formalised as an aspect of co-operative retail practice and the buyers schooled in what is involved in fair-trade supply chain relationships. Such practices go well beyond the fair-trade standards because they involve technical support in improving production, processing and packaging, as well as long-term commitments to the partners.

For retailers following this second path, there should also be a transparent policy on margins. The French fair-trade company Ethiquable has reached an agreement with the continental retail giant Carrefour to lower their margins on fair-trade production to 25 per cent, and this commitment is included on the packaging. UK retailers should now adopt a similar principle.

Another possibility would be to provide incentives on the shelves not just as price discounts to consumers – usually paid for by fair-trade suppliers – but extra premium payments to the producers. Modern smart cards, such as those used in the Lincoln and Chelmsford Co-ops, would allow the transfer of premiums to be itemised for every town and every consumer, tracing it through to the producer co-ops at origin.

Corporate partnerships

I am arguing here for a shift in retailer-supplier relations from one of dependent subordination to one of collaborative partnership. A similar partnership model relevant to fair trade has been developed by Muhammed Yunus, the founder of the Grameen Bank. He was approached by Franck Riboud, head of the French multinational Danone, who told him that he thought large corporations could no longer ignore social issues yet were strangers to the social economy. Riboud asked him if he would work with Danone on a project to reduce poverty. Yunus agreed, but on one condition: that the project should be driven by its social and environmental imperatives not financial ones. That was the founding principle of the partnership. Grameen Danone Foods was established in Bangladesh as a social business yielding no profit to Danone.

The two parties decided to make use of Danone's product specialism and produce a nutritionally fortified yoghurt that was cheap enough for the rural poor. Yunus insisted that rather than the normal centralised plant, it develop micro yoghurt factories that could be located near to the villages because it would mean less of a journey for the 'yoghurt ladies' from the villages who would do the selling. (Because the units were not centralised they could dispense with much of the expense of refrigeration, which also meant the yoghurt ladies using cooler bags on their regular runs to the villages.) He also insisted that the containers should be biodegradable and edible. All these ran against the grain of the normal. But Yunus found that when pressed Danone had the capabilities to apply its know-how to produce radical socially oriented technical innovations. He has become a strong advocate of such social-private partnerships to harness modern technology for social goals.[1]

With the growth of environmental concerns, and with the expansion of fair trade to complex manufactured products, such partnerships could become increasingly important. In rubber products, for example, there is a need to develop the properties of smallholder latex so that it can compete effectively with petroleum-based synthetic rubbers, and to substitute dyes and other hazardous substances used in the production of latex-based products, such as shoe soles or rubber gloves. (Another example is in paper production, using renewable resources such as straw. The barrier here has been a solution to the problem of 'black liquor' produced during the processing of straw. Its pollution is causing much of the rice straw production in India and China to be closed down, with the resulting pressure of virgin forests and a rise in imported waste paper. The UK social company Bio Regional has been working for more than a decade in partnership with commercial paper companies to find a solution to this problem, and then diffuse the know-how cheaply. It represents a form of fair trade in reverse and has echoes of the fair procurement that was an initial driver of fair-trade companies like Twin Trading.)

As with the retailers, corporations ready to act in this way should have the producers' fair-trade companies working as part of a joint team rather than as a subordinate supplier. It would be a way of raising the bar, not just for individual projects but more generally by embedding fair-trade practice within large corporations. There would be a case, indeed, for establishing an association of corporations ready to partner in this way. The association would have its own supplementary codes of practice that would distinguish it from 'tick-box' fair traders.

Fair-trade innovation

Technical innovations of this sort are only one type of innovation relevant to the next phase of fair trade. There are organisational innovations – how to strengthen the management and governance of the first- and second-level producer co-ops, and the third-level international co-ops and networks that have emerged as a result of fair trade. Fair-trade companies in the north need to develop mechanisms for closer collaboration. And there are supply chain innovations required with respect to traceability and the capacity to track fair-trade products back to the farms and localities.

Advanced commercial logistics technologies would be valuable here. But there is also the question of processing flexibility that would permit short runs of products from specific villages and localities. NASFAM [National Smallholder Farmers' Association of

Malawi], the peanut co-operative in Malawi, has been working on its collection and quality control systems that now allow its peanuts to be identified down to a cluster of twelve to twenty farmers. The challenge is how to maintain that degree of specificity through processing and packaging so that the consumer (and the quality controller) can identify these growers.

But there is also the question of new product development. It is a long process. Kuapa Kokoo in Ghana took five years to establish as a co-operative that was able to operate the collection and merchanting functions in Ghana. It took its branding company Divine a further four years to break even and expand. Cafédirect and Liberation Nuts had similar early life spans. Like trees, robust supply chains take time to grow.

Not all fair-trade products are generated in this way. There are now over 3000 products that have a Fairtrade mark. Many of these use materials and ingredients from established co-operatives, purchased on the fair-trade commodity market. On the demand side, Britain is rich in the skills of product design and market testing to make desirable products. The challenge is on the supply side – issues of sustainable crop management, generic quality issues like aflatoxin in peanuts, new types of micro processing and strong producer co-operatives to manage all this. These all require producer-oriented innovation.

All these can be used to promote fair-trade innovations and could be hosted either by a small independent fair-trade innovation lab or by the Fairtrade Foundation itself.

Alongside the above, there needs to run a source of early-stage innovation finance that is driven not by prospective financial rates of return (as with most venture capital) but by the goal of launching successful products and the deep taproots that supply them. A fair-trade innovation lab could be linked to a seed fund to finance prototypes and beta testing. Promising projects could be taken further through community of interest companies (CICs). This company status has proved valuable for financing fair-trade projects because it allows charitable funds to be channelled into start-up ventures (as in the case of Liberation) and maintains the fair-trade mission as primary.

A fair-trade college

I have discussed a number of economic mechanisms that can expand and enrich fair trade. But the development of a common culture of fair trade is even more important. Culture is a wide term. It covers festivals, language, performance, films, music and the many types of electronic media. In a sense it is what is at the core of life itself. There is scope for extending fair trade into such services and for establishing a network of fair-trade cultural centres that could showcase these many forms of culture from the developing world, and provide a place where fair trade becomes more a way of life than a narrow economic transaction.

Here I want to focus on one particular cultural issue. It is how fair trade learns about itself and generates a common understanding. It is one of the features of successful civil economic movements that they develop their own structures of education. The British co-operative movement, for example, established its own college in 1919 that developed successive generations of co-operative staff and managers. The retail co-ops all ran their own education programmes. The Mondragon co-operatives in Spain started from a training course and now have their own university. The remarkable Sekem project in Egypt, which has pioneered biodynamic farming and the conversion of 85 per cent of Egyptian cotton to organic production, has established its own Sekem academy in Cairo. Such colleges are the source of vitality and renewal in any movement. Like a hidden attractor, they shape the patterns of activity and make coherent the disparate living centres that make up a movement of this kind.

Fair trade lacks a college. Those engaged in it have not had a space to stand back and reflect. From the farmer right through to the importer and brander, the focus has been on the product, getting it from field to plate via a supermarket, in the right shape and at the right time. In the south there has been some training in the running of co-operatives and in the business of trade. But in the north there has been almost nothing that is plugged into and informs practice. The new generation of fair traders has been formed on the job but without a wider context. Those in the commercial and cultural world who engage with fair trade – the buyers, the marketeers, the journalists, even the board members – have little substantive induction beyond the generalities of principle. Fair trade has been a movement of the hand and heart. It has not paid enough attention to the reflective head.

The intellectual challenge is this. Fair trade is not just business as usual conducted for an ethical end. It is a looking-glass economy; like Muhammed Yunus's Grameen Bank, it discovers the limitations of the normal practice and reverses it. It partners with small farmers in marginal communities rather than large plantations. It shifts risk in the trading chain from the farmer to the importer. When world prices fall it raises the price it pays. It advances credit to those who have no collateral to give. It shares ideas rather than hides them.

It is these reverses that have resonated with consumers and investors. For, like Grameen, they show that another kind of economy is possible. It is an economy of reciprocity, based around what we have in common rather than the antagonisms of the private market that keep us apart. Fair trade shares these features with other parts of the rapidly growing social economy. But the mechanisms and laws of such an economy are still too little understood.

This is where a college comes in. Its first task is to expand this understanding beyond the celebration of individuals and examples of ethics-in-practice. Adam Smith's theory of markets was more than a theory of entrepreneurs.

A second task is to develop a shared perspective and set of principles for operating successfully in this economy. For in this other kind of globalism, where the number of farmers scattered across continents, cultures and languages supplying Cafédirect is greater than the workforce of Ford or General Motors, a shared outlook is the binding necessary for such a dispersed movement to cohere.

A third task is to develop particular skills and methods that embody the principles of this different kind of economy. It is sometimes said that social business is 90 per cent conventional business and 10 per cent a social topping. In our experience the two should not be split apart in this way. Fair trade needs distinct management-information systems, marketing approaches, HR policies, organisational structures – many shared with the most innovative firms in the wider economy. It needs its own type of business school.

Last, the college needs to provide a space for those engaged in fair trade to take time out and reflect – what Donald Schon, the farsighted American management theorist, called 'reflective practice'.[2]

A college to carry out these tasks should be a college without walls and with many centres. It should be modelled on the Open University, which was founded on the principle of people studying where they work and live, supported by local tutors and fellow students, and gathering together annually. It was a model of decentralised and networked learning that shared many of the features of the great institutions of adult learning in twentieth century Britain, such as the education programmes of the Co-operative Retail Societies and the co-op-inspired Workers' Education Association, whose tutors took themselves and their book boxes on the road.

The internet has allowed this principle of a decentralised college to grow exponentially. The Open University now has 180,000 students interacting with it from home. There are 16,000 conferences, 2000 of them moderated by students, with 110,000 participants. Its student-guidance website has 70,000 hits a week. This is a measure of the power of web-based education.

A fair-trade college would link existing resources (in the Co-operative College in Manchester for example) with a multiplicity of study groups. Its principle would be that of the Open Source movement – the free posting of curricula and content on the web coupled with their constant upgrading in response to comments and submissions. The fair-trade college would run some central courses – an action-research degree for some, shorter courses for new buyers or recruits to the companies. But much would be distributed, both for producer co-ops in the global south, and those wanting to engage with fair trade in the north. Such an open college should become one of the main drivers of the next stage of fair trade.

Extending the social movement

In many ways the axis of the fair-trade economy in Britain in 2010 has shifted from the complex architecture of markets to the gathering force of a social movement. It is this movement that will fuel the widening and deepening of fair trade. If we think of fair trade as a mix of philosophy, politics and economics, we can see that both the philosophy (in terms of the ethic of fair trade) and the politics (in the form of the fair-trade towns, schools and municipalities) have become key parts of its economics. The idea of the college is to develop the philosophy. What are the ways of sustaining and strengthening the social movement?

The growth phase has focused on products. Local groups have campaigned for shops and cafes to take fair-trade goods. They became the local champions of the iconic fair-trade brands owned by the small farmer co-ops. But a chocolate bar has its limits. It is direct relationships with the farmers that really matter. Fairtrade Fortnight has provided resources and a framework for connecting. Visiting farmers have travelled all over the UK, addressing meetings, appearing on local television, being welcomed in town halls. Occasionally the annual assemblies of the fair-trade companies have led to memorable occasions – with fair-trade fairs and dances. But for the most part, fair-trade activists have been separated from the producers.

In other countries, consumers are more directly connected to producers. In Italy, the leading fair-trade company Altermercato is part of a network of 500 One World co-operative shops. They are run largely by volunteers who engage with producers not just through the multiplicity of stories attached to the products on the shelves but through campaigns that emerge from these stories, such as the repression of the brazil nut producers in the Pando province of Bolivia, or the olive oil producers in Palestine.

Similarly in Japan, Altertrade, the fair-trade company owned by and supplying the large consumer co-ops, organises regular exchanges between consumers, who stay in the homes of small banana producers in the Philippines, and the farmers who return visits to the co-ops in Japan. Altertrade refers to this as 'people to people' trade, and as with Altermercato, it is direct trade between producers and consumers.

In Britain most fair trade is not direct. It is sold predominantly through mainstream retailers, subcontracted category managers and private merchants. They are multiple curtains that stand in the way of the direct and continuous relationships that the fair-trade movement needs if it is to sustain itself.

How to develop more direct links? Retailers could, like Altermercato, encourage groups of consumers to connect directly to their suppliers. This is most likely to happen through the British One World shops, or through Oxfam, and the online retailers (like Traidcraft and the Ethical Superstore) or through some of the Co-operative retailers.

The 100 per cent fair traders and the Fairtrade Foundation could encourage twinning – of the kind that has begun with schools in England and Ghana, and which could be greatly extended between fair-trade towns in the UK and villages in the global south. Twin Trading and its partners in the regions of Kilimanjaro in Tanzania and Cusco in Peru have launched a tourism project for visitors from the north to live among coffee farmers. There are initiatives to provide training and placements for members of southern co-operatives in the UK. There is also scope to greatly expand volunteering and technical support, and for all those involved, as in Japan, to speak about their experience when they return.

But it is to the web that we should turn for a step change. As with education, the world of the web radically alters the conditions for connecting. To date most of the websites of fair-trade companies have taken the old form, of content presented for passing readers. They have carried abbreviated stories and pictures about particular producers, and directory entries about producer organisations. But few have been interactive or have had the real-time immediacy of Facebook or Myspace. (Divine is a partial exception, particularly its Dubble website, www.dubble.co.uk, connecting young people in Britain and Ghana.)

With the growth of broadband and mobile phone technology, closer connections are on the horizon. What is needed is a platform that enables such interaction. Actively hosted, it would mean that fair-trade products need no longer be merely a symbolic connection between consumers and producers, but a bridge connecting the two directly.

Across that bridge much could flow. There are few producer co-ops whose stories do not have a dramatic character, faced as they often are with the opposition of the local political and economic interests that they challenge. It is the detail of these stories that gives meaning to fair-trade products in the shops, but that gets lost in the abbreviations of conventional marketing. The web is a medium that thrives on detail, on exchange and reciprocity, and the spread of the immediate. And it is a medium that allows the local to become global and transparent.

Such a hosted platform would best be established by a consortium of the 100 per cent fair traders in conjunction with those active in the fair-trade movement. In addition to facilitating north-south exchanges, and helping to spread an awareness of the conditions and activities of marginal farmers, its aim would also be to fuel the many new initiatives now being developed by fair-trade activists in the north, such as the opening up of fair-trade walking trails. Fair trade would no longer be merely a means for transferring small sums of money across the lengthy chains of international trade, but a platform for direct exchange and a common mobilisation. Fair trade now has the potential to enter fully into the information age.

The pioneers

What role is there for the 100 per cent fair traders in this next phase of fair trade? One course would be to accept the logic of the increasingly crowded fair-trade market and wind themselves up, their job done. Or, like Ben & Jerry's, the Body Shop or Green & Black's, they could seek to work as an ethical implant within mainstream corporations.

Yet these companies remain key players in the wider agenda that I have set out. As producer-owned companies, they are a principle conduit for producer engagement in the development of a fair-trade web platform, a fair-trade college and the many fields of innovation. But to play this role the 100 per centers need to radically change themselves from companies primarily focused on the development of particular products and services to be the hubs of wider networks.

On the one hand, this means rationalising their own operations by merging their organisations or forming consortia to provide backroom services more cheaply. While in the initial phase it made sense to have separate companies, each with their own drive and identity, now they should consolidate, not least in marketing, to provide a stronger voice for the 'fair trade plus' model, and to develop their role as fair-trade hubs.

On the other hand, they need to turn outwards and actively connect to the potential partners in the new agenda – to the fair-trade towns, the Fairtrade Foundation, to those with specialist skills, to sympathetic corporations, and to the environmental and co-operative movements. This means a shift in focus and governance from closed to open fair trade.

Conclusion

Social and environmental innovations like fair trade are often initiated by imaginative groups driven by a social cause. But the path of their growth has its pitfalls. If successful they can be absorbed and shackled by the mainstream, sometimes by the state (in the field of mental health for example) or by large players in the market. In recycling, for example, large waste companies have crowded out the community innovators and lowered their standards. In organic food, US organic farmers have had to develop a new quality kite mark because the large corporate food producers used political pressure to water down the official organic standards. In both cases, more has meant worse.

Fair trade need not go down this route. It controls its own standards. The governing body that sets the standards, the Fairtrade Foundation, represents many of the interests that want to enrich fair trade rather than dilute it. The FAIRTRADE mark has its competitors and faces its own pressures to relax the standards. But these are counterbalanced by the growing strength of the fair-trade towns and of consumers at the checkout.

In this context the pioneers are far from done. They have an established place in the market and are seen as embodying fair trade's aspirations. They have much to live up to, both as standard bearers and innovators, and much still to do once their own economic position has been secured.

So the further diffusion of fair trade can be one of enriching its practices rather than reducing its standards. There are strong currents running in its favour. But to make the most of them the multiple springs of activity that have up till now followed their own courses need to link more closely as partners to further a common programme of initiatives. The small rivers of fair trade that have already begun to reshape the contours of an impoverished economic landscape could together take on the force of a flood.

Notes

1 Muhammad Yunus, *Creating a World Without Poverty: Social Business and the Future of Capitalism*, BBS Publications, 2007.
2 Donald Schon, *The Reflective Practitioner: How Professionals Think in Action*, Basic Books, 1983.

Co-operatives

11

Taking stock, looking forward

This is an abridged extract from Robin Murray's chapter in Ed Mayo (ed.), The Co-operative Advantage, *New Internationalist, 2015. Reproduced with permission.*

A daily economy

This book breaks down the landscape of the British economy into contours that we can recognise. The great national aggregates of GDP, employment, the rate of inflation and the balance of trade are the data of those who control the macroeconomic levers in London. They obscure the specific character of the economy of our daily lives – the shops, the buses, the farms and the streets of a city. The chapters here come down to a human level and describe the hidden structures and forces that are shaping the economy as we experience it. In doing so they allow us to think how things could be done differently and map some of the promising paths opening up for co-operators to follow.

What we learn

Three features of these sectors stand out. First it is striking how many of them in Britain are dominated by a few large firms. In energy it is the big six, in banking the big five, as it is in housebuilding. We learn that the twenty-four passenger rail franchises are in fact owned by six or seven parent corporations. The top four supermarkets account for three-quarters of grocery sales. We would find a similar picture in other sectors – the oil companies, the press, book publishers or pharmaceuticals. Economists refer to this as oligopoly. It appears as an inherent tendency of market competition. In Britain it has been naturalised as an inescapable way of life.

Here is the bind. We depend on these companies yet they abuse their position. The banks are the overwhelming case, not just for the calamities of 2008, but for the successive scandals of mis-selling and market manipulation. The oil companies and the electricity majors have been intensifying the problems of climate change, not resolving them. In the press it has been the scandal of phone tapping. British house-builders have produced smaller houses, at poorer quality and at higher prices than those in Holland and Germany, principally because the money in the UK is to be made in land. All these companies have contributed in their own way to tax avoidance and the growing inequality that, as Thomas Piketty records,[1] is approaching levels last seen in the early nineteenth century. There is a consistent pressure driving a wedge between the public and the private interests.

The second striking fact is that in many of the sectors the traditional role of the state of counteracting this divergence has been eroded. In some of the sectors the wedge has deepened as a result of the privatisation of public assets. In social care, for example, privatisation has reached the point where the sector is now dominated by private providers, many of them owned by private equity companies, that have cut pay and the quality of service in order to generate their returns. In education we see the emergence of large quasi-corporate chains of academy schools. Public land is being returned to the speculative private market in spite of the need for social housing. Nearly two million council houses have been sold in the past thirty years, and there has been a long-term shift to private renting. Now health care is being opened up to a private market. Far from counteracting the wedge between the public and the private interest [the state] appears bent on expanding it.

Third is the significance of new technology in shaping the future of these sectors. In many of them a battle has already been joined between the use of information technology by the old majors to strengthen their position and new entrants with disruptive online alternatives. In banking there has been an upsurge of online banking innovation – so called Banking 3.0 – whose upstart companies threaten the foundations of the old banking models, as they are already doing in Africa and the Far East. In retailing, Amazon is surging into one sector after another, leaving traditional retailers struggling to catch up. The Kahn Academy and massive online open courses (MOOCs) have the capacity to transform school and university education respectively. There are similar trends appearing in health care, in food production, and above all in energy, where renewable energy technology provides the scope for each village, and even each house, to become its own power station. Just as iTunes has changed the record industry, so these innovations are threatening the foundations on which the old oligopolies have been built.

There is a common pattern. The innovations open up spaces for distributed production – where a multitude of small producers are connected through common platforms, grids and protocols. Apple is a new giant, but it has provided the platform for more than a million apps. Coursera, the first MOOC founded two years ago, now has 10 million worldwide students receiving 839 free courses supplied by 114 institutions. The renewable energy co-ops in Germany are now pressing for smart grids to support their local systems. Solar technology is set to be even more distributed. The forecasts are that it will be so cheap by 2030 that, like the computer, we will find it on every home and building.[2]

The picture that emerges is of a private economy that is out of sync with the major issues of our day, and in many cases is making them worse. Climate change, the relentless growth of hazardous materials, pollution and waste, of chronic disease and obesity, of inequality, and most starkly the wider uncoupling of wellbeing and growth – all these described by those within them as time bombs – are intensifying rather than being defused.

To put it mildly, this is not an economic system at ease with itself. And the state, faced with mobile capital and an eroding tax base, appears paralysed, insisting on seeing the problems of ever-increasing corporate economic and political power through the prism of nineteenth-century free-trade market liberalism. It has all the marks of a Shakespearean economic tragedy, the principal characters unable to escape from their tragic flaw.

Waves of co-operation

Where does this leave the movement for co-operation? Faced on the one hand with large, often global corporations, how can small co-operative Davids hope to hold their own against the Goliaths that command the main spaces in the economy? On the other hand, there are the social and environmental 'time bombs' – the intractable issues, and the ever-more evident wedge between the public interest and the private giants on the path. It is this space – the space of the wedge – that co-operation in its very purpose and ethic is designed to close.

The Hungarian economic historian Karl Polanyi, analysing previous periods of what he called market utopianism – when governments legislated about land, labour and money as if they were no different from bread and potatoes – said that the crises that followed their new policies would trigger a counter movement, a political response demanding an alternative. For Polanyi what was demanded was a democratic and interventionist state. Writing in 1943, he saw the Chartists in the 1830s making such demands, just as he witnessed demands for state management of the economy and then the welfare state in the 1930s and 1940s.

What is fascinating is that these moments of economic and social crisis were also ones for the growth of co-operatives. They were the economic parallel of the democratic political initiatives. The Rochdale Pioneers came out of such a counter movement in the 1830s. There was a surge of co-operation in the 1880s and 1890s in Europe and the US in the wake of the long depression, and of rural electricity co-operatives in the US in the depression of the 1930s. Standing back we can see that just as there have been long waves of economic prosperity and crisis, so there have been long waves of co-operation.

Now may be a point for the emergence of a new wave of co-operation. The multiple crises of the mainstream economy are unresolved. There are demands for alternatives. The question is how the co-operative movement, representing a new moral economy, can develop its networks so that it is able to grow within the hostile world of the private market.

To answer this question requires two things. First, a close study of the potential economies of co-operation and how successful systems of co-operation have realised such economies. Second, how the potential for distributed production and collaborative consumption opened up by information technology can be used to the advantage of co-operative growth.

Viral co-operation

When the history of co-operation in twenty-first century Britain comes to be written, the remarkable growth of co-operative schools over the past six years may have the same inspirational place as that of the Rochdale pioneers in the mid nineteenth century.

There is the same sense of wildfire growth in them both, of a model that is at the same time visionary and practical, one that is tangibly of the moment. The co-operative movement has from the first highlighted the importance of education. It is the fifth of the seven co-operative principles. The new co-operative schools in England have taken all seven principles and embodied them within the educational process itself. In 1844 the necessities were bread, butter and porridge. Today's necessities in the information age are the values, the capacities of thought and creativity, which are the bread and butter of a school.

The first co-operative school at Reddish Vale – significantly in Greater Manchester, like Rochdale – had no idea that it would be the spark that led to a wildfire. Those who started it did not have a sector strategy, any more than did the first twenty-eight pioneers in Rochdale. What they had were strong values, and a model of how a self-governing school could work. They had a keen sense of unfolding the future. At each stage Reddish Vale and the many schools that followed moved forward along the paths of possibility, establishing new initiatives, as they were needed. Some were within the school and their communities, some with other co-operative schools.[3]

Where might this remarkable contemporary story of co-operation lead? There will certainly be more schools and opportunities for the extension into other spheres of education, particularly for further education colleges (some of which are already partnering with their local co-op schools). But the possibilities go wider.

Education is only one of many relational services. In a relational service the quality of the service depends critically on the relation between the frontline staff (the teacher in the case of a school) and the user (the pupil). It also is shaped by the communities in which each are involved (the home and its communities, other users, and the service professions). Multi-stakeholder co-operatives are proving to be a remarkably effective model of governance for services of this kind.

Social care is a case in point. Health, particularly wellbeing and the care needed for those with chronic disease, is another. There is the remarkable story of social co-operatives in Italy. From a few hundred in 1990 their numbers have grown to 14,000 today. Many of them, like the English schools, are multi-stakeholder co-operatives. They involve the carers, the families of those being cared for, volunteers, and funders. Cities like Bologna now have 80 per cent of their care services organised through co-operatives of this kind.

There are now 120 health co-operatives in Japan, running eighty-one hospitals and 350 health centres. They are rooted in a network of 26,000 small local groups that promote health care and healthy living. Many of them have developed as offshoots of food co-operatives that sprung up in the late 1960s and 1970s in response to a succession of food scandals, and sought to re-establish food as a relational service linking consumers back to local organic producers.

I first learnt about these remarkable food co-ops through fair trade. The Green Co-op in Japan had fostered a project for displaced sugar workers on the island of Negros in the Philippines. The ex-sugar workers formed a co-op to grow bananas which they would ship to the Green Co-op's 300,000 members. The producers visited the local Green Co-op chapters to raise finance, and once the trade was established delegations from the Green Co-ops paid return visits to stay with producers. It was called 'people-to-people trade' rather than fair trade, a reminder that fair trade arose out of projects to reintroduce direct relationships between the small farmer co-ops in the South and consumers in the North. The Japanese and the Italians, with their large consumer co-operative networks independent of supermarkets, have been most successful in maintaining these links.

Food and fair trade are cases where co-ops are demonstrating relational alternatives to mass commodity industries. There are others. In finance, it is the local co-operative banks that spread so rapidly in continental Europe and Canada in the second half of the nineteenth century that still comprise a major part of retail banking in many countries. There was a similar expansion of co-operative renewable energy co-ops in Denmark and Germany over the past twenty-five years, with 750 being created in Germany in the past five years.

The strategic point is that all these are growth sectors. Relational services like health and education are taking an ever-greater proportion of GDP in the post-industrial countries. There is a rising demand for a return to relational services – from banking to tourism.

The overseas examples of co-operative growth, like that of the English schools, reflect these trends and show that co-ops, and in particular multi-stakeholder co-ops, have a structure and culture particularly suited to relational services. In each case they have become major players in their respective sectors. They are evidence that co-operative systems work, and that co-ops as a form of enterprise are not confined to the margins but provide an alternative human-centred model for much of the economy.

That said, the examples of viral growth have been specific to certain countries and regions. The social co-ops have taken root primarily in Italy and Canada. Community banking has been strongest on the continent and is now growing rapidly in the US. By far the largest consumer-farmer food co-ops are in East Asia. The challenge is whether these successful co-operative systems can be replicated in this country. Although the conditions in which they are flourishing are different, are there some lessons we can draw that would contribute to co-operative growth in Britain?

Creative instruction

The first thing to note is that many cases were the result of social movements usually sparked by some crisis or threat. Some were movements of those marginalised by the market – small farmers or tradesmen, ill-housed tenants, those without access to equitable finance. They have been part of Polanyi's counter movement. Others are modern movements that question the trajectory of growth and its impact on wellbeing and the environment.

Second, these co-operatives have grown organically. The idea and the methods of one successful initiative inspire others. There is a distinctive 'co-operative multiplier'. In some cases the multiplier remains informal. But there are many ways it can be actively promoted. In Italy, each new social co-op is helped to its feet by an existing co-op, but on the understanding that once it is up and running it will become the foster parent of a new co-op. They refer to this as the 'strawberry patch' principle.

Third, as the numbers multiply, the system grows in complexity. The cells remain distinct, but they increasingly collaborate. Many establish intermediary support organisations – the Italians refer to them as consortia – to provide market intelligence, or finance, or shared standards, or political advocacy. For the retail societies and village shops, the collaboration is for purchasing. For the milk producer co-ops of Parma, it is for the branding and quality control of their Parmesan cheese. In all cases, the intermediary or second-level co-ops are controlled by the first level. The result is an inversion of the customary pyramid.

Fourth, these co-operative networks have found a way of achieving sufficient economies of scale and specialisation through such networks of collaboration without undermining the quality of relationships that lie at the heart of the co-operative advantage. This balance is critical. The strength of the Goliaths of the mainstream is based on economies of scale, of scope and specialisation. Co-operative collaboration can limit their advantage but cannot hope to match it. Where co-operatives have the edge is in realising to the full the 'economies of co-operation', and these depend critically on maintaining the quality of the relationships as experienced by all those involved.

There is a continuing tension between the two forces. Co-operative history has many cases where the drive for scale and the shift in balance from the local co-ops to the central service providers have led to the weakening of the economies of co-operation and the re-absorption of co-operative enterprises into the mainstream commercial economy. Some have characterised this in terms of an S curve, where a period of rapid co-operative growth comes to a point where the core relationships are lost and degeneration sets in.

The successful ones have resisted re-absorption. Each have fascinating histories of how they mixed and matched so that they hold their own in the market, while maintaining their central ethic and sets of relationships. When their size threatens to create too great a distance from the ordinary members, they split up their organisations rather than consolidate them, or work to reach a consensus of every branch and level. The Desjardins bank in Quebec took ten years to negotiate a consensus balance between the primary, the secondary and in their case the tertiary levels in order to maintain their relational core in the face of liberalised financial markets.

What they have taught us is that co-operatives have to give equal priority to expanding their economies of co-operation as to driving down their costs through scale and specialisation. The care of members, the nurturing of relationships and a deepening of a shared co-operative ethic are not supplementary but the precondition for successful co-operation.

Co-operative sector strategies

Any sector strategy needs to keep the above lessons in mind as it assesses the possibilities for co-operative expansion. The purpose of a sector strategy is for those actively involved in the sector to understand its structures and the contending currents shaping its future in order to inform its own choices and plans. It provides a map for the traveller.

One element of a co-operative strategy will be similar to that of any cluster of small and medium firms (SMEs) – how to find spaces where they can compete against the large firms. Thirty years ago it was still thought that competitivity depended on scale. That remains the case in mass commodity and service industries. But in the post-Fordist era, mass markets have fragmented and new sources of competitivity have opened up. Design, innovation, specialisation, speed of response and service quality have all underpinned the growth of SMEs in this period. So too has the growing significance of ethical and sustainable production.

Most co-operatives sail in these seas. Their position is much like that of other SMEs. They need their distinctiveness and quality. They also need to collaborate with others to provide some services that would be available to a large firm internally. Many of these are to do with information – market research, technical intelligence, sales representation and branding. In Italy and Spain, the consortia to provide these services comprise co-ops and small family firms – such a model of firm-to-firm co-operation is of ever-growing importance today.

The co-operation may be between individual producers, or members of the so-called precariat. In tourism and agriculture, it is collaboration Italian-style. In Wales the traditional farmer-purchasing co-ops have been declining in the face of large-scale private competition. But there are growing number of small farm-to-farm producer co-ops that have been flourishing with their own specialist products, their joint processing and branding.

The message is that co-operation by itself is not enough. Co-operatives on their own or in sectoral collaboration need their specialisations, and their capacities for design and innovation, to succeed in the new competition. This is the material dimension of strategy. It has to run in tandem with the relational strategy. For co-operatives the two are intertwined.

Economies of co-operation

Co-operatives have an added edge in the material field as a result of distinct 'economies of co-operation'. These economies are at the core of the economics of co-operation. They stand in contrast (and often in tension) with economies of scale. They are discussed in terms of the 'co-operative advantage'. But whereas economies of scale are delivered by machines and the systems surrounding them, economies of co-operation depend on people and relationships.

Motivation is one of these economies. Long-term commitment to the co-op is another – particularly significant in the case of workers with key skills. But in an information age it is the nature of 'co-operative intelligence' that has the most far-reaching significance. A collaborative culture encourages the generation and sharing of ideas within co-operatives. It is one of the features of successful workers' co-ops, such as Suma or the scientific instruments co-ops in Wales. But it also applies to the sharing between co-operatives, which gives them a marked potential advantage over private firms, concerned as they are with their patents and confidentiality clauses.

The open-source movement has taken the principle furthest. Two-thirds of the world's software is now based on programs developed by co-operators, working voluntarily and giving away what they have collectively produced. They are not formal co-ops because they don't need formal enterprise structures. But they provide a paradigm for the principle of co-operative working in the information age.

The parallel developments of crowd sourcing, crowd searching, crowd funding and citizen science highlight the advantage co-ops have in accessing the collective intelligence of their members, and of others inspired by the work of the co-operative and sharing its values. The core idea of openness – of sharing information between collaborators who do not abuse that sharing – is the driving idea of the new peer-to-peer movement and feeds into the idea of open co-operation.[4]

It means that eco housing co-operatives share their development knowledge with new projects. The same has happened with mini-hydro schemes, organic farmers and among farmers' markets. In state-funded services it points towards the establishment of public-social partnerships with open accounting and the joint sharing of knowledge for service improvements. Co-operation allows private knowledge to become social.

It also generates trust. The link between information and trust is at the heart of the success of local co-operative banks. The banks are rooted in their localities. Their managers may have been at school with the customers and local businesses. They know each other in a way which the statistical assessments on which large banks depend cannot hope to match. As a result, co-operative banks have consistently had higher loan rates to small and medium businesses, lower default rates and greater resilience in periods of economic crisis.

What distinguishes co-operative sector strategies then is that they are concerned both with material strategies and relational strategies, and how to maximise the collective 'economies of co-operation' among co-operatives. That will also influence the sectors and the spaces in each sector where the co-operative advantage will count for most. The knowledge sectors stand out, as do relational and environmental services. Then there are those sectors, like housing, that have been badly affected by land speculation and where co-operative ownership of the freehold not only secures affordable land but also the future of valued facilities, and shares any gains among members and their communities. All these are sectors where there is that growing gap between the public and the private interest, which co-ops are in a position to bridge.

There is one other economic trend where the moral economy of co-operation gives it a potential advantage. In a growing number of sectors, users/consumers are playing a substantial part in the production of a service. They have become 'producers'. For example, 98 per cent of the care of people with diabetes is provided by themselves and their family and friends rather than the NHS. In some measure this is the case with much chronic disease, of care services more generally, of much education, transport, leisure and personal finance, as well as today's environmental management of the home.

The modern producer requires skills, some tools, but above all s/he requires support. A new support economy is emerging that provides advice, information and help in assembling a customised package of services. The processes reintegrate what are otherwise siloed services around the needs of the user. The support has to be independent with no other interest than that of user, for it is a relationship that depends centrally on trust.

While there are some private firms and social enterprises that are seeking to provide such services, it is consumer and multistakeholder co-ops that have the principles of member needs and trust encrypted in their structures and guiding principles. In some services it is individual packages of support that are required. In others it is packages for members that might not otherwise be available.

The co-operative economy has certain hubs that are well placed to play this role of advice and assembly. The retail societies are one, co-operative GP surgeries another. Some of the co-op schools are beginning to perform this function. This is a field of ever-expanding opportunities as public services are aware that they are constricted by their silos, and the private market and much of the charity sector is experienced as such. Along with other economies of co-operation, these particular opportunities should be on the strategic agenda.

Co-operative innovation

The importance of innovation for the future of co-operation has been a principle theme of this book. It is a further dimension of a co-operative sector strategy. One of the features of successful co-operative economies is that they have institutionalised the capacity to innovate. The Mondragon group of co-ops have their own research and development laboratories to support innovation in their member co-ops. The light industries in Emilia Romagna have established consortia that scour the world for the latest technology on behalf of their members. A visitor to the small furniture workshops of Emilia Romagna will find the latest equipment for producing specialised parts or processes. The ceramic co-operatives of Imola have become European leaders on the back of their innovations in the design, machinery and quality of their tiles.

There are examples of 'hard innovation' in products, services, processes and the formal codes (as against the tacit knowledge) governing those processes. All sectors need to consider how to promote and share such innovations as part of their material strategy. There is no single technological path. Co-ops may develop a distinct one. There is the example of Mydex, the company that designs software so consumers control their own data – a small-data response to the rise of big data. There are similar initiatives in developing patient control of their data in health. These are human-centred paths of innovation that are particularly appropriate to co-operatives.[5]

Material innovations such as these are, however, only one kind of innovation. There are other 'soft' ones. One that recurs is relational innovation – the adoption of a co-operative culture and a structure that reflects that culture. This is the kind of innovation that generates the economies of co-operation. Co-operative schools exemplify the liberation of energy that comes from such a change. The criminal justice proposals carry a similar promise. Fans-owned sports clubs, co-operative wind turbines, village pubs and shops are all examples where the major innovation is a change in the ownership and governance of an enterprise, and the change in culture that goes with it.

A second kind of organisational innovation is that which is at the core of the 'enterprise systems' developed by the viral co-operative networks described earlier. It transforms the twentieth-century model of the corporate pyramid, which was itself a major organisational innovation. The pyramid model was based on the principle of compartmentalisation, that management-like work could be broken down into separate self-contained parts. Each part could operate according to rules established from above and co-ordinated by those at the top. It was a model suitable for mass production, and was developed first for private corporations and then for the state.

Yet it is a model that is quite unsuited to the complexity of modern production. Now the demand is to increase the autonomy of the front line, and break down the silos that have traditionally divided them. If Fordism was about compartmentalisation and centralisation, post-Fordism is about reintegration and decentralisation. The silo walls are being dismantled.

The employee-owned business Ove Arup organises its 10,000 worker-owners on the basis of projects, not organograms. The same happens in IBM, or in film production. Teams are now taking the place of divisions. And organisations are becoming open, involving their workers, their suppliers and their customers in the development of strategy, and the generation of new ideas. Firms that have developed these new ways of working have been outcompeting those still bound to the twentieth-century pyramids.[6] It has been one of the primary innovations of the past forty years.

The successful co-operative systems have been pioneers of this new latticed model. They combine autonomy of the parts with integration of the whole. Their threads of connection are lateral. Common service consortia are controlled by their members. Information is open and shared. The critical binding is one of a shared ethic.

One of the most remarkable examples is the Japanese Seikatsu co-op with 350,000 members. Their basic cell is the *han* of six to ten households that are organised into nineteen districts which, although they are independent, collaborate in the sharing of knowledge and political advocacy nationally. The result is an enterprise system of great complexity. The autonomy of the parts means that each has been able to control its own operations and their direction of development (including what new products to develop, who should produce them, and how quality is controlled and improved). It has also meant that they have been able to use their resources as springboards into other services. Seikatsu means 'life' and the co-op, like other similar networks in the country, has diversified into those fields which their members see as necessary for a good life.

Organisations of this kind are not blueprints that can be simply transferred and copied. They face continuous changes in technologies, the wider society and the needs of their members to which they must always be ready to respond. They are in this sense open systems, and how to develop them needs to be part of the relational strategies in any sector.

The spread of the internet is introducing further changes in open organisational models. Web-based technology is opening up new ways for consumers to combine. There are the peer-to-peer sharing sites that have mushroomed over the past few years. There is the case of collaborative purchasing of insurance, and of crowd funding future services in advance. These examples point to the potential for new types of co-operative enterprise system in which the co-operative is responsible for a platform that promotes informal collaboration.

Finally, there is innovation in how complexes of production are organised – so-called 'productive systems'. Community food has developed as a counter movement to industrialised food. It emphasises the centrality of healthy and nutritious food (and how it is produced and shared) to health and wellbeing. It has promoted local and organic production, and connected directly to consumers through box schemes and farmers' markets. In the more developed systems, it has led to co-operative processing industries, 'closed loop' composting, distributed technologies and community food preparation and eating. In parts of Japan, this system has outcompeted conventional supermarkets and intensive farming.

Similarly, the emerging system of distributed renewable energy plants has led to the development of technology for energy storage and smart grids, and for new methods of reducing the need for energy in the home, in transport and in industry. This is a quite different model to that of capital- and carbon-intensive centralised electricity systems that developed in the twentieth century. As with community food, co-operative and local ownership is a central feature of the new renewable energy system. It confronts the giants on the path of all such transitions – from technology and finance, to the large corporations and regulatory regimes of the old systems.

What emerges from this discussion is that co-operative innovation is many sided: from the generation of new co-ops with the cultures that encourage 'economies of co-operation' to the establishment of the outlines of new systems of production. The soft relational streams run alongside the material ones, each with a distinctive character in co-ops. In each case the strategies for innovation are often best pursued by co-ops in collaboration as part of a wider sector strategy. The sixth principle, of co-operation between co-operatives, is the guiding one for an innovation-driven co-operative sector strategy.

Next steps

This book is the launch of such a process. The chapters provide a first sketch for those engaged in the sector to develop. The process should be open and involve those researchers with knowledge of the sector, as well as co-operative practitioners from overseas. The value of this book goes further. Because it looks at fifteen sectors together, it identifies the opportunities for cross-sectoral collaboration. It moves beyond the sectoral boundaries to connect the threads of a wider co-operative system.

For the kind of growth we have witnessed in co-operative schools, much will depend on changes in the policy envelope within which each sector is operating. What is clear is that national policy and the regulatory system in every sector – whether it be agriculture, energy, planning, housing, health or banking – can be more or less friendly to co-operative development. To date it has largely been less. Trentino and the other co-operative regions in Italy, with their 'co-operative effect', show what can happen if it is more.

Notes

1 Thomas Piketty, *Capital in the Twenty-First Century*, Cambridge, MA: Harvard University Press, 2014.
2 Jeremy Rifkin, *The Zero Marginal Cost Society*, New York: St Martin's Press, 2014.
3 It took nearly twenty years for the early retail societies to establish the Co-operative Wholesale Society (CWS) in 1863 to purchase collaboratively. The first fifteen co-operative schools set up their CWS – the Schools Co-operative Society or SCS – in three. Like the CWS, the SCS is a source of advice and support and acts as a 'lifeboat' for any member in difficulty.
4 For the extent and richness of the new peer-to-peer economy see the website of the P2P Foundation: http://p2pfoundation.net/
5 These examples bring out the point that material innovations are not solely technical. They embody and shape relationships in both production and use. There is a strong current of work on human-centred technology which looks at skilled work as life to be enhanced by tools and machines rather than replaced by them. For a recent introduction to the literature and applications to the practice of technological innovation, see Adrian Smith, 'Technology networks for socially useful production', *Journal of Peer Production*, Issue 5, October 2014. An influential early text was by Mike Cooley, *Architect or Bee*, London: Hogarth Press, 1987. The social perspective of technology has a close fit with the idea of co-operative innovation.
6 For a detailed comparison of the two, see Ted Piepenbrock's 'Toward a theory of the evolution of business ecosystems: Enterprise architectures, competitive dynamics, firm performance & industrial co-evolution', MIT thesis, 2009.

Platform Economy

12

Post-post-Fordism in the era of platforms: Robin Murray talks to Jeremy Gilbert and Andrew Goffey

This interview appeared in the journal New Formations, *Issue 84-85, Winter 2014-Summer 2015, pp5-19. Available online at https://www. lwbooks.co.uk/new-formations/84-85*

Introduction

This issue of *New Formations* is concerned with a complex of issues around the politics of networks, 'control' and 'security' societies as defined by Deleuze and Foucault respectively, and post-Fordism. In fact Maurizio Lazzarato, for one, has explicitly linked the latter two phenomena, understanding post-Fordism as more or less the direct consequence of new techniques of power and governance as described by Foucault, being deployed in the context of processes of capitalist production.

Today the 'post-Fordist' hypothesis seems more or less irrefutable. While some of the key features of 'Fordist' capitalism – such as assembly-line production – remain central to global manufacturing (above all in China), they are no longer bundled with the other key features of 'Fordism', such as a strict gendered division of labour and a macro-economic policy committed to maintaining high aggregate demand within the same nation state in which production is concentrated. Industrial automation, market differentiation, corporate disaggregation, labour market specialisation, just-in-time production and the expansion of the retail, IT and service sectors have transformed economies beyond recognition, not just in the old industrial heartlands of Northern Europe and North America, but in differentiated ways on a global scale. What's more, these changes have been bound up with profound cultural, social and political changes, as commentators such as David Harvey were already discerning at the end of the 1980s. It is worth bearing in mind, then, that when the hypothesis was first advanced at the end of the 1970s, the idea that such changes would have any significant results at all was widely regarded as controversial, and was much resisted.

Robin Murray has been one of the UK's leading radical economists for many years. An expert on co-operatives, social enterprise and institutional and technological innovation, he was Director of Industry for the Greater London Council during the 1980s. This was the period during which the GLC, led by Ken Livingstone, was enacting one of the most radical progressive programmes of any major governmental body in British history. Directly influenced by this experience, Murray wrote two celebrated articles for the British monthly *Marxism Today* on the subject of emergent 'post-Fordism' in the second half of the 1980s. These two essays 'Life After Henry' and 'Benetton Britain' were key in introducing the concept of post-Fordism to the wider left in the UK. New Labour would later take up the idea of post-Fordism as dictating a narrowly individualist culture and an approach to economic management and public-service reform which was wholly informed by neoliberal ideology. But this was never Murray's conclusion. Instead he has argued consistently that the new technological and organisational forms of contemporary production are adaptable to classic democratic socialist objectives, and facilitate collaborative creativity, democratic self-management and co-operative production. In this interview Andrew Goffey and Jeremy Gilbert discuss these issues with Robin Murray.

Post-Fordism in practice

Jeremy I was hoping that initially you could say a bit about the idea of post-Fordism, and its reception in this country, because you were one of the first people writing about it, at least in a context that was widely read.

Robin Well, for me, it originated in our experience at the GLC, not from any writing. Throughout the 1970s, and right up until the drafting of Labour's London Manifesto for the 1981 municipal elections, the predominant economic paradigm was Fordism: left economic industrial strategy was based on the idea of scale and rationalisation. The critique of industrial Britain across the political spectrum was that it was backward. It had too many old family firms, who under-invested and weren't good at managing. What was needed was to modernise them, by encouraging amalgamations, increasing investment and appointing professional managers. That approach underpinned industrial policy in the 1960s, but it was then given a 'leftward flip' in the 1970s, when Tony Benn (a key figure of the Labour left in the 1970s and 1980s) took it up, with the idea of marrying these modern 'forces of production', with greater democratic control. He, and the left of the labour movement more generally, had been much influenced by the Institute of Worker's Control, which was formed in the mid-1960s and remained strong until the mid-1980s.

The GLC's manifesto in 1981 was in part drafted by Stuart Holland, who had been influential in shaping Labour's Alternative Economic Strategy in the 1970s; and the GLC Manifesto reflected this established 'Left Programme', but at the level of London. So the GLC was to have a public investment bank, it was to promote enterprise planning and co-operatives, and develop plans and strategies for the London economy as a whole. Our little unit was established with the task of setting up and running all this.

This was at a time when many companies in London were being undermined because of Thatcher's policy on the exchange rate. London had nearly half a million unemployed. All the way up the Lea Valley companies were falling like ninepins. On our very first day I remember being called into his office by the Industry and Employment chair, who told us about the owner of a furniture factory who had come in to see him and was desperate. Could we save them? And this man was just the first of many others. Once our new bank (the Greater London Enterprise Board) was established, our idea was to rescue such companies from the receiver, amalgamate them, and do all the things we were expected to do under the left Fordist model.

One of the companies we rescued was a firm in East London that made workwear and was one of the last surviving clothing firms of any significance in the area. We took it over, installed new machinery, appointed a new and well-qualified woman to run it, and introduced public ownership and workers planning. That was the recipe.

One day, a member of our unit, who was chair of the Board of this municipal company rang me and said, 'Listen, the company is a bit short of markets, and I see that there's a GLC contract out for different kinds of work-wear. I'm going to really pare the price down so we get the work. Can you speak to the Supplies Department?'. Well, there are strict laws on municipal purchasing. But generally, in this kind of situation, if you come within two or three per cent of the lowest offer a council can accept the tender on the basis of a variety of wider social and economic reasons. So I spoke to the head of the GLC supplies department about this, and when the tenders were in he rang me back. 'We've had thirty tenders', he said. 'Yours was number 3'. 'And the difference between our bid and the lowest?' 'Let me just have a look', he said. 'The best bid is 34 per cent cheaper'. We thought this must be based on clothes made in China just being badged, but when we investigated we found out that the winning tender wasn't from China, but it was from a firm in the UK called Alexandra Workwear, in Glasgow. Alexandra Workwear used computer-aided design. They could embroider a little badge saying GLC Fire Brigade, or GLC Road Sweepers, at a negligible cost. They had a warehouse in Bristol, produced just-in-time, and therefore had very low stocks. It was a better product at two thirds of the cost.

At the same time, another member of our unit, Michael Best, was meeting similar challenges in furniture. We'd amalgamated three big furniture factories, and yet were still up against major competitive pressure from Italy so Michael went over to find out about Italian production. If our new London factory had about 3000 workers, we thought the Italian companies must have 10,000. Michael went first to Poggibonzi, a Tuscan town that was one of the centres of Italian furniture-making. He found that the largest firm had 45 workers, not 10,000. But there were 85 other furniture firms in the town, each specialised and interconnected, so that together they more than matched the size of our three factories.

In Italy, Michael met a Harvard researcher, Chuck Sabel, who was writing a book that came out soon afterwards called *The Second Industrial Divide*. The argument of the book was that what Sabel called 'flexible specialisation' – such as was happening in Poggibonzi – was the way forward for competitive manufacturing. Michael invited Sabel to come over to the GLC, and we spent two days with him at the bank, as he outlined a completely different model of production, one that we found difficult to take in. Evidently the Communist Party in government in Emilia Romagna were the promoters of this flexible, small–firm approach – which we had at first seen as a form of Thatcherism.

Chuck Sabel's book was transformative for us. It gave numerous examples of the success of this model, from food and engineering to airlines. Instead of pushing its products or services onto a mass market, it was flexible enough to respond to increasingly differentiated demand. Sabel helped us to re-read our own experience in London's industries, and see how the model he described was driving many of the old mass-production firms into the low-margin, 'commodity' sectors of the market.

The first piece I wrote on it was in 1985, and it was called 'Benetton Britain' – because of course Benetton was one of the companies that had grown suddenly out of the small local Italian milieu of the Veneto to become a big operation. At that time, it was emblematic of the changes.

The origins of Post-Fordism

Jeremy So what was the key driver behind the shift into this new paradigm – was it the new technology? Or new types of competition? Was it broader social changes? Is that something you've got a view on?

Robin What is fascinating is that '68 – we'll use that as a shorthand – seemed to come 'independently': the new subjectivity just 'burst up'. How do we understand that? In part I see it as a reaction, or countermovement, to Fordism, both amongst manual workers and then amongst the 'cognitive workers' of various kinds; they were finding the very same structures that they were resisting at work in many of the other institutions they experienced. This was reflected in the institutional critiques of writers like Marcuse, Illich, and Schumacher.

But there were also other changes happening at this time. And because information technology and information more generally, is central to this story, we should go back to look at what was happening in production. In manufacturing the early movers were Toyota and its chief engineer Taiichi Ohno. Ohno was really the Henry Ford of this new phase. He and his colleagues had gone to look at an American supermarket and saw the potential of applying the same retailing principles to cars. With hindsight, we can see that it was supermarkets who were the pioneers of the new systems.

The reason for this is that retailers had to handle a great variety of goods (even in the smaller shops), many of them perishable. Their goods came from a multitude of suppliers and were sold to a multitude of customers, each with their own individualised shopping basket. Faced with such complexity, the supermarkets had a great need for information. The first commercial computer developed in this country, the LEO, was produced in 1951 by J. Lyons & Co in order to monitor its Swiss rolls. Lyons spun off the computer operation into a separate company in 1954, and finally sold it to International Computers Limited (ICL) in 1962.

In the UK retail trade, the Co-op had been easily the most dominant retailer in the later nineteenth and first half of the twentieth centuries. The first supermarket was introduced by the Co-op in London during the Second World War, and that supermarket model of 'self-help' by the customer had spread. Sainsbury's had started in 1867 and Tesco in the 1920s. But their growth had been limited because they couldn't run themselves on a national level in the same way as the Co-op, which was a decentralised distributed system whose parts were linked in all sorts of ways: it actually rather modern, without the modern technology.

In the 1950s, however, the Co-op was slow to adopt the emergent information systems, whereas Sainsbury's and Tesco began to gradually expand their range. And this was when, what are now the two largest retailers in the world, started. Walmart was established in 1962, and the French Carrefour in 1963. They rose on the back of these new systems. Once they had good information technology, they went worldwide, and today each of them has over 10,000 branches, and handles over 100,000 different products. This is an extraordinarily complex system, with all these suppliers and logistics, and its organisation is a remarkable technical feat, one that is impossible to think of without IT.

So, as you can imagine, when Ohno saw this new system he thought 'now, how can we do it for cars?'. He spent the next thirty years studying in detail how the flow of products to and through a supermarket could be applied to the flow of materials to and through a car factory. And in so doing he upended Taylorism, because he realised that you couldn't have all of the information centralised and concentrated in management. He saw that you had to have the frontline workers analysing and adjusting the things they knew about. The moment you go into one of these Japanese factories, you can see (and not just in Toyota) real-time information displayed everywhere. It is often handwritten – for example, the number of parts done in an hour – it isn't computerised at all at the beginning, because they want to start with the human: Toyota never jumped first to technology.

For Toyota, one of the big statistics that limited the potential extent of flexible production was change-over times, particularly for presses. Ford's first change-over, in 1927, took nine months and he nearly went bust, because he had to manufacture a whole new bank of bespoke machines. For the presses that shaped the car bodies in the Ford factory, the changeover time was about fourteen hours as late as the 1980s. Toyota, when I visited them in Japan in the late 1980s, had got it down to 4 minutes. That is a revolution. They did it by focused concentration by teams of workers, figuring out what the holdups were at different points in the process.

A fascinating footnote is this: the Formula One racing car company McLaren, has set up a number of subsidiaries, and a consulting company, that take their methods to other industries. So, for example, when a toothpaste manufacturer was having trouble, McLaren consultants analysed it in exactly the same way as they would their racing car; and they found that the toothpaste could be produced at much less cost with a greater flow in production. It's all about *flow*, from single product to multiproduct flow.

That's the heart of it. Why Formula One? Because it's the most intense form of competition – racing every two weeks in the season, with innovation between each race: this is where 'just in time' and 'flow' becomes the key aspect of the whole thing. McLaren is now the third largest conglomerate in the UK. It is fascinating to see the principles that the supermarkets and Ohno developed spreading into every pore of capitalist production.

Jeremy So it seems from all this that there's a kind of convergence historically, between, on the one hand, the revolt against Fordist discipline and, on the other hand, the superseding of some of the limits of Fordist production in consumer retail and industrial production; and there's also a history of a network of organisations which you've traced back through the history of the Co-op. There's a convergence of these different processes in that they are all technologically accelerated by the IT revolution.

So, one of the things that's really striking now, for me at least, is that when I read 'Benetton Britain', probably just a few years after you wrote it, it was still very contentious across the wider left to say that this was the shape of the future, that this was how the entire capitalist economy was going to be restructured and that the culture was going to be restructured along with it. So were you conscious of this at the time, that what you were saying was controversial?

Robin Well what was interesting about the GLC was that our unit, which expanded because of its role as a kind of 'wedge' within traditional bureaucracy, did contain just about every group there was on the left, many of whom had strong political identities. But one of the things that working in the unit brought home to me was that, whereas if you're an intellectual, you distinguish yourself by difference – by developing a position in argument that forms your intellectual identity – the moment you get into production, you've got to cooperate. You can discuss strategy and what you're going to produce but the demands of practice means you have to collaborate. In the unit everyone had their own tasks, but on the whole the Communist Party people and the members of a whole range of Trotskyist groups lived and let live. Everyone was focused on their projects and trying to understand the nature of territory we found ourselves working in. My writing was merely a contribution towards this process of reflection, and by and large was received as such.

One thing that became clear from that period was that you cannot mix Fordism with democracy. It seems so obvious now, but it wasn't to us then. There were so many attempts on the left to democratise Fordist institutions. It was the project of the Institute for Workers Control, and of many in the co-operative movement. But in a large Taylorised factory how can you have substantive democracy, when the whole project depends on stripping workers of any autonomy? Democracy in a Ford factory was about resisting, on the shop floor, the management's attempt to treat manual workers as cogs in a machine. It was not about developing enterprise plans while the front-line war of production was raging. Similarly with co-ops. Once you've got a big co-op which has become Fordist in its structure and its production processes, the attempt to have democracy within it is delusory. Democracy has to start with the labour process, whether that is an assembly line or the running of a shop.

So, in terms of attacks, I was aware that people were producing critiques, but for me it felt as if we were trying to create something new in the space that was opened up by these systemic and technological changes.

Jeremy So to what extent were you influenced by the wider movement for workers' self-management and the experience of self-management in Yugoslavia – was that one of your reference points?

Robin Oh yes. One of the unit's original members was Mike Cooley, formerly a designer and chair of the technical union TASS at Lucas Aerospace. Mike had led the celebrated campaign to resist closures and instead convert Lucas's military plants to the production of socially useful products. After a long struggle, the Lucas management managed to dismiss him for spending too much time on union business and 'concerns of society as a whole', but the Lucas Plan produced at the time by the workers, and the campaign around it, had great influence. Hilary Wainwright, another of the original unit members, had worked with the Lucas stewards on the Lucas plan, and later with the Vickers shop stewards on Tyneside to produce a similar plan. I had written about the Yugoslav experience for the Institute for Workers Control as part of the campaign around the occupation of Upper Clyde Shipbuilders, in the early 1970s. This wider movement underpinned the GLC Manifesto commitment for workers' self-management and enterprise plans. Hilary's section in the GLC was called the Popular Planning Unit, and many of its eventual thirty-five members had been shop stewards and involved in various kinds of struggles for economic democracy.

But you will notice that the industries at the centre of the workers control movement – such as the shipyards and military factories – were not Fordist. Indeed, the problems at Upper Clyde were the result of Japan having applied Fordist principles to shipbuilding while the UK industry remained centred around bespoke ships produced by highly skilled workers. Workers' self-management was a quite different matter in these industries. Conditions there differed vastly from those in the mass production factories that had been the basis for the growth in London since the 1930s.

Jeremy How did the changes you were experiencing get reflected in your strategy?

Robin The GLC Manifesto proposed that the new unit should first produce an Industrial Strategy, and then put it into practice. Our suggestion, once we started up, was that we would first engage with the crisis facing London's economy, and then develop a set of reflective papers as we went along, gathering them together as a strategy informed by experience and not just by data and documents. As a result, the London Industrial Strategy we produced in 1985, covered not only some of the productive changes in manufacturing I have mentioned, but also industries that we could see were to play a major role in the next phase of London's economic growth, such as the information and knowledge sector, health, and many branches of what have come to be known as the cultural industries. These emerging sectors reflected many of the features of post-Fordist production.

A number of issues in these sectors provoked significant internal debate within the unit – for example whether to focus on pressurising the BBC to pay more attention to black music and musicians, or instead, on supporting the multiple initiatives of small producers. Or whether to save NHS hospitals under threat from Thatcher, as against supporting numerous community health initiatives that addressed particular conditions When I now re-read the 1985 London Industrial Strategy, what is most striking is the central role that labour had in our thinking. We called the whole model 'Restructuring for Labour'. It was reflective of the 1970s, and the influence of the strong economic productionism of that period.

One interesting case that signalled the turn that took place after 1985 was in the food industry where our initial focus had largely been on saving food-producing factories. When we interviewed for a new unit member in this sector, one of the applicants clearly came from the countryside. He didn't quite have corn in his hair, but that was the impression he gave. He turned out to have been a farmer who had been living in Spain. His name was Robin Jenkins and he had written a book on his struggles there over land. He started the interview by saying 'I think you've got it all wrong. It's not "labour", it's consumers who will force change'. And he outlined a Ricardian position about the way the earth was being exhausted ... This was not at all in tune with the approach we had been taking, but his commitment and vitality meant that we immediately appointed him. As soon as he joined the unit he began to organise, around school meals, and the grassroots food initiatives that were emerging. And, thanks to him, we managed to set up the London Food Commission in 1985, before the guillotine came down (when the GLC was abolished by Thatcher's government in 1986). Robin appointed Tim Lang, a former hill farmer, to run it. Within three or four years the Commission's work had led to at least four major food scares and the resignation of a cabinet minister and had changed the tempo of the whole food movement. Sainsbury's and other supermarkets were some of the first to respond to this, and Tim became something of a food celebrity.

I give you this as an example of a change from a focus on labour as the only subject of social processes, and as the only set of interests the left wanted to defend, towards a realisation that radical politics had to have a wider compass – and a recognition as legitimate and important of the various social movements in a whole number of fields which were not worker-based.

At the same time, things like the International Workers Committee (IWC) were losing ground as Thatcher's economic policies were decimating the unions. Some people characterise the change as a re-orientation from production to consumption, but I think this is too narrow and reflects only one side of the change. In production what we were seeing was a shift from 'Fordist push-through' to 'post-Fordist pull-through' centred around the user. And the more you could disaggregate the user, identify them, first by forecasting their behaviours and then in real-time (and all of the technological innovations were helping with this), the closer you could get to genuine mass-customisation. That was only the first change, but it underlay what in those days we called 'post-Fordism'.

Post-Fordist pessimism and neo-Fordist hopes

Jeremy That's really useful, because I think that speaks to the next thing I wanted to ask you about, which is the shift from pessimism to optimism in the understanding of the implications of these changes. The very early literature on post-Fordism seems to be from a left perspective that is very optimistic about what this all might mean for workers insofar as it might seem to resonate with the objectives of worker self-management etc. On the other hand, the situation more recently, since the 1990s, has been one in which a much more pessimistic account prevails of what this means for the workforce. The consequences are often seen as quite negative, ultimately resulting in precaritisation. In fact those two different aspects seem to be connected in some way insofar as the shift towards the empowerment of people as consumers matches up with a situation in which there is a difficulty in workers being able to exercise any degree of agency *qua* workers.

Robin Well, I'm not sure if this entirely answers the question, but one of the things that was being enabled by this new technology was the unbundling of the corporation with the growth of subcontracting. The state's version was privatisation, but, as we know, it had also been happening in firms. I'd become aware of this when I was working at the Institute of Development Studies at Sussex

University, because in the post-colonial period the big multinationals had begun to do this in primary production. It was their way of somehow finding a new mode of control: moving from the disciplinary period in which populations were directly governed to establishing control through contracts and their domination of technology and markets. Maureen Mackintosh, one of our colleagues at the GLC, had undertaken detailed studies in Senegal of this movement to nominally independent smallholders in the late 1960s early 1970s. For the firms it was a way of resisting the danger of unionisation in the period after colonial independence.

From the 1980s there was a similar pressure for corporations to 'slim down', and for the Fordist operations to move to the periphery. There had always been 'peripheral Fordism' – the kind of 'fag-ends' of Fordism that had marked much of the import substitution industrialisation of post-war Latin America and parts of Asia. But these formerly peripheral locations then became, contrary to our expectations, the great centres of global Fordism. In the 1980s and 1990s, once production processes could be codified, they could be moved East and South – both in manufacturing and then services, leaving stripped-down corporations with their strategic, research, design and financial functions in the core countries.

So it wasn't that Fordism had disappeared, but it had been removed as the dominant paradigm in the North. It was exported under various headings as 'development prospects' for the South, creating a new proletariat, with all that that implies.

I don't know if you can really talk about 'optimism' in these circumstances, but we can say that there's no way the Chinese will be able to resist the rise of a labour movement, when they have as many as 40,000 workers in a single factory.

What does this mean for the workers who remain in the old 'centre'? Well, when you have the proliferation of products and the transformation of processes that results from the IT revolution, there is intense pressure to innovate. That's why all management schools (and national industrial strategies) put so much emphasis on innovation. You can no longer freeze products and processes as Henry Ford had to do after producing the Model T in 1908.

What we have to ask is: 'what kind of innovation?' Some of that innovation is in processes and products; but a great deal is in the cultural sphere, and in what we might call the 'attention economy'. In many consumer industries, marketing in its widest sense has become the majority of company spending.

It was always significant in the Fordism era, but at that time it was 'mass' culture, a kind of battle for mass attention in which the brand was central. Now I am not so sure. I wonder whether the brand is not a mark of Fordism, and whether we're moving beyond the traditional brand, which is after all merely a summary form of information. It's very condensed. It's information-thin and association-heavy. Now the internet is blowing open the mass brand and putting it on the defensive. A fault in a Toyota, or a food poisoning from a Master Chef, becomes news worldwide. McDonalds takes the offensive and sues, but McLibel becomes the costliest marketing mistake in mass brand history.

The proliferation of products, together with the internet, means that there is so much more granular information that consumers can take in and choose from. It can be discussed and ranked. As with physical products, the consumer becomes part of the production process of marketing. They are canvassed, asked for feedback, and for ideas. Firms target opinion makers, and 'lead' consumers. They pursue strategies of 'viral marketing'. The company brands start to fragment. Rather than disappear, we see each product becoming its own brand, above all new products promoted and targeted through the internet. Of the estimated $600 billion global spend on advertising in 2015 (itself only a part of total marketing expenditure), one third will be shortly be digital, and one quarter will be focused on mobile phones alone. This is a new world of post-Fordist consumer culture.

The result is an uninterrupted growth in the numbers of people working as cultural producers – market researchers, designers, writers, film makers, ethnographers, advertisers, musicians and web-makers. Alongside them are the systems managers – such as financiers, accountants, and lawyers – and the researchers and developers. Some of this growing workforce of immaterial labour is employed directly by the large corporations. But many are independent and become brands in themselves. As one web designer put it, every font, every statement, every CV, a freelancer puts on their website has to be seen as part of an integrated personal brand.

Guy Standing sees these freelancers as an important part of a growing 'precariat'. I take the same approach as André Gorz. Cognitive labour is now central to all of these immaterial processes; and the fact that one condition of effective production is now cognitive labour produces various openings and paradoxes. The year I spent at the design council, working with designers, suggested a tension at the heart of this form of work. In one sense the means of production have been internalised within labour and cannot be entirely appropriated *from* labour. Capital is always trying to codify this knowledge, but there are always things that cannot be codified. In an era of continuous innovation, there are limits to automating the immaterial in order to deskill cognitive labour. Capital has to readjust to this, find a new accommodation with its cognitive labour.

Young designers will look at a project or company and say to themselves, 'I'd like to go and work with them. They're an interesting group. I will learn there and make interesting contacts. I will accumulate knowledge and experience within myself which I can then use in various ways and return to the market'. Employers have to take this on board. They can't just offer the Taylorist deal of higher pay for less skilled work. So you get firms like Innocent who make a work-life pitch. When I passed the Innocent head office the other day, you can see the workers there playing table tennis and sitting on sofas – a kind of Google lifestyle – and this is Innocent's attempt to create a place that is more like home than a workplace. I think that is a decisive shift.

Jeremy I think that formulation you offered there is very useful, about the problem posed for capital by the fact that some of what it needs remains, as you say, 'inside' labour. For me the implication is partly that what has to be developed under these conditions of cognitive and communicative capitalism is a set of potentialities which capitalism requires labour to develop, but which can't be fully expropriated to the extent that they could under the industrial model. But capital is always looking for ways to expropriate it fully.

Andrew I think that's one of the issues about languages. Language is a really big area for people developing computer software – how to extract patterns of information from natural language: you see it in healthcare for example. I think that chimes very much with what you're saying, about these forms of tacit knowledge that workers possess, which are something that is shared through language. I wonder if there aren't processes of codification and extraction potentially within software that are really trying to address that problem.

Jeremy This is the argument about automation isn't it – that we're about to see this massive wave of automation of various tasks, like accountancy, low level legal work etc.

Andrew Well a lot of that stuff is already outsourced.

Robin I think this whole area is one of the key practices for capital now. It is a central part of the infrastructure of business: the means of control. Information systems are central here. If these can be codified and privatised, it is possible to set parameters for labour throughout the system. You can see their importance in the developments in education, with the growth of private chains that are taking over school after school. The school becomes merely a branch office for those controlling the back-office systems. The same is happening in social care. The progressive alternatives have focused on the 'front office' part of these systems, not on the back office and systemic control elements.

Having said that, not all can be codified. In many industries there is a constant interplay between creativity and codification. I recently read a study of a Danish firm called Unimerco. It was a machine tools company, the kind that has been undercut by China and the Far East, since producers there can now copy any machine tool automatically using 3D printing and make it more cheaply. Faced with this challenge, Unimerco converted themselves from machine production to servicing. They found that their advantage was that they were close to their manufacturing customers, they know them, they know the kind of equipment that they want, they are on hand to sort out glitches, they can anticipate along with the customer what the next move in the industry will be. Unimerco's role became that of being on top of the global development in machine tools. This is an informational function. So they went to the world trade fairs, brought back the intelligence and said to customers: 'This is where it's happening; we could develop it like this; we needn't do it ourselves, we could actually get the Chinese version and then customise it for you'. What they recognised explicitly is that they were, at their core, a firm of cognitive labour, in which there is a constant process of development. They always looked to see if knowledge could be codified, yet always knew that you had to have tacit knowledge to apply and customise the codification. That tacit knowledge might itself be codified. But that too needs further tacit knowledge. And so on. It was a constant movement of codification plus the tacit, never the eradication of the tacit. The moment you lose the tacit, the living labour, the codification atrophies.

Jeremy So are there implications of that for forms of social and political organisation?

Robin Yes. Unimerco issued shares to workers in the firm. I visited a similar company, an Italian workers co-op, in ceramic machinery. They too had become a service organisation – the Chinese couldn't do it because they couldn't speak or relate to the customer. We were taken into the 'boardroom' where the members of the co-op would go, every month, to hear from the management whom the workers had appointed, how it was going. I asked them 'How many members are in the co-op?'. They replied: 'we've got 175 members out of about 1,200 in the workforce'. The members have to be between twenty-five and forty years old. They buy their way in, and then can cash in when they leave. When I asked: 'Are these skilled workers?' the reply was that they were. And this made me realise that the co-operative structure was a way of locking the skilled worker and their knowledge into the firm. It allowed the co-op to develop a sustained body of skilled and experienced workers, which had made it the leading ceramic machine maker in Europe. 'What about management, are they members?' I asked. They answered without pausing: 'Oh no, our current managing director's forty-five and so he can't be a member, and anyway sometimes we like to sack our MDs – we sacked the last one.'

I found a similar thing when I was a member of the Welsh Co-operative Commission last year. In Wales one of the places where there had been an expansion of co-ops was in instrument companies, high tech ones, which mostly employed cognitive labour. We met with four of these new co-ops. Each had been started as a private venture, but when it had come to the founder's retirement the children hadn't wanted to take over, and had said 'let the workers buy you out and we'll take the money'. These firms then turned into worker co-ops. The people running them were peers. They sounded more like people in university departments in the old days, except the professors would have been elected. That, I think, is one way in which this shift towards immaterial labour will be reflected.

Jeremy Do you mean a generic rise in co-ops, or in different forms of management?

Robin Not necessarily strict co-ops. It can be different forms of mutuality. Workers like this want some engagement, some involvement, some stake in the thing, which is reflected in start-up companies, when people are given an equity stake. So it needn't be a cooperative stake, but it is a sense of stake.

The era of the platforms: post-post-Fordism

Jeremy And in terms of periodisation, are we still in the post-Fordist moment?

Robin No, we've gone to post-post-Fordism.

Jeremy And what's the difference between post-Fordism and post-post-Fordism?

Robin Well post-Fordism was about the production process, and its transformation: the sudden switch in gravity and magnetism, from the push to the pull; and the various subjective changes that went with that. The new subjectivity and the new post-Fordist production started dancing together, each finding interesting aspects of the other and sometimes crossing over.

So we saw the emergence of the consumer as producer as a developing feature of post-Fordism. There has been a growth in the DIY economy. With some products the parts are assembled by the consumer according to the design of the manufacturer (as with flat pack furniture or with standard Lego); or they are assembled by the manufacturer according to the choice of the consumer (as with Dell computers;) or assembled by the 'produser' according to the design of the produser (as with advanced versions of Lego). Toyota even applied these self-design principles to housing.

What has now grown out of this is the era of platforms. The decisive date was 2003. This is when Silicon Valley realised that they had to move from content to platforms. Just as traditional money has no concern with the content of the commodities whose exchange it enables, so platforms present themselves as innocent of content. They enable others to share content (Google) or exchange content (eBay and Amazon), or simply communicate (Facebook and LinkedIn).

As it has turned out the new platforms are far from innocent of content, but they relate to content in a different way. They may not have to produce content. That can be delegated to others, like a modern version of the putting-out system. But they have great interest in the substance of the content and the identity of those who are using the platform. Because it is that kind of information which for many of them is their main source of revenue. EBay and Amazon may take a cut from the exchanges they enable. But Google and Facebook make their money as intermediaries for the advertising industry. They have become core suppliers and hosts to the attention economy.

In this they are similar to many modern forms of money. Credit cards act not only as mediums of exchange and sources of credit, but also as sources of laser information: about who is exchanging and what is exchanged. It as if all our coins no longer simply carry the queen's head on them: they also have a microchip within them, one that can watch our every transaction.

That is the capacity of a platform, and, just as the informational role of money has led to the proliferation of currencies (in such forms as store cards, loyalty cards and air-miles), each of which is an enclosure of information for the use of competition in the attention economy, so platforms too are specialised, but they hold within them the hunger to extend. It is no accident that Amazon has moved into banking functions offering national and international payments systems, and in 2013 introduced its own currency, Amazon Coins.

For post-post-Fordist capital, it is less the control of bounded systems that is important, but the control of platforms and their information in distributed populations.

What are the implications of this new phase? What has it done to social relations, to forms of exploitation and the accumulation of capital, and to the possibilities of resistance to and autonomy from capital? Michel Bauwens, an inspiring lead theorist and promotor of the new commons movement, frames the issue in terms of value. He sees users of the platforms as creators of value, part of which is appropriated by the owners of the platforms. For this reason he refers to Google and Facebook as 'netarchical capital'.

My feeling, however, is that it is not about value in a Marxist sense, nor about the exploitation of labour. Platforms are a new kind of economy, in which you can talk about labour, but it isn't labour in the sense that we once conceived it, nor is the relationship between user and platform that of capital and labour. The time I spend in looking something up on Google is not creating value from which Google takes a cut. Google makes its money, like a bank or a merchant, from taking a slice out of the value embodied in the commodities or services which I might buy as a result of seeing the sales pitches from companies in the 'real economy'.

Michel Bauwens proposes another category of appropriating capital, which he calls 'anarcho-capitalists', as exemplified in a currency like Bitcoin or a platform like Kickstarter. The latter kind of platforms are based on a quasi 'dating agency' model – matching one person to another, or one bit of information or bit of finance to another. Uber works on the basis that it tells the mobile user 'I've got a cab – You're there – I'll pick you up'. Sites such as Airbnb and couchsurfing allow people to operate and synchronise with each other. They encourage civil collaboration. And these different types of relationship are both being enabled and at the same time being used for profit by those controlling the platforms.

If it is not direct exploitation, what then is going on? One lens through which we could view this is that of the socialisation of labour, a concept that was central to Marx's account of capitalist development, and in particular to his theories of technology, and the concentration and centralisation of capital. He traces the expansion of this direct socialisation from simple co-operation to manufacture through to machinofacture; and we could add systemofacture.

Contemporary capitalism has in many ways tried to reverse the movement to direct socialisation by fragmenting labour. Capital may not have read Marx but it recognises his point only too well. So it has changed strategy, through sub-contracting, automation, partnerships, or moving production to places where it will take time for the direct socialisation of labour to lead to industrial and political resistance.

Jeremy Isn't that the key thing? It seems to me that on one level the socialisation hasn't stopped, it's even intensified, but the key problem for them is to find modes of allowing that socialisation to continue and intensify without it actually having political ramifications.

Robin It may help if we recast Marx's discussion in terms of the socialisation of information. Labour no longer has to be in a single factory or firm. It can talk together and organise across spatial and organisational boundaries. The internet has greatly extended the space and capacity for labour's responses to capital.

It also opens up the potential for collaboration. The key word is open: open source, open knowledge, open learning, open data, open innovation, open production. The internet has enabled a platform like Wikipedia, or joint project like Linux, at the same time as it has given birth to Google.

This leads straight into the issue of the 'commons' because the socialisation of information, and its sharing, creates the potential for an autonomous collective intelligence on a planetary scale. In this new economy of the commons, the form of licence becomes a key area of contest, about who owns what, who has access to the collectively produced knowledge and so on.

This in turn leads to a third form of socialisation, which we might call 'civil socialisation'. I would like to distinguish it from the socialisation of information, for it is about the capacity of us as civil beings to socialise directly, to act directly, to discuss directly, to produce directly: to produce not only ideas but also, say, an open-sourced car, by collaborating. Bauwens has established a core platform for this new collaboration, the P2P Foundation. The extent of peer to peer collaboration is already remarkable. It is bursting through the bounds of the old form of socialised civility – which tended to be bound by space – yet is still able to link this new 'collaboration without boundaries' back to specific places.

We talk about optimism, but it's not a question of pessimism and optimism. It is a question of where are the possibilities, and, through understanding the contours and modes of operation of the new economy, whether or not we can collectively organise ourselves as so many communities of interest, including labour, in other words as directly socialised citizens.

I'd like to draw a key distinction between the current phase and what has gone before. As Marx pointed out, time economy was at the core of capital. Saving time has been the driver of technological innovation and capital accumulation. Speed has now reached the point that US stockbrokers site their offices near servers rather than Wall Street in order to gain a second or two advantage over their trader competitors. Time is measured in femtoseconds or billionths of a second.

Platforms are about space rather than time. Geographically they reduce space, but their aim is to expand in the social space of those using their platforms. They act as a socialisers of this social space, and although netarchical capital then connects this economy of social space back into the conventional commodity economy of time, the possibilities of an alternative 'social space' centred round platforms on the global scale is quite new. Given the many other material planetary constraints on the ungoverned growth of capital, I think we can see emerging a new economy of space that potentially challenges the prevailing current industrial economy of time.

Jeremy Can I ask you both – where do Edward Snowden's revelations relate to this, or what do they tell us about the state's response to this? I will start off with a suggestion which you can respond to.

Partly I've been thinking about the Deleuze control essay – and it's so minimal and suggestive that everyone has their own version of it – but the version of it I use when I teach is that there are several key aspects. The argument is that, compared to disciplinary society, which we could say matches up almost identically to Fordism, system management is inherently less concerned with content, less concerned with the ideas in people's heads, less concerned with norms. It's more concerned with mapping and managing relationships and with anticipating behaviours, and so the Snowden thing always seems to me to be a really interesting illustration of this, in that, compared to the way the state was operating throughout the Cold War, they don't really care that much about the content of what people are saying. They're not trying to map that too much, and they're not trying to force what people think into particular patterns. What they're trying to do is make sure they know absolutely everything about who's talking to whom. Rather than knowing about the content of the messages, they're bothered about the metadata, and they're bothered about trying to anticipate patterns of behaviour. So I think that seems to say something about the way the state, or institutions of government – whether that's corporate government or state government – are increasingly concerned with this question of relationships, and mapping, understanding and pre-empting relationships. I was thinking when you were talking about that 'dating' model, that, essentially, the function of the system or platform is to generate links, to generate connections, to generate relationships, to anticipate likely relationships between different units of information ... So there's something there, and I suppose the thing I'm wondering about is the extent to which – just as the disciplinary state at one point in its history becomes the mechanism by which capital is itself disciplined, arguably, during the high years of Fordist social democracy – it might be necessary to think, to some extent, about institutions of government in the twenty-first century, even progressive ones: that they are going to have to operate according to similar mechanisms; that they're also going to have to be about the facilitation and anticipation of relationships.

Andrew I wonder whether mapping is really the right term. It seems to me it's more about modelling relationships – that would provide the conceptual bridge between something like the Snowden revelations and other areas in which IT is a big deal, such as the whole 'big data' thing. The excitement about 'big data' is really an excitement about this possibility of perpetually generating models for how relationships are taking place and then using that information: in recommending things, etc, etc. So it's not really about mapping, it's more about modelling. And that would tie in with all this stuff you get around behavioural economics, nudging people, pushing people in certain directions: and, yes, the precise details, or the precise content, are unimportant really.

Jeremy I'm really struck by the idea that it's not about content, it's about the platform ... I mean that arguably sums up the nature of the shift from 'disciplinary' to 'control' society, doesn't it?

Andrew Isn't there an argument that if you can control the infrastructure, if you can bring people into a platform, then you can shape the platform around them once they're in, which is what tends to happen. For example, you get somebody into Facebook, then you start changing the platform around them, and so you shape what they can do, you run little experiments on how you think people should be relating to each other and so on. So controlling the infrastructure is the key thing there.

Jeremy And also, crucially, you have to allow them a latitude, because what you really want them do to is to generate data for you, that is useful, that represents value or potential in some way.

Andrew And I think also the thing about platforms is that you move from a situation where people are buying a phone, to one where it isn't actually a phone: it's a very powerful computer. But you don't programme it: you buy applications and then you're tied in to Apple's infrastructure, and then there's a closing down of possibility there

I think, at the same time as the infrastructure affords all sorts of possibilities. That's a Jonathan Zittrain argument about 'generativity', and the way in which tech corporations are responding to the possibilities that people are exploiting with file sharing and so on, which is to make it difficult by bringing them into enclosed technological spaces. So I suppose there's an issue there around the interest in infrastructure and the interest in the platform: that the platform is easier to control in some respects.

Robin I think the idea of enclosure is a useful one here: the battle for enclosure – that's where I think the commons discussion has taken us. I'd like to answer your Snowden question by distinguishing the private economy from the state, and the state's concern for some kind of discipline/control.

As regards the private sphere: my starting point is the one I mentioned earlier about the significance of the economy, at a time when we have so many things, too many things, and so much on offer. When there is such a ridiculous amount of choice, and a *huge* quantity of information about those choices, quite apart from all the other aspects of daily life, the question for any particular corporation is, how do I get people to pay attention to my product.

To return to Google. Google is about producing not intermediate goods but intermediate information for those who are engaged in trying to get attention. It is not itself concerned with trying to get attention, nor with the objects it is dealing with. It is concerned with its clients and the data it gathers. The image I have of it is of the farmer harvesting her or his crop – they are concerned with fertility and the generation of more and more granular information, so that they have more to sell in the form of charging for advertising.

I don't know if you've seen Shoshana Zuboff's work: her current work is on what she calls 'surveillance capitalism'. She thinks we are at a new stage because firms like Google and Facebook are in the business of creating a twenty-first century version of the panopticon. She gives the example of Google's electric car project. When I first read about this I thought 'well, they've got so much money, they're putting it into green projects, that seems like a good idea'. Her reading of it is that what they want to do is to track all our movements, where we go, with how many people, how fast we drive, and so on. Their over-riding interest is to get into every aspect of our lives – it could be via Google glasses, or wearable clothes, or the beds we sleep in, it could be ... anything. They want to generate data about *individuals* – it's more than just relationships. For them the data needs to be at the cellular level – because it can then be assembled and sold and resold in different ways and packages. In this sense they have an interest in individual content to the extent that it can be 'commoditisable' or valorised. On the other hand, I think you're right to say that their interest in content is in other senses neutral, and that what they are concerned with is patterns, and the sale of wide ranges of data to those who wish to use it to shape behaviour.

It is an extraordinary project, and it means that we are entering into a further form of alienation. For Marx, in a market society, social relations appear in the form of commodities, which represent so much alienated labour. In this new era, our own knowledge about ourselves, how we live our daily lives, where we go, what we read and write, even what we say, is appropriated by corporations like Google and returns to us in the form of commodity promotion.

On the question of who will take over, in the great battle of the Titans, my sense is that it will be Google rather than Apple who wins out. The key cards are possibly in their hand.

I think you're also both right to say that the state has an interest in patterns, and the shaping of behaviour, in this case for the sake of social steering and control rather than the promotion of particular commodities. One of the features of the neoliberal era is a shift from direct regulation to the use of market signals as policy instruments (in relation to the environment for example). But, as Andy suggests, the nudging can take other forms, such as the state's own entry into the attention economy, through publicity campaigns and what is often called 'public education'. What this approach shares with the market version is the idea of the individual as the free agent, responsible for their own decisions and actions.

On the other hand the state does in some fields have a direct interest in content – for example, whoever uses a particular word or visits a particular place or website can then be identified and brought within the traditional physical forms of state control. Snowden's revelations showed the extent to which the top internet companies had been drawn into the state's interest in control. The most celebrated is the PRISM programme, which required top internet companies to hand over information about suspected external threats. Further disclosures have revealed how the overlap of interests between the US state and the companies goes much wider, with formal co-operation agreements having been made between the NSA and the internet corporations, including one with Google in 2010. The extent of the imbrication between the corporations and the state is the basis of Shoshana Zuboff's argument about the new phase of 'surveillance capitalism'.

I recently saw a piece in the *Guardian* about 'Smart Cities' – and I would previously have thought this was a positive idea. But in the light of Shoshana Zuboff's work, I could see that its implications went far beyond the positives. By assembling together data not just from platforms, but the growing internet of things, a 'Smart City' could match Google and Facebook in creating a modern panopticon. The article discussed the ways in which such a system could be controlled in more democratic ways, for example through a kind of social contract, but the effectiveness of that control could all be down to the way it is developed and who controls the information.

Jeremy Can you say something more about the arguments in your 2010 paper 'Co-operation in the age of Google'?

Robin I was asked to offer some perspectives for the co-operative movement in the coming decade. The co-operative economy in this country had been inspired by the 1844 Rochdale Pioneers, and the working-class co-operative network that grew from it, to become by the 1880s one of the largest set of enterprises in the world. Many of the co-ops from the early period had had difficulty in keeping pace with scale-based Fordism, but over the past twenty years there has been a new wave of co-ops that have some of the features of the Italian industrial districts like the one in Poggibonzi. The question I looked at was what the future holds for the new and older strands of the UK's co-operative economy.

My starting point was the potential for more lateral and democratic forms of production and circulation as the result of the internet and growing civil socialisation. The potential for co-operation is startling. If anyone says to me, 'co-ops are over', the response has to be 'What about Linux?'. Open source is a contemporary form of cooperation. With open source projects you don't need to set up a co-op, because there's nothing bought or sold. But if you think that the majority of software in the world is now dependent on open source, co-operation has now reached a scale that William Morris could scarcely have dreamt of.

How does this translate into the material world of food and energy or expanding services like education, or health and social care? All these have the potential to develop as distributed post-post-Fordist systems. Already Germany's remarkable growth in renewable energy has been driven by local energy co-operatives (as was Denmark's wind industry). Similar patterns have emerged in social care (in Italy, over 14,000 social co-ops involving families, care workers and volunteers have been established in the last twenty-five years). In Japan, food co-ops, based on box schemes, now involve 12 million households, organised around local cells of 6-12 households. These food co-ops have now diversified into health, social care and a myriad of worker co-ops.

In all these systems, and in similar ones in the wider social economy, platforms, grids and common services are crucial to the effectiveness and economy of the constituent parts. What marks them out is that the infrastructure and support services are directly controlled by the productive 'cells' they are there to service. So the first recommendation of my study was to move away from the pyramidal structures that marked many of the larger twentieth–century co-ops, and towards developing such platforms and common services for distributed co-operative systems.

Secondly, if co-ops are driven by wider social and environmental goals, what holds everyone together and ensures that democratic structures remain inclusive and constructive? This has been a problem for the co-op movement. As co-ops grow in size, you can see a common tendency: after initial enthusiasm and expansion, pyramids based on knowledge often develop, with power moving to technicians and managers. In Fordist co-operatives, the managers tend to be sucked in to the methods and ideologies of their corporate competition. The economies of system clash with the economies of cooperation. How to marry the two?

The distributed systems of German energy or Japanese food are one answer. Another is ideological. The Mondragon network of 220 worker co-ops (with 85,0000 workers) has a Lego-like structure, with the individual co-ops encouraged to remain small and specialise, and spin-off operations as they grow. But their distinguishing feature is their emphasis on education, or 'formación' as they put it. Launched in 1956 from a training course, Mondragon now has a university serving its members, whose purpose is both technical and ideological, so that the values of co-operation are embodied in all its parts. Its founder, the priest Jose Arizmendierreta, when asked why they place such importance on education in an economic project, replied 'No, no – this is an educational project with an economic component'.

Another post-post-Fordist feature of the co-operative landscape is the appearance of co-operative platforms as a way of marrying autonomy and scale. The One-Click platform allows you to set up a co-op or other social venture in ten minutes, and then enables members to come in and out of discussions normally reserved for a Board according to each person's time and interest. What is fascinating about how it works in practice is that there's rarely a non-consensus decision. If there are differences those involved are encouraged to sort it out offline and return online to take formal decisions. Charles Armstrong, who developed One-Click, describes it as 'emergent democracy'.

One way of looking at these developments is to focus on how knowledge and information are generated and shared. One of my arguments in 'Co-operation in the Age of Google' was that co-ops with social and environmental goals have an incentive to share their knowledge with other social organisations with similar goals. We can think of it as a potential cooperative commons of information. This is one element of the economics of co-operation, and it gives co-ops, like others in the social economy, a decisive advantage over private corporations,

I also suggested a number of ways in which the movement as a whole could establish systems for the collection and sharing of their information and knowledge, as one part of a wider strategy for the British co-operative movement to embrace the emerging features of post-post-Fordist production – distributed systems, platforms, formation, and open information.

I also raised the issue of developing a cooperative currency. As Amazon and Google have both recognised, currency is a great tool for socialisation. As with 'open source' collaboration and its social-isation of information and knowledge, so a co-operative currency is a way of directly connecting (that is 'socialising'), the different parts of a co-operative system.

Jeremy Is cryptocurrency a harbinger of this?

Robin I've been to Bitcoin meetings, and I know some progres-sive people who are involved. Almost all of them regard Bitcoin as prototype. For them, it's not the Bitcoin, it's the encryption and the blockchain that are the important technologies. Already there are about fifty blockchain-based crypto currencies in circulation. There is a confidence in those meetings that these new forms of currency will undermine the key operational systems on which the major banks have based their monopoly. Again, there is the possi-bility of a progressive inflection of this monetary technology.

Jeremy Are these things that you think the government could play a positive role in facilitating?

Robin No, these directions in co-operative self-organisation have nothing to do with government.

Jeremy Is there anything you think government can do in this context to facilitate social progress, or democratisation?

Robin Well, a lot of what we are talking about can be applied to government itself, to make it more open, distributed and demo-cratic. This would enable closer relations between the growing civil economy, including co-ops and the state. We might say that this would widen the scope of democracy from discursive to productive forms.

Jeremy I suppose what I'm wondering, just to conclude, is: are polit-ical orientations still important in how people are approaching this? One of the obvious challenges from any kind of progressive perspective is that many of the mechanisms you're describing are primarily being used to maximise the rate of exploitation in various contexts, and I would like to ask if you think it's important to retain anything like a class perspective on these issues?

Robin How do we define class? How do we define the battle lines, and its key points? I return first to the Gorzian propositions on immaterial labour. My experience of working with those in the 'post-post-Fordist' culture involved in social innovation, and with those involved in the commons movement, is that there is an emergent cognitive class (of which we are members). Their material basis is the knowledge and information which is now at the heart of the new economy. The talk is not yet about class but about control, power, where the key sites of power lie, and how they can be democratised. Among those I have worked with there is a widely shared view that successful innovation has got to be deeply socially embedded. There's a kind of hostility to big capital but not small capital.

There is a gulf between the left and its analyses in class terms, and that of this widening post-post-Fordist strata. I think they would be fascinated to hear a talk by you on class. They are quite eclectic, and there are things which I am sure would resonate. They wouldn't want to enclose themselves.

Jeremy There's actually been very little work done, I think, on the basic notion that there is a global historic hegemonic block, and it is based on venture capital and Silicon Valley: they are the people who are occupying, in classic Gramscian terms, the position of hegemony, in that they are the people determining the direction of travel. It seems to me that the key mechanism by which they're doing it is through the implementation of platforms. And, again, the status of content is really interesting here. One of the phenomena observed in recent years by critics who are interested in cultural content has been this sense of stasis, the sense that fashion and music haven't really changed in noticeable ways in the past twenty years, except very superficially, and my argument would be that it's the same twenty years during which you can say actually *this* particular group have consolidated themselves as global hegemonic faction. And the fact that they are uninterested in content is kind of paradigmatic in some way.

For example, you can consider the role of Apple with the music industry. The old music industry cared to some extent about content, it had an interest in homogenising tastes, but that itself also gave people something to kick against. Whereas Apple, you know they can make the same amount of profit per unit sale from someone who sells a hundred of their files, as from someone who sells a million, so they're completely indifferent to content. But their indifference to content somehow becomes culturally lucrative; and so musical innovation just sort of stops. If you think about the whole era of the iPod: today music just sounds the same as it did when it started ... But hardly anyone talks about this. There's lots of Marxist denunciations of Apple, but they don't get to considerations of culture.

Robin I don't know if you've read the earlier book by Shoshana Zuboff and James Maxmin, *The Support Economy*? Their central thesis is that the individual now has become the centrepiece of the economy. Like any producer, each person requires all sorts of systems, tools, knowledge, advice, etc, suited to their specific needs. They refer to this as a support economy to manage the complexity of information that exists.

This is a powerful idea ... and again you can illustrate it by thinking of Lego. The way I think of Lego, as opposed to Ford, is that Ford had purpose-made machinery, with standardised outputs, whereas Lego has standardised inputs, namely the bricks, to produce customised, outputs – and the central thing is you've got to trust the adviser. And if you don't have the trust ... well, it's no good. So in health, for example, you can't just have an NHS adviser with a script, who is low down on the hierarchy, you have to have someone who is, as it were, your partner – who then scours the world and helps you make your decisions.

Jeremy Like a personal shopper.

Robin If you like, but more like a personal producer, who knows exactly the kind of thing that's necessary in order to do whatever it is. And as relational services become an ever greater part of the core economies – in education, health and social care – then the idea of a support economy, resting on democratically controlled platforms and collaborative relations, becomes a powerful alternative to that of post-post-Fordist capital. It provides a contrasting possibility to what you've said about Silicon Valley and all of these people being hegemonic. The 'social innovations' movement could be seen as seeking to use new technology to foster a socially oriented economy, even if it hasn't fully worked out the wider implications.

How do we see such a citizen-oriented economy in terms of class, save as a contradiction between such an economy and the netarchical capital of Google and Facebook?